THE INTERACTIVE HISTORY OF BRITAIN

igloobooks

igloobooks

Published in 2013
by Igloo Books Ltd
Cottage Farm
Sywell
NN6 0BJ
www.igloobooks.com

The measurements used are approximate.

SHE001 0713
2 4 6 8 10 9 7 5 3 1
ISBN 978-1-78197-541-1

Printed and manufactured in China

CONTENTS

Introduction

Britain has had a truly **amazing history**. Thousands of years ago, it was covered in ice and joined to the rest of Europe. Then the ice melted and Britain broke off to become the group of islands that we know so well today.

Battles, wars and conquests

The sea that surrounds Britain has never discouraged people from moving around. Over the centuries, lots of peoples – including the Celts, Romans, Vikings, Anglo-Saxons and Normans – have arrived in Britain from overseas in order to make a new life for themselves here.

People from overseas have often wanted to conquer Britain, and fierce battles have been fought throughout England, Ireland, Scotland and Wales. The Romans occupied Britain for a while, and then returned home,
but the Vikings, and later still the Normans, also settled here. All of these different people brought their own customs and ways of life with them.

The British have also fought many battles with other countries over the years. As Britain is an island, these battles were often fought at sea. Foreign countries that had once been our friends sometimes become our enemies. When the war was finished, they became our friends again.

Even in the 20th century, Britain fought two world wars against Germany, but now we think of them as neighbours and allies. For a while, Russia was regarded as an enemy to be feared. Today, countries like Iran and Iraq seem like dangerous places, but people used to go there on holiday.

Inventions and social change

It isn't just wars and political upheaval that have helped to shape Britain into the country we know today. British people have also invented lots of useful things and found new ways of working. For example, the Romans laid down roads in Britain. Much later, canals and railways were built in order to help industrial goods and people move around more easily.

Once most people had electric lighting and heating, life in Britain became more comfortable. Before the invention of these luxuries, however, life was often very difficult for many people. Up until relatively recently, most ordinary people had to work very hard to grow their own food and there was no television to keep them entertained in the evenings. Before there were machines to do all the washing and cleaning, rich people would have to employ servants or even slaves to do the work for them, often for little or no pay.

History is all around us

When you look at the buildings in Britain, do you ever wonder why they were built or who lived in them? The purpose of the huge stones at Stonehenge in Wiltshire, for example, is still a mystery, although they have probably been put to a number of uses over the years. In our towns and cities there are also plenty of old buildings that have seen all manner of events – royal visits, hangings and other punishments, religious services or sometimes just big parties. Even the houses we live in today might have seen many changes over the years.

How do we know so much about history?

Before people wrote things down, they probably told each other stories around the fire about what had happened long ago. Later on, people began to write these stories down. They started keeping diaries and writing letters, and there were also books and reports in newspapers. Archaeologists also find objects of interest on digs that can tell them a great deal about what life was like for earlier people living in Britain.

We are always finding out new things about the past and we now know far more than can be contained in a single book. Once you have read this one, why not see if you can find out more about your favourite parts, whether these are life-changing periods such as the Industrial Revolution or one particular historical figure like Henry VIII or Sir Winston Churchill.

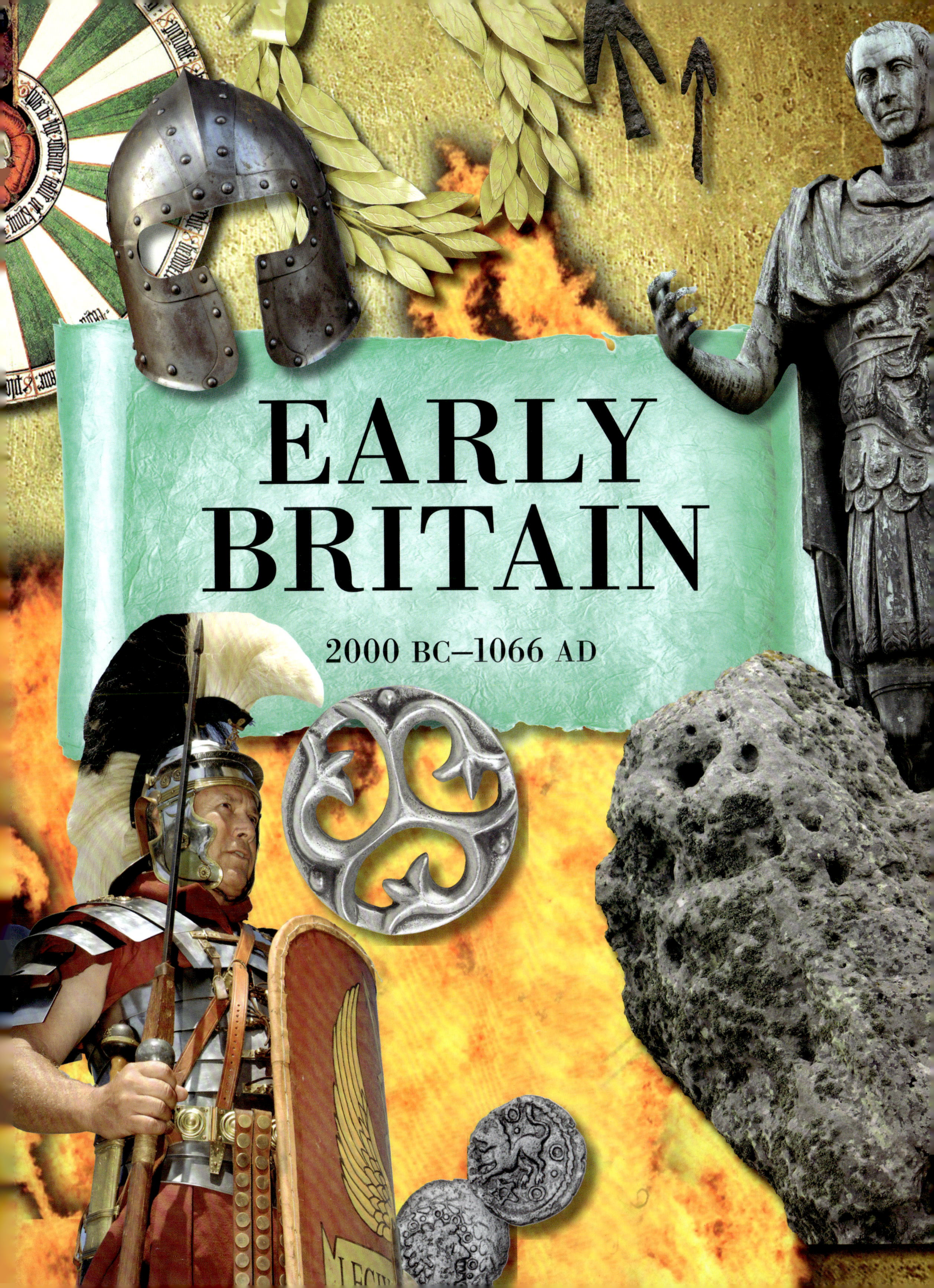
EARLY
BRITAIN
2000 BC–1066 AD

c.3000 BC: Work begins on a large-scale stone monument at Stonehenge.

c.2600 BC: Stone replaces timber to build Stonehenge.

c.2280–1930 BC: The bluestones are rearranged at the site of Stonehenge.

STONEHENGE

A circle of large stones, Stonehenge is one of the most important historic sites in the world. Archaeologists continue to disagree about the function of the stones but the site has probably been put to a number of uses during its long history.

SCAN ME

Instructions on page 5

AWESOME FACT

The monument was privately owned until 1918 when Cecil Chubb, a local man who had purchased it three years before, gave it to the nation. The number of visitors to the site has gradually increased from 38,000 per year in 1922 to over 900,000 today.

THE BUILDING OF STONEHENGE

The stones are situated in a field near Salisbury in Wiltshire. The exact date when the stones were put in place is unknown, but it could be anything between four and five thousand years ago. The chances are that the site had already been used for rituals, burials and celebrations for many centuries before that. Like a large cathedral, it was probably made over the course of many centuries.

THE STORY OF THE STONES

The first stones to be erected were bluestones, which were arranged in a double circle. These were later replaced with a series of sarsen stones in the shape of a horseshoe. Each pair of these huge stones had a stone laid horizontally across the top to connect them. A ring of sarsens surrounded this horseshoe, also connected to each other at the top.

The monument was later expanded by the addition of two bluestone rings, one inside the horseshoe and another between the horseshoe and the outer ring.

Over the centuries, many of the stones have been taken away, probably for use in other buildings.

c.1136: Geoffrey of Monmouth refers to the stones in his *History of the Kings of Britain*.

1540: Henry VIII gives the monument to the Earl of Hertford.

1918: Cecil Chubb, a land owner, gives Stonehenge to the nation.

THE SOLSTICES

The longest day of the year occurs around 21 June. This was a very significant date for early peoples. On that date, the sun rises above a sarsen stone known as the heel stone. At midwinter (around 21 December, the shortest day), the sun sets between two large stones – one of which has now fallen.

Knowing when these dates occurred allowed ancient peoples to decide when to sow and harvest crops. The solstices were usually a time of celebration. There would always be a feast in midwinter, rather as Christmas is celebrated today.

COOL FACTS

- There are several other stone circles throughout Britain but Stonehenge is the largest and has always been the most famous.
- The biggest stones, known as sarsens, are up to 9m (30ft) tall and weigh 25 tonnes on average.
- The smaller stones, referred to as "bluestones", weigh up to 4 tonnes.

INTERESTING

What is a "Henge"?

A henge is basically a ring of raised earth, roughly circular or oval, with a central ditch. There are usually one to four entrances. They were often used for burials.

An artist's impression of Stonehenge showing what it may have looked like when it was first built.

Stonehenge today

c.2500 BC: The Bronze Age begins in Britain with the emergence of the Wessex Culture.

c.2280–1890 BC: Copper mining begins at Alderley Edge in Cheshire.

2049 BC: "Seahenge" is constructed near Old Hunstanton on the Norfolk coast.

THE BRONZE AGE

In Britain, the Bronze Age lasted from about 2,500 BC to 800 BC. During this period, people from mainland Europe arrived in Britain, bringing new customs and ways of living.

WHY THE BRONZE AGE?

This period is called the Bronze Age because copper and bronze (a mixture of copper and tin) were used to make tools, cooking pots and jewellery. Farming began around this time, too – rather than hunting for wild animals, people started to keep them in enclosures and grow crops in fields for bread-making.

It is widely thought that bronze was first brought over to Britain by the Bell Beaker people (or just the Beaker people), who originated in Portugal and then spread throughout Europe.

INTERESTING

What is Bronze?
Bronze is a mixture (or "alloy") of copper and tin. On its own, copper is a very soft metal. Adding tin (about 10 per cent) makes the metal much harder.

Both metals were widely available in Britain. Tin was found in streams in Cornwall, while copper was mined mainly in North Wales. The molten metal was poured into moulds to make tools, weapons and other objects.

AWESOME FACT

Beaker People
The Bell Beaker people were so named because they made bell-shaped pottery drinking cups.

1692: Abandoned Bronze Age copper mines are reopened at Great Orme in Wales.

1959: The Isleham Hoard, a collection of bronze objects, is found in Cambridgeshire.

1993: Excavations in Leicestershire uncover the Lockington Gold Hoard.

BURIAL MOUNDS

Mounds, or "barrows", are found throughout the southern part of Britain and were made to contain the remains of the dead. Alongside the remains would be placed various precious objects that would be of value in the afterlife. These grave goods included stone battle axes, metal daggers with elaborately decorated hilts, and various ornaments made of gold and amber. Some of these are very similar to objects found in Ancient Greece, suggesting that even in these early times international trade was common.

DAILY LIFE

Houses were usually built in a round shape using mud and other natural materials. In the centre was a hearth for a fire. The roof may have been grassed over to help keep the heat in.

Trees were chopped down in forests to create fields where crops could be grown. They were divided up with stone walls, some of which can still be seen today. The best examples are on Dartmoor in Devon.

Water was very important, and most settlements were made near rivers, streams and bogs. Religious ceremonies were held there, and various offerings to the gods have been discovered, including jewellery.

COOL FACTS

- In the later Bronze Age, people learnt to weave textiles. Both men and women wore tunics and cloaks, with woollen hats for extra warmth. Women had long skirts, while men had knee-length skirts like kilts.
- People in the later Bronze Age also developed pottery-making and used cups and bowls for eating and drinking.
- Later Bronze Age people did not bury their dead, but cremated them instead.

c.900–600 BC: The first hill forts are made as a means of defence in Britain.

c.500 BC: Celtic peoples start to appear and settle down in Britain.

c.450 BC: An agricultural settlement appears in Danebury in Hampshire.

IRON AGE BRITAIN AND THE CELTS

The period from around 750 BC to 43 AD, when the Romans conquered Britain, is often called the Iron Age. During this time, people started to use iron instead of bronze.

A CELTIC IRON HELMET

CELTIC COINS

IRON VERSUS BRONZE

Although bronze is a very beautiful metal, iron is much harder. Objects made from iron were stronger, and tools could be made with sharp edges. While bronze was melted and poured into moulds, iron objects are made by hammering the hot metal against an anvil – a technique called smithing. Iron was used to make ploughs, knives and other tools, for shields and helmets, and for coins. Iron-age people became very skilled at all kinds of metalwork. Many beautiful objects have been found in archaeological digs.

Smithing is the technique of hammering hot metal against an anvil ready for shaping.

CELTIC SHIELD

c.100 BC: Coinage appears in Britain, mainly in the south-east of England.

c.50 BC: The Romans occupy France and trade with Britain increases.

2012: A huge hoard of Celtic coins is found in Jersey in the Channel Islands.

WHO WERE THE CELTS?

The people who lived in Britain at this time are often called Celts. The Celts were a tribe of people who originated in Europe. Around 500 BC, some of them migrated to Britain. Today, many people in Britain claim to be Celtic, especially in parts of Wales, Scotland, Ireland and Cornwall.

INTERESTING

People had dogs during the Iron Age, mainly for hunting and to help herd other animals, and perhaps to act as guard dogs. But they may have treated them as pets as well.

WHAT DID THE CELTS LOOK LIKE?

The Celts were very conscious of their appearance. They used berries and other parts of plants to make dyes, so their clothing would have been quite colourful. Men wore tunics with a belt over loose trousers with a cloak for extra warmth. Women wore long dresses fastened with brooches.

According to some later Roman writers, who encountered the Celts when they invaded Britain, British soldiers used white lime to spike up their hair, a bit like hair gel. Or they would tie their hair up in a ponytail.

HOW DID THE CELTS LIVE?

People lived in small communities of individual roundhouses, which were often sited on top of hill forts. Each house might have a small garden, probably used for growing vegetables and herbs. The herbs would have been used not only to cook with, but also to make medicines and dyes for wool.

Most people at this time would have been farmers, growing crops such as barley, rye, oats and wheat and keeping a few animals. They had cattle, sheep and pigs, exactly as we do today. Horses were used to pull carts and chariots.

AWESOME FACT

The word **Celt** comes from the Greek ***keltoi***, meaning **"barbarians"**.

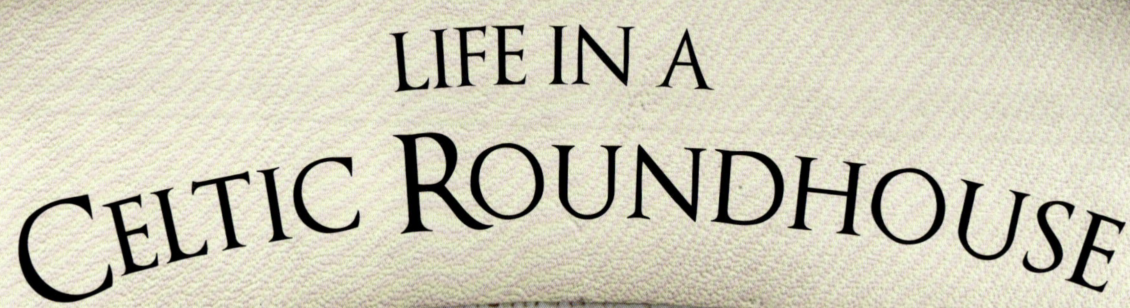

LIFE IN A CELTIC ROUNDHOUSE

Most houses at this time consisted of a single round room. The roof was cone-shaped and covered in a thatch – lengths of dry straw tied together. Alternatively, it might have been covered in turf instead. In the centre of the room was the fire, so there would be a hole in the middle of the roof to allow the smoke to escape.

BUILDING WITH WATTLE AND DAUB

This is an ancient building method found in many parts of the world and one that was used for building Celtic roundhouses. A basic framework is made from planks or tree trunks. Then thinner branches are woven between them, rather like making a big basket. This is the **wattle**.

The gaps in the wattle were filled in with a **daub**, which is a mixture of earth, straw and animal manure. The walls would be very thick, keeping the house warm in winter and cool in summer. Daub could also be baked into rough bricks and cemented together with wet daub.

Wattle-and-daub houses continued to be built until medieval times, when brick and stone became more usual. Today, houses made from wattle and daub can still be found in Devon and Cornwall.

AWESOME FACT

Salt

Salt was used not only to spice up food but also to preserve meat and fish. Another way of preserving was by smoking in front of the fire.

SMOKE RELEASED THROUGH A HOLE IN THE THATCH SO NO NEED FOR A CHIMNEY

HIGH-BEAMED ROOF FOR SMOKING MEAT AND FISH

UPRIGHT LOOM FOR WEAVING

OPEN FIRE FOR COOKING

LARGE TIMBERS TO MAKE FRAME

DAUB

WATTLE

INTERESTING

All in a Day's Work

The Celts spent a lot of time each day on the practical tasks they needed to carry out to survive, including:

- Growing crops
- Tending livestock
- Building and repairing
- Collecting firewood
- Hunting
- Weaving
- Dyeing clothes
- Making jewellery

THE CELTIC DIET

Iron-age people had a surprisingly varied diet that is not so different to what most people eat today.

- As well as meat and fish, people in the Iron Age used the crops they grew to make bread, porridge and beer.
- Cows would have provided milk.
- Iron-age people collected berries and nuts from the forest and probably also ate leafy vegetables and roots.
- Some people kept bees for their honey, which was used as a sweetener, as there was no sugar.
- Iron-age people cooked their food in clay ovens.

50s BC: Julius Caesar refers to Druids in his *Commentaries on the Gallic War.*	**1st century:** Roman emperors Tiberius and Claudius try to ban Druidism in Britain.	**835 AD:** All Souls' Day moved from 13 May to 1 November – the same day as the end of Samhain.

Celtic Culture and Beliefs

The Celts worshipped many gods and goddesses, mainly concerned with nature and the changes in the seasons. Some of their superstitions linger on today when we celebrate Hallowe'en.

CELTIC RELIGION

The Celts probably worshipped many gods, who were associated with lakes, rivers and bogs, as well as the sun, moon and stars. They often made sacrifices to them, and many precious objects have been found in bogs, preserved in the mud. Animals and even people were sometimes sacrificed.

Celtic religion was overseen by people called Druids, who were like priests. They were well-educated, respected members of society and were in charge of religious ceremonies.

DID YOU KNOW?

Bog Bodies

Many bodies have been found in peat bogs. The peat acts as a preservative, so the skin and clothing are often intact. They may be people who were sacrificed to the gods. A well-known example is the Lindow Man, found in Cheshire. Investigations showed that his remains were around 2,000 years old. He was strangled, hit on the head, and then had his throat cut. He was put in the bog face down.

1200s: The Isle of Man incorporates the triskele into its coat of arms.

1593: Shakespeare refers to Hallowe'en in his play *The Two Gentlemen of Verona*.

1984: The body of a man is discovered and examined in a peat bog in Cheshire.

JEWELLERY AND OTHER METALWORK

The Celts were fond of jewellery, which would have been made of iron and other metals. It was decorated with animal shapes and faces or complicated patterns. Important members of the tribe wore a torque, a kind of solid necklace, made of gold, silver or iron. Brooches, buckles and pins were used to hold garments together.

Warriors had elaborately decorated helmets and shields, which may have been used in ceremonies rather than actual combat. The helmets might have been decorated with birds or animals, or have two horns, making the wearer look like a bull.

COOL FACTS

Celtic Religious Festivals

There were four major Celtic festivals:

- **Imbolc** celebrated spring.
- **Beltane** was the great May festival.
- **Lughnasadh** was the Harvest Festival.
- **Samhain** was celebrated at the end of October when the days were getting shorter and the nights longer. Celtic people thought the dead could come back as ghosts and spirits at Samhain.

INTERESTING

Triskeles

A popular Celtic motif is the triskele, made up of three interlocking spirals. A form of triskele can still be seen today in the flag of the Isle of Man, which has three bent human legs joined together. Triskeles often appear on Celtic shields and brooches.

AWESOME FACT

The Green Man

The Green Man is the god of spring and summer, usually depicted as a face surrounded by leaves, sometimes with leaves coming out of his mouth. Green Man carvings are often found in old churches or in stained-glass windows.

55 BC: Julius Caesar leads an expedition to Britain, but is forced to turn back.

43 AD: The Romans led by the Emperor Claudius conquer Britain.

60–70 AD: The Romans build a temple at *Aquae Sulis* – now Bath.

ROMAN BRITAIN

Around 2,000 years ago, Rome was the most important city in the western world. The Romans had a vast empire, which they were always looking to expand. They invaded Britain several times.

THE ROMAN INVASION

In 55 BC, the Roman general Julius Caesar led an expedition to Britain across the English Channel from Gaul (nowadays France), but was forced to turn back. The following year, he returned with an army of 30,000 men, but soon decided that it was not worth attempting to conquer Britain. He was more interested in going back to Rome, where he planned to take control of the Roman Empire.

The Romans did not try and conquer Britain again until nearly a hundred years later, when, in 43 AD, the Emperor Claudius sent over an army to take control. At this time, Britain was divided into many smaller areas, each with its own tribe and ruler.

Although many battles were fought, the Romans were able to occupy Britain until 410 AD.

Roman soldier

AWESOME FACT

The Romans invaded other countries as well as Britain. Their empire covered much of Europe and parts of North Africa and the Middle East.

180 AD: Most of the Romans' important road-building programme is complete.

410 AD: The Romans return home after a few centuries of occupation.

2013: Archaeologists dig up 10,000 objects from Roman London.

ROMAN TOWNS

Before the Romans arrived, most British people still lived in circular houses in clusters, as they had done for centuries. The Romans built real towns, with streets arranged in straight lines like a grid and with a central space (the "forum") that could be used for markets or meetings. Some had public baths and outdoor theatres. They gave the towns Latin names.

- **Chester** was *Deva Victrix*
- **St. Albans** was *Verulamium*
- **London** was *Londinium*
- **Bath** was *Aquae Sulis*
- **Colchester** was *Camulodulum*

Colchester was the main town, but by 100 AD London was the biggest town in Britain.

What the Romans Brought to Britain

Many things we take for granted today were unknown in Britain before the Romans introduced them.

- The calendar
- Cement
- Glass
- Plumbing
- Apples
- Carrots
- Grapes

DID YOU KNOW?

ROMAN ROADS

Before the Romans came, there were no proper roads in Britain. They built many long straight roads, making it much easier to get from town to town. It was important that they could move soldiers rapidly around the country. The Roman foundations can still be found under many roads in use today. Important Roman roads were:

- **Watling Street**, running from Dover, through London to St. Albans, then on to Wroxeter
- **Ermine Street** from London to Lincoln and then York
- **The Fosse Way**, linking Exeter to Lincoln, via Bath, Cirencester and Leicester

INTERESTING

As well as many legions of soldiers, the Romans also brought government and a new way of life to Britain. Many buildings, roads and forts from the time of the Roman occupation still survive to this day.

c.60 AD: Under Boudicca, the Iceni and other tribes rise up against the Romans.

c.98 AD: The writer Tacitus gives a description of Boudicca in his *Agricola*.

c.122 AD: Work begins on the building of Hadrian's Wall in the north of England.

RESISTANCE TO ROME

Although many of the British ruling classes enjoyed great prosperity under the centuries of Roman occupation, there were pockets of resistance from local tribes throughout Britain.

BOUDICCA AND THE ICENI

Boudicca, sometimes called Boadicea, was queen of the Iceni tribe, who lived in what is now East Anglia. She was the widow of King Prastagus, who had been allowed to continue to rule in harmony alongside the Romans. But after his death, the Romans seized the Iceni's property and had Boudicca whipped.

In around 60 AD, the Iceni rebelled, gaining the support of other British tribes. Led by Boudicca, they attacked the Roman cities of London, Colchester and St. Albans. The Romans were finally able to win a victory at the Battle of Watling Street in the Midlands. According to some accounts, Boudicca took poison after the defeat and died.

AWESOME FACT

Boudicca is often depicted as a warrior queen driving a chariot. There is a bronze statue of her near the Houses of Parliament in London.

INTERESTING

Iceni Body Art

It is often said that the Iceni painted their bodies with woad, a blue dye they got from plants, perhaps to make themselves look more fearsome in battle. But they may have used the dye simply as a kind of antiseptic on wounds.

1902: A statue of Boudicca is given to London.

1987: Hadrian's Wall is named a World Heritage Site because it is an area of such historical interest.

2012: Hadrian's Wall is illuminated as part of the London 2012 Festival.

SCOTTISH RESISTANCE AND HADRIAN'S WALL

Although the Romans occupied Britain for several centuries, they never conquered Scotland (which they called Caledonia). They made a few attempts, but were always driven back by the Scottish tribes. To prevent these tribes from attacking the part of the country they did control, the Emperor Hadrian had a long stone wall built from coast to coast that could be patrolled by Roman soldiers. It was probably started after Hadrian's visit to the country in 122 AD.

Along the wall were milecastles (gatehouses that allowed soldiers to cross over from either side of the wall) and turrets. The soldiers lived in 16 forts along the wall. Parts of the structure can still be seen today.

Once built, the wall marked the most northerly boundary of the Roman Empire.

COOL FACTS

- Hadrian's Wall is the biggest thing the Romans ever built.
- The wall was 117km (73 miles) long and stretched from the North Sea on the east side to the Irish Sea on the west side.
- It was up to 3m (10ft) wide in places and around 5m (16ft) high.
- The wall was built by three Roman legions stationed in Britain.

LIFE IN A ROMAN VILLA

Roman villas could be very luxurious. Today, remains of villas can be seen at Fishbourne in West Sussex, Chedworth in Gloucestershire, and Piddington, Northamptonshire, as well as many other places occupied by the Romans.

HOW WERE ROMAN VILLAS BUILT?

A villa is really a **complex of houses** – a big house for the owners, with smaller wooden ones for servants and farm workers, along with **barns and stables**. The main house would have been airy and spacious, and built of stone. Some were just long rectangles, perhaps with a corridor to one side with doors into each of the rooms. The grandest were square or rectangular, with a central **courtyard**. The villa at Fishbourne had around a hundred rooms.

The **floors** would be tiled, often using colourful mosaics, either in elaborate patterns or depicting Roman gods. There would also be **paintings** on the wall. Underfloor **heating** would keep the house warm. Floors were supported on stacks of tiles. A furnace outside would circulate hot air in the spaces between the tiles. The heating system was called a *hypocaust*.

Stone columns supporting the ceiling might be intricately carved. Instead of thatch or turf, the **roof** would be covered with terracotta tiles.

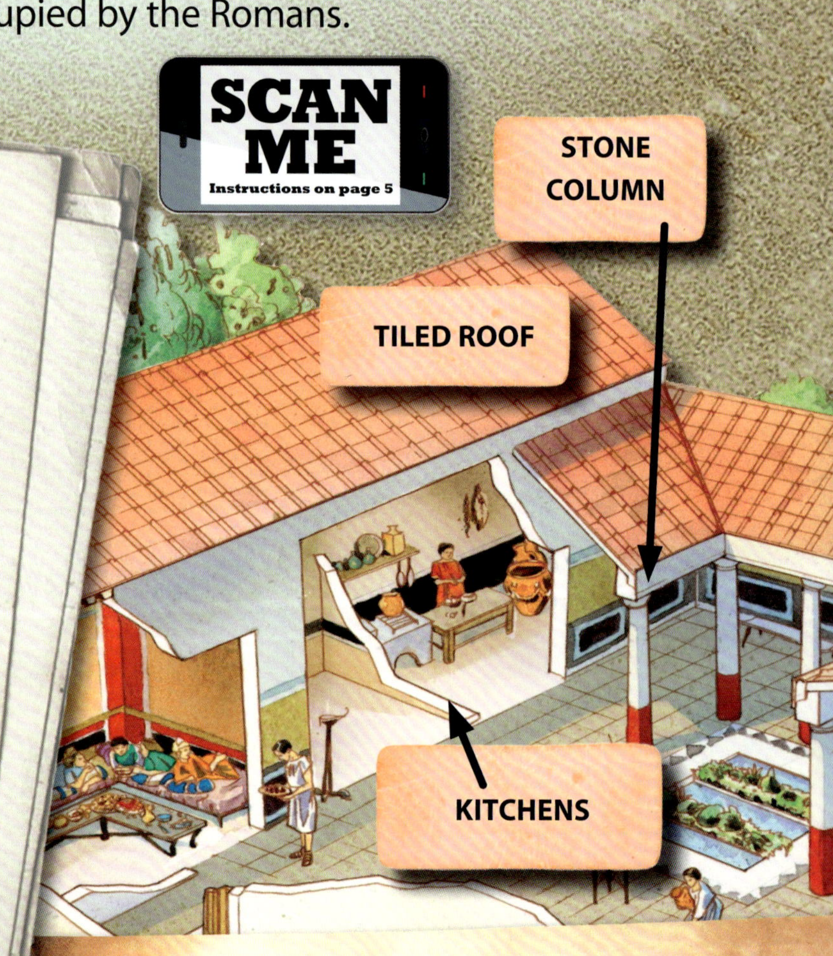

Roman Baths

The Romans were very keen on personal hygiene and bathing could provide an opportunity for relaxation and meeting friends, as well as keeping clean. Bath-houses comprised various rooms. A hot room, called a *caldarium*, was like a sauna, designed to make you sweat. A warm room was called the *tepidarium*. After spending time in these, you could, if you were brave enough, jump straight into a cold plunge pool in the *frigidarium* next door.

INTERESTING

Keeping Clean

To get rid of dirt, Romans would apply perfumed oil to the skin. Then a slave would scrape them down with a strigil – a small, curved tool like a narrow shoe horn, usually made of bronze.

Roman Toilets

The Romans had proper toilets that you would recognise today but, instead of having separate cubicles, you were expected to sit in a line with other people. Nobody seemed that bothered about privacy!

The toilet was made of a bench with holes cut in it placed over a sewer. The toilets were flushed with water from a channel, so could be kept clean. Instead of toilet paper, people used sponges on sticks.

AWESOME FACT

Window on the World

Glass was used for the windows in a Roman villa. Before the Romans, people would have used animal skins or rough blankets to keep out the draughts.

COOL FACTS

Roman Slaves

- Wealthy Romans had slaves, who could come from any part of the Empire, including Britain. Even children were used as slaves.
- Slaves were bought and sold in slave markets in the big towns. Young slaves were more expensive, as they had many years' service ahead of them.
- Some slaves were treated very harshly, but others had a decent life.
- In a villa, slaves would help the master and his family dress and bathe, clean the house, and prepare and serve the meals.

563 AD: Columba is granted land for a monastery on Iona.

597 AD: Augustine arrives in Kent to convert the English.

604 AD: Augustine dies and is buried at Canterbury.

CHRISTIANITY IN BRITAIN

In early times, most people in Britain worshipped a number of different gods and goddesses. Each new wave of invaders brought their own religion with them.

A NEW RELIGION

The new religion of Christianity began to spread into Western Europe in the first century. It is not known exactly when Christians first arrived in Britain, but there is a legend that Jesus's uncle, Joseph of Arimathea, came to England in 63 AD.

Early Christians were often persecuted. By 313 AD, Emperor Constantine in Rome became more tolerant, and Christians no longer had to worship in secret.

By the time the Romans left Britain, many people had converted to Christianity. But new invaders still worshipped their own pagan gods. Christianity was only one religion among many, and was practised mainly in Wales, Ireland and western Scotland.

735 AD: Bede dies at Jarrow in Northumbria.

1899: Pope Leo XIII declares Bede a saint.

2012: St. Augustine's shrine is re-established in Ramsgate in Kent.

St. Augustine

The monk Augustine was born in Rome. The pope sent him to convert the people of England to Christianity. He arrived in Kent in 597, where he impressed King Ethelbert, who gave him a church at Canterbury. Later, he built the first cathedral at Canterbury and a monastery, which became the most important in England. The Pope made him the first Archbishop of Canterbury. He died in 604 AD.

DID YOU KNOW?

"Non Angli sed Angeli"

St. Augustine is supposed to have seen some English children in the slave market in Rome. Struck by their blonde curly hair and blue eyes, he asked where they had come from. Being told that they were "Angles", he exclaimed *"Non Angli sed Angeli"* – which means "Not Angles but Angels".

INTERESTING

St. Columba

St. Columba (c. 521–597) was an Irish monk who spread the Christian faith through Ireland and Scotland. Aged 42, he landed on Iona and built a monastery there that became world famous. He converted many pagans to Christianity.

The Venerable Bede

Bede (673–735) was probably born in Durham. At the age of seven, he was entrusted to the care of Benedict Biscop, the founder of the monastery of St. Peter at Wearmouth. In 682 AD, Bede moved to the monastery at Jarrow, where he spent the rest of his life. Bede wrote many books. His most famous is called *Historia Ecclesiastica Gentis Anglorum* or "The Ecclesiastical History of the English People", which he finished in 731 AD.

Most of what we know about early British history is in this book.

COOL FACTS

- Bede wrote around 40 books on theology and history.
- Bede's *Historia* is the first history book in which the AD system – meaning "in the year of the lord"– is used for writing dates.
- The church in Canterbury that was given to St. Augustine is still in use today. It is called St Martin's.
- Justin Welby, the current Archbishop of Canterbury, is 105th in the line of succession from Augustine.

410 AD: The Romans leave Britain to defend the city of Rome.

447 AD: Vortigern gives Hengist and Horsa the Isle of Thanet in Kent.

556 AD: Seven separate Anglo-Saxon kingdoms are established across Britain.

Angles, Saxons and Jutes

The Romans left Britain in 410 AD. Their empire was too large to manage easily, and there were several wars between rival groups who wanted control. The soldiers were needed back home to defend Rome.

THE ROMAN DEPARTURE

Britain was still made up of a number of smaller kingdoms, each with their own ruler, who had managed to live happily alongside the Romans. During the occupation, there were raids from across the North Sea, but they were always forced to return. Without the Roman soldiers to defend the county, invasions became more frequent and eventually, from around 450 AD, the invaders were able to form settlements.

WHO WERE THE ANGLO-SAXONS?

Angles, Saxons and Jutes are three separate groups of people, who are sometimes just called the Anglo-Saxons because the Jutes came in much smaller numbers. They came from the Netherlands, Jutland (modern Denmark) and the northern part of Germany. They crossed the North Sea in small boats to raid Britain many times but were finally able to settle here.

It is thought that they wanted to come and live in Britain because their own countries kept flooding, making it difficult to grow crops. In Britain, there was plenty of land suitable for farming. Although there were probably several battles, the invasion was mainly peaceful.

ANGLO-SAXON RULE

The Anglo-Saxons ruled Britain for the next 500 years. They never left, and many people in Britain today are descended from them. The part of Britain where the Anglo-Saxons made their homes became known as England. They did not manage to make settlements in Wales, Cornwall and Scotland, which is why many people in those areas today claim to be Celtic.

INTERESTING

Anglo-Saxon Settlements

- **Angles** settled in East Anglia, the East Midlands and Northumbria.
- **Saxons** settled in Sussex, Essex, Middlesex and Wessex (which is now south-west England).
- **Jutes** settled mainly in Kent, Hampshire and the Isle of Wight.

617 AD: Northumbria becomes the Supreme Kingdom.

757 AD: Offa becomes the King of Mercia.

1971: Offa's Dyke Path, one of the longest National Trails, is opened.

Hengist and Horsa

Hengist and Horsa were two brothers from Jutland who are sometimes said to have led the first bands who settled in Britain. They wanted control of Kent, but Horsa was killed in battle. After further fighting, Hengist managed to drive out the Britons.

There are many stories about the brothers. Hengist had a beautiful daughter named Rowena. He offered her as bride to the Kentish king, Vortigern, but this angered Vortigern's sons, so there could never be peace between the two sides. We do not know much about what actually happened, because few people could read or write down the story.

Offa's Dyke

Rather like Hadrian's Wall, which was built by the Romans, Offa's Dyke was made to defend a boundary. The kingdom of Mercia (which today is the West Midlands) was ruled by King Offa in the second half of the 8th century. The dyke is a ditch and a wall of earth, dug between 757 and 796, marking the border between Offa's kingdom and the Welsh kingdom of Powys.

COOL FACTS

Anglo-Saxon Names

- Place names that end in "ham" were once Anglo-Saxon settlements. "Ham" means "village" In Anglo-Saxon. Cheltenham, Wokingham and Birmingham are good examples.
- "Wic" or "wich" meant "farm" or "village". Ipswich, Droitwich and Greenwich were Anglo-Saxon settlements.
- Lots of Anglo-Saxon words are still used in English today, such as ache, baby, earth and hole.

1116: The most recent Anglo-Saxon Chronicle is written in Peterborough.

1485: Thomas Malory's tales of King Arthur, *Le Morte d'Arthur*, are published.

1939: The burial mound at Sutton Hoo, in Suffolk, is excavated by archaeologists.

ANGLO-SAXON LIFE AND LEGENDS

The Anglo-Saxons lived in small settlements, often made up of only a few families. They spent their time clearing land for farming and tending crops and livestock. Early Anglo-Saxons were pagan and superstitious. Several of their burial mounds can still be seen in Britain today.

LIFE IN ANGLO-SAXON BRITAIN

As well as establishing their own settlements and villages, the Anglo-Saxons also made towns inside the old walls of Roman cities.

They built their houses of wood with a thatched roof. As in Celtic times, most just had a single room, with a fire for warmth. In a village, several small houses might be grouped around a larger hall where the most important family would have lived.

Men wore tunics over tight leggings that were tied with strips of cloth or leather. The women had long dresses and wore metal brooches.

SUTTON HOO BURIAL MOUNDS

Sutton Hoo in Suffolk is the location of several burial mounds. In one of them, archaeologists uncovered the remains of an Anglo-Saxon ship that may have belonged to a 7th-century nobleman.

Only the overall shape of the ship could be seen, as the wood had rotted. But there were many objects made of gold, silver, bronze and iron buried with it that had survived. These included a sword, a shield and a beautiful helmet.

The helmet is made of bronze coated in tin. It was in pieces when discovered but has since been reconstructed. The helmet was decorated with boars' heads, a dragon's head and a bird with its wings spread. Panels on the helmet depict warriors, one on horseback. The helmet was probably used for ceremonial purposes, not actual fighting.

The Anglo-Saxons were often buried with their possessions. Men were buried with knives and spears, while women's graves included tools for sewing and weaving.

1958: T. H. White writes an Arthurian fantasy, *The Once and Future King*.

1976: Investigation dates the Winchester Round Table to the 13th or early 14th century.

2001: A new visitor centre opens at Sutton Hoo, the site of an Anglo-Saxon burial mound.

THE LEGEND OF KING ARTHUR

A legend grew up about a British king who fought bravely against the invading Anglo-Saxons. King Arthur is supposed to have won a great battle at Mount Badon in 518, but he may not even have existed. Most of the stories about him were written down much later.

Arthur is supposed to have lived in a castle called Camelot, where he had a big round table where all his knights would meet. A story has it that if Britain is ever invaded again, Arthur and all his knights will reappear to defend it.

AWESOME FACT

King Arthur's Round Table
A large round tabletop hangs in Winchester Castle, which many people believed was the original round table. But we now know that this was made around 1250–1280. It was painted during the reign of Henry VIII.

INTERESTING

The Anglo Saxon Chronicles
We know much less about this period of British history than we do about Roman Britain. The Romans wrote about what happened and their writings were kept in great libraries. The Anglo-Saxons did not write things down.

The people who wrote the chronicles had to rely on stories that had been passed down over the centuries. These stories were later written down in the late 9th century – they are known as the Anglo-Saxon Chronicles.

849 AD: Alfred the Great is born at Wantage in Oxfordshire.

871 AD: Alfred defeats the Vikings at the Battle of Ashdown.

878 AD: Alfred defeats the Vikings at the Battle of Edington.

The Vikings

Britain was invaded again in the 8th century by people from Denmark, Norway and Sweden. These people were called the Vikings. Unlike the Anglo-Saxons, they also moved into Scotland and Wales.

WHY DID THE VIKINGS INVADE?

Some Vikings just wanted to raid Britain, but others were more interested in living there. There were many battles between the Vikings and the English. Finally, Alfred the Great managed to win a number of important victories and make peace with the invaders.

The Vikings were not only great travellers, they were also great traders. In a Viking market, you could find goods not only from other parts of Britain, but also from Scandinavia and even the Middle East.

COOL FACTS

Landings and Invasions

- The name "Viking" comes from a Norse word meaning "pirate raid".
- Viking boats were called "longships".
- Besides landing on the mainland, Vikings also came to the Orkney and Shetland Islands and the Isle of Man.
- During the invasions the Vikings, who were not Christians, stole from many churches and monasteries.
- Apart from Britain, the Vikings also went to Iceland, Greenland, France and Russia. They even went as far as the Mediterranean, Turkey and North America.

886 AD: Alfred arranges a treaty with the Vikings.

899 AD: King Alfred dies and is buried at Winchester in Hampshire.

1102: Slave trading by the Vikings is stopped.

York – a Viking stronghold
York was an important town for the Vikings – they called it *Jorvik*, which later became "York". Around 15,000 people lived in the town. The remains of many of their homes were found in what is now Coppergate.

AWESOME FACT

Viking Slaves
The Vikings had slaves just like the Romans, and they were made to do all the dirtiest jobs. They captured slaves in raids and sold them in markets.

DID YOU KNOW?

Some Viking words are still commonly used today, including crawl, husband, leg, ugly and window.

KING ALFRED THE GREAT

Alfred (849–899 AD) was born in Wantage, in Oxfordshire. After all his successes in battle, he divided the country in two. The northern part of England was controlled by the Vikings, while he ruled the southern counties and the Midlands. He built up an army and navy and created a system of laws by which the country would be ruled.

A famous story tells of how he once had to take shelter in a cottage. He was asked to keep his eye on some cakes that were baking while a bed was being prepared for him. However, he was so worried about a forthcoming battle that he paid no attention and the cakes were burnt. Not knowing he was the king, the cook gave him a ticking off. Realising that the cakes were ruined, Alfred meekly apologised.

793 AD: Vikings sack the monastery at Lindisfarne in Northumbria.

866 AD: York is captured and becomes a Viking stronghold.

876 AD: Vikings settle permanently in England and spend their lives farming.

VIKING LIFE AND BELIEFS

Although they could look quite fierce when ready for battle, many of the Viking settlers were content just to be farmers. Christianity was already widespread in Britain, but they carried on worshipping their own gods and goddesses.

DAILY LIFE

Most of the Vikings who settled in Britain were farmers. In the fields, they grew oats, barley and wheat, using iron tools to harvest the crops. They used the grain to make flour, porridge and beer. They grew vegetables such as onions, beans and cabbages and kept pigs, sheep, goats, cattle, geese and chickens.

The Vikings' clothes were similar to Celtic clothes. Men wore tunics over trousers while women had long dresses.

Viking toilets were less pleasant than Roman ones. They just used a ditch, dug some distance from the house, and collected river or stream water for washing.

INTERESTING

Like Celtic houses, Viking houses usually consisted of just one large room. Bigger houses might have had an entrance hall and separate kitchen and bedrooms. They could be made of wattle and daub, though they sometimes used stone instead. The floor would be dug out, so you stepped down into the house.

1984: The Jorvik Viking Centre is opened by the York Archaeological Trust.

2008: Archaeologists excavate a Viking burial pit near Weymouth.

2011: Fragments of a Viking chieftain's burial ship are found in Scotland.

A HEALTHY DIET

Apart from meat, both from the animals they farmed and the wild ones they could hunt, the Vikings ate fruit and vegetables, which they grew themselves, and nuts and berries that they could find in the forest. They made bread from rye and barley flour and made cheese from cows' milk. Vikings also kept bees and used the honey not only as a sweetener but also to make mead – a strong alcoholic drink. They sometimes drank this out of cow horns.

TOYS AND GAMES

Children had dolls and toy boats to play with and also played football. Toys were made out of wood or animal bones. Grown-ups liked swimming, wrestling and horse-riding. Everybody could play *hnefatafl* ("king's table"), a board game that was a bit like chess.

VIKING RELIGION

The Vikings worshipped a number of different gods and goddesses.

Odin was the chief god. **Thor**, god of thunder, was one of Odin's sons. **Loki** was something of a troublemaker – but he was clever and often solved problems for the other gods.

Odin's wife **Freya** was the goddess of war and death. As the goddess of spring and youth, **Idun** was especially important. The goddess **Hel** ruled over the land of the dead.

ODIN

THOR

DID YOU KNOW?

Mead made from honey was the Viking god Odin's preferred drink!

VALHALLA

Vikings believed that warriors killed in battle were taken to a great hall named Valhalla, where they were waited on as they feasted at a long table. Odin sent the Valkyrie, who were warrior maidens, to gather up the dead from the battlefield.

AWESOME FACT

The dead were often buried with some of their belongings. If the person was a chief, these might include jewellery and weapons, and even dogs and horses.

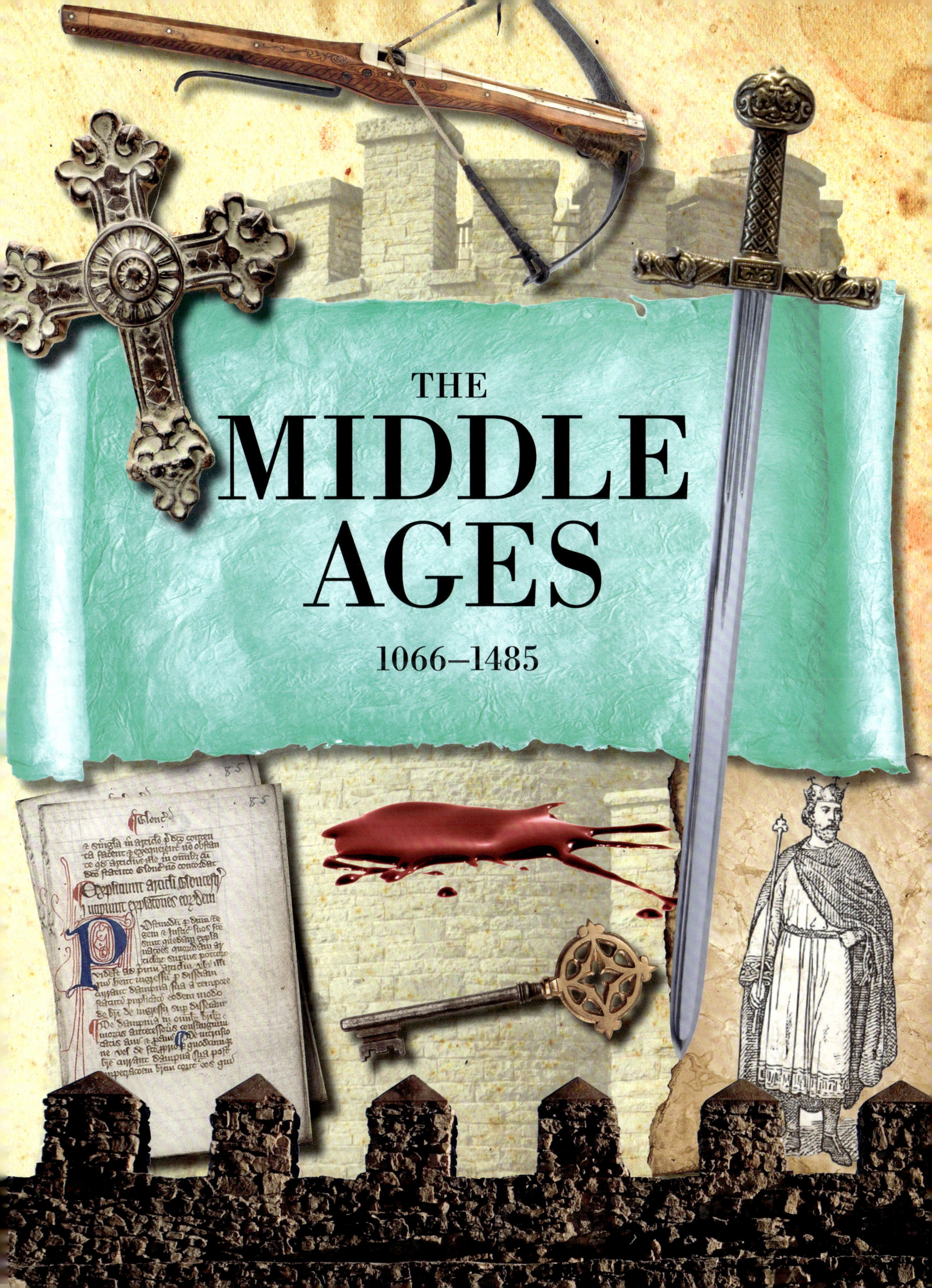
THE
MIDDLE
AGES
1066–1485

1066: William of Normandy invades England and wins the Battle of Hastings.

1072: Having conquered England, William invades Scotland.

1081: William the Conqueror enters Wales on another military campaign.

The Norman Conquest

The Normans, who came over to Britain from northern France, did much to change Britain. Not only did they introduce new words to the language, but they also created a new aristocracy and way of life.

WILLIAM THE CONQUEROR

In 1066, Edward the Confessor, King of England, died. He had no children of his own, and so Harold, Earl of Wessex, was crowned as his successor. However, William, Duke of Normandy (c.1028–c.1087), who was a distant cousin of Edward's, claimed that Edward had promised him the crown instead. He decided to invade England and seize the throne for himself.

THE BATTLE OF HASTINGS

William landed in England in 1066 and set up camp near Hastings. At the same time, England was invaded from the north by Harold Hardrada, the King of Norway. The English Harold headed to York to meet him. Hardrada won the first battle, at Fulford, but a few days later Harold defeated the invaders at the Battle of Stamford Bridge. Harold returned south to confront William. On 14 October 1066, the English and Norman armies met on the battlefield.They fought all day but the English lost when Harold was killed, and William was proclaimed king.

COOL FACTS

- William was very tall for a man of this period – about 175cm (5ft 10in).
- He was crowned on Christmas Day 1066 in Westminster Abbey.
- William never learnt to speak English properly, so French was spoken at his court.
- Later in life, William put on weight – some people said he looked as though he was about to give birth!

1083: Matilda of Flanders, William the Conqueror's wife, falls ill and finally dies in November.

1086: King William orders the Domesday Book to be compiled. It is completed in little more than a year.

1087: William I dies at the priory of St. Gervase at Rouen in France.

The Bayeux Tapestry
This tapestry tells the story of the Battle of Hastings. William's half-brother Odo had it made to celebrate the Norman victory in Britain. Famously, it shows how Harold died in battle – an arrow entered his brain through one of his eyes.

AWESOME FACT

A Story Told in Stitches
The Bayeux Tapestry is actually an embroidery, not a tapestry. At 70m (230ft) long, it is the longest piece of embroidery in the world.

INTERESTING

A New Nobility
William created a new governing class made up of the Norman aristocracy and some prominent English people. Even today, many titled people claim to have "come over with the Conqueror".

A NEW ERA

William was determined to bring stability to Britain. He invaded Scotland in 1072 and made a truce with the Scottish king. He entered Wales in 1081, creating "Marcher" counties along the borders. Once he had established a government he felt he could trust, he returned to Normandy.

The Domesday Book
In 1086, as a further mark of his authority, William ordered a census to be carried out. This was to be a record of who owned what in the country, so there could be no arguments over how much tax they should pay. The information was written down in the Domesday Book. The book survives to this day in the National Achives at Kew, in London.

LIFE UNDER
THE FEUDAL SYSTEM

Life in the Middle Ages was organised around what is known as the feudal system. Once William the Conqueror had taken control of England, he divided it among his supporters, but made sure they had certain duties to perform.

THE FEUDAL SYSTEM

The feudal system was introduced to Britain following the invasion of the country by William the Conqueror in 1066. It had already been used successfully by the Normans in France for many decades. Although all the land was ultimately owned by the king, it was granted to the barons and knights in return for their loyalty and money.

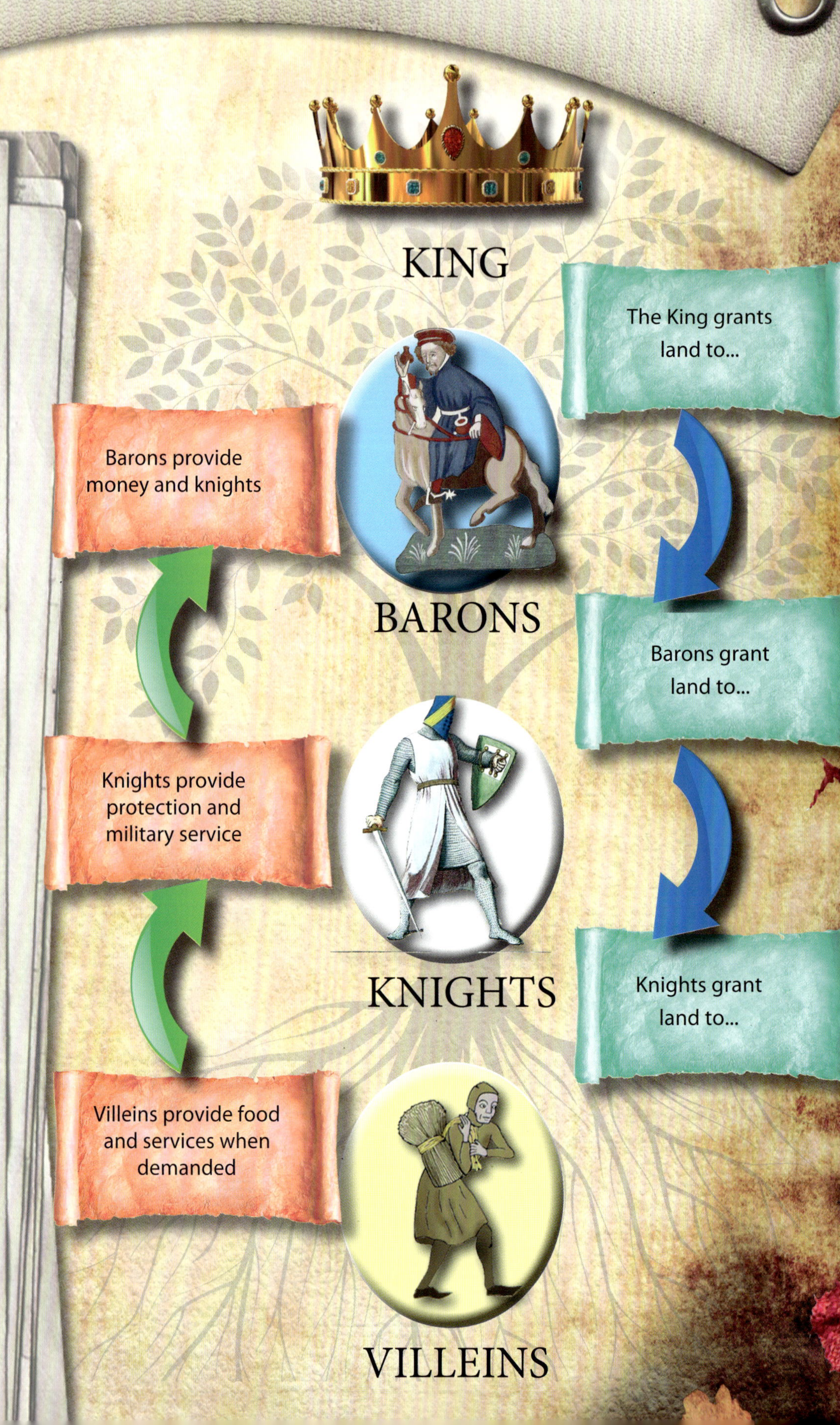

BARONS AND BISHOPS

People to whom William gave areas of land were called **Tenants in Chief** or **Barons**. In return for the land, they had to swear an oath of allegiance to the king – in other words, promise they would always support him. They also had to provide knights for the army for 40 days a year. This meant that nobody could ever build up a big army of his own and try and overthrow William. Some barons did not provide knights but paid the king a tax instead – this was called **shield money**.

Bishops also owned land and became very rich and powerful.

KNIGHTS

In turn, the tenants in chief divided their land into smaller areas that they granted to **knights**, who had to promise to serve in the army for 40 days a year.

The knights shared their land among the villeins, who farmed it. In return, the knights promised to protect them.

WHEN EVERYONE KNEW THEIR PLACE

The feudal system kept everyone in their place and allowed William to raise an army whenever he needed one without having to keep soldiers permanently at court.

Under the feudal system, barons were able to become very rich. They could mint their own money and impose taxes on all the people below them. But they also had to pay rent to the king and offer him hospitality as he travelled around the country.

Knights were also rich, but not as rich as the barons. They had to protect the baron – and the manor – from attack.

VILLEINS – A LIFE OF SERVITUDE

The **villeins**, also known as serfs, did all the work. Mainly working in the fields, they provided the knights with food and service. They were allowed to keep a small amount of the food they produced to feed themselves but otherwise had no rights.

While it was a hard life for most of them, some were able to earn money by becoming carpenters, bakers or blacksmiths.

THE POWER OF THE CHURCH AND MONASTERIES

At this time, the Church was immensely rich and powerful. Although kings ruled countries, it was believed that all the land actually belonged to God. As God's representative on earth, the Pope was therefore the most powerful person in the world and could tell kings what to do. Bishops and archbishops had great influence, as there was always the chance that they might one day become the Pope.

AWESOME FACT

Wealthy Monasteries

While monks were fairly lowly, the monasteries often owned vast areas of land, managed by the abbots, who became very rich.

1075–79: A keep is built in London that later becomes the Tower of London.

1083: Work begins on Ely Cathedral.

1093: The cathedral at Winchester, in Hampshire, is consecrated.

GREAT NORMAN CASTLES AND CATHEDRALS

The Normans were great builders. William had hundreds of castles built to help maintain his control and authority. At the same time, work started on several important cathedrals throughout the land.

CASTLE CONSTRUCTION

Castles were built on hills or on specially made mounds called mottes. This made it easy to spot invaders from all sides. The sides were steep, so the enemy would find it difficult to climb up – especially as arrows would be raining down on their heads from soldiers inside the castle.

There would usually be a central look-out tower, which was often square, called a keep. At the bottom of the motte would be a circular area called the bailey, where all the workers lived in small huts.

Around the motte a ditch would be dug that could be filled with water – this was a **moat** for keeping enemies out. Most Norman castles survive only as ruins.

ROCHESTER CATHEDRAL

CORFE CASTLE

DURHAM CATHEDRAL

People who lived in a castle would come in and out by means of a drawbridge over the moat that could be pulled up once they were safely inside.

1118: Building work starts on a cathedral at Peterborough in Cambridgeshire.

1121: Henry I marries Adela of Louvain at Windsor Castle in Berkshire.

1180s: Henry II commissions White Castle in Monmouthshire in Wales.

AWESOME FACT

William the Conqueror's son, William Rufus, was buried in Winchester Cathedral in 1100.

COOL FACTS

Prominent Castles and Cathedrals

- **Rochester Castle** has the tallest keep in England at around 35m (115ft). The walls are up to 4m (13ft) thick in places.
- **Pickering Castle** in Yorkshire was used by later kings as a holiday home.
- **Corfe Castle** in Dorset was built on the site of an earlier Saxon hall.
- Work on **Ely Cathedral** began in 1083 on the site of a convent. Many statues, carvings and stained-glass windows were destroyed when Henry VIII dissolved the monasteries after breaking from Rome.
- **Peterborough Cathedral** was originally called St. Peter's Cathedral. Building began in 1118 and took 120 years to complete.
- **Rochester Cathedral** was begun in 1077 and contains a crypt that still bears the graffiti left by Simon de Montfort's soldiers when they attacked the building in 1264.
- **Durham Cathedral** was begun in 1093 and largely completed within 40 years. While most cathedrals have been added to and rebuilt over the years, Durham's is the only one in England that has kept almost all of its original Norman craftsmanship.
- There has been an important church in **Winchester** since the 7th century. After the Norman Conquest, William's royal chaplain, Walkelin, had the old building demolished and replaced with a new one. The new cathedral was consecrated in 1093 with a great ceremony attended by nearly all of England's bishops and abbots.

"Will no one rid me of this turbulent priest?"
Thomas Becket was Henry II's Chancellor and good friend. Henry made Becket Archbishop of Canterbury in 1161. But Becket started to live a simpler life and stood up for the church in disagreements with the king. Late in 1170, four knights, believing they were acting on the king's wishes, murdered Becket in Canterbury Cathedral.

INTERESTING

Thomas Becket was made a saint in 1173 and his shrine in Canterbury Cathedral was often visited by pilgrims.

The murder of Thomas Becket in Canterbury Cathedral.

LIFE IN A NORMAN CASTLE

Norman castles were built to last and to stand up to attack. They had very thick stone walls and narrow windows. For a lot of the time, they would have been very cold, draughty and dark places to live.

HOW WERE CASTLES ORGANISED?

The lord or knight lived in the **keep**, which was the strongest part of the castle, with his family. The keep had several floors, with spiral staircases in the corners for going up and down. The peasants or serfs who did all the work lived in huts around the castle.

The **ground floor** was used for storage. The most important room on the first floor was called the **hall** and served as the main living room. **Bedrooms** were on the upper floors. There could be a private **chapel**, or religious services could be held in the hall. Large rooms were sometimes divided up with screens to keep out the draughts.

High up in the keep would be **toilets**, in little alcoves, called **garderobes**. These consisted of wooden seats over a long chute over a cesspit or the moat.

Furniture was very simple. The windows would be closed with shutters or covered with animal skins or **tapestries**. Large open fires would be lit for warmth and people used candles for lighting. Instead of carpets, rushes or herbs would be strewn on the floor.

The Castle Kitchen

Lords and ladies who lived in castles liked to eat well. The kitchen was an important, often large, room where there might be several fireplaces used either for roasting meat on spits, like a big barbecue, or for cauldrons – big iron cooking pots that were filled with water. There would be an outside **scullery** for washing.

In the **bailey** outside, fruit, vegetables and herbs were grown. There might also be a fish pond and a few animals for slaughter.

Norman Banquets

Magnificent feasts were sometime held in the great hall. The lord and his family – as well as any important guests – sat at a separate table, which was raised above all the other tables.

The Normans did not use forks. They ate their food with a knife and spoon. Also, instead of using plates, their food was served on slices of stale bread, called **trenchers**. After the food was eaten, the trenchers might be given to the serfs – the closest they ever got to a decent meal.

COOL FACTS

Norman Food Words

Many words that we use for cooked meat today are Norman in origin, including:

- **Beef**
- **Pork**
- **Veal**
- **Mutton**

INTERESTING

Garderobe means "guard robes", because people also kept their clothes in these alcoves. The bad smells kept the moths and fleas away!

1199: Richard the Lionheart dies after receiving a fatal wound in battle.

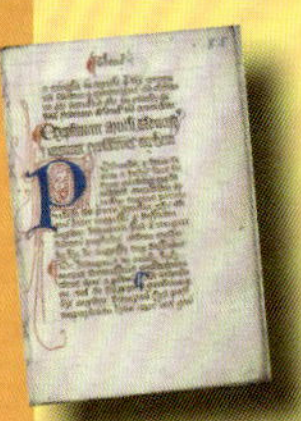

1215: The Magna Carta is presented to King John at Runnymede in Surrey.

1216: King John dies at Newark Castle, possibly as a result of deliberate poisoning.

KING JOHN AND THE MAGNA CARTA

The Magna Carta is probably the most important document in British history. Magna Carta means "Great Charter", and it established that the king had to obey the law just like everyone else.

RICHARD THE LIONHEART

Richard the Lionheart (1157–1199) is a famous king who ruled from 1189. However, he spent most of his reign outside England, fighting battles in the Middle East and France. He died from a wound to his shoulder in battle.

King John signing the Magna Carta.

King John (c.1167–1216)

KING JOHN

When Richard died, his brother John (c.1167–1216) became king. He too fought many battles, for which he needed increasing amounts of money. He expected the nobility to pay larger amounts of tax and confiscated church property, and then sold it back to the bishops.

The nobility felt exploited and decided to rebel. They took control of London and confronted the king. The Magna Carta was presented to him at Runnymede on 19 June 1215.

1219: The Magna Carta is translated into French. It was originally written in Latin.

1776: The American Declaration of Independence reveals the lasting influence of the Magna Carta.

1957: A monument is erected at Runnymede in Surrey to honour the Magna Carta.

THE MAGNA CARTA

The Magna Carta is a list of rights. The nobles thought that the king should follow the laws of the land just like everyone else. They told him that unless he agreed, they would no longer provide him with an army. He would no longer be able to arrest or imprison people, or take away their possessions unless they had been tried by their equals. This prepared the way for trial by jury, the system still in use today.

The Magna Carta established the principle that the people of England could limit the power of a king if he was not running the country properly.

Besides listing existing rights, the Magna Carta also added new ones. It guaranteed the rights of the Church and curbed some of the king's abuses of the feudal system.

Copies were made and distributed around the country. Four of these have survived.

Quote from The Magna Carta
"No free man shall be seized or imprisoned, or stripped of his rights or possessions, or outlawed or exiled … except by the lawful judgement of his equals or by the law of the land."

INTERESTING

The Legend of Robin Hood
Many stories are told about Robin Hood, who lived in Sherwood Forest, near Nottingham. According to legend, he robbed from the rich and gave to the poor. He is usually portrayed in green clothes and with a band of followers – his so-called "merry men".

While Robin remains a popular folk hero, he may never have actually existed.

1254: Edward I marries Eleanor of Castile. He becomes king in 1272.

1265: The Battle of Evesham is fought on 4 August in Worcestershire.

1270: Edward I leaves England in order to join the Eighth Crusade.

EDWARD I (1239–1307)

Although he is said to have been a sickly child, Edward I grew up to be a very strong-minded king. He was determined to establish law and order throughout Britain and fought many battles.

A groat containing Edward I's head.

EDWARD BECOMES KING

There were many uprisings during the reign of Edward I's father, Henry III (1207–1272). Edward was held captive for a while by the rebel leader Simon de Montfort. But he was able to escape and later won the Battle of Evesham, where de Montfort was killed.

Edward I (1239–1307)

EDWARD CONQUERS WALES

Henry died in 1272. As the new king, Edward was determined to get the better of the rebels, starting in Wales. He invaded Wales in 1277, defeated the Welsh leader Llywelyn ap Gruffyd, and built a ring of castles to help him defend the country. But many Welsh people still wanted to be independent, and there were more uprisings. Gruffyd was killed in battle in 1282 and Wales came under English control.

INTERESTING

Edward I was a tall man, about 188cm (6ft 2in). He had long arms and legs, and was often known as "Longshanks".

EDWARD INVADES SCOTLAND

In 1290, Margaret, Queen of Scots, died without leaving an obvious heir to the throne. Edward was asked to help find a new king, and he suggested John Balliol. However, the Scottish became unhappy about the alliance with Henry and made new one with France. Edward conquered Scotland, despite fierce fighting.

Edward I died on his way to fight Robert the Bruce on 7 July 1307 and was succeeded by his son Edward II.

1290: Edward I expels all Jewish people from England in the Edict of Expulsion.

1292: Edward names John Balliol as the future king of Scotland.

1301: The king's first-born son is proclaimed the Prince of Wales. He goes on to become Edward II.

WILLIAM WALLACE

William Wallace (c.1270–1305) was the leader of a rebellion against Edward I in 1297. He quickly gained supporters. After a battle near Falkirk in 1298, he escaped and went abroad. The leadership of the rebels passed to Robert the Bruce and John Comyn. Wallace returned to Britain in 1303 and was eventually captured, tried for treason and executed.

William Wallace
(c.1270–1305, executed)

ROBERT THE BRUCE

Robert the Bruce (1274–1329) had never supported John Balliol as king and allied himself with William Wallace. Both he and John Comyn had claims to the throne. Some time after Wallace's departure, they quarrelled and Robert stabbed John to death. He was then pronounced king, but Edward's armies forced him to flee. He later returned to Scotland to fight further battles.

DID YOU KNOW?

Edward II was very unpopular in England and he was eventually deposed in favour of his son, Edward III, who made peace with Scotland.

INTERESTING

After Wallace was executed, his head was placed on London Bridge and his limbs displayed in Newcastle, Berwick, Stirling and Perth.

THE BATTLE OF BANNOCKBURN AND AFTER

In June 1314 at Bannockburn, Robert defeated a much larger English army under Edward II (Edward I's son). But Edward refused to give up his claim to the throne, even though all the Scottish wanted Robert as king. In 1320, the Scottish earls sent a letter to the Pope, declaring that Robert was their rightful monarch.

1337: Philip IV of France confiscates Aquitaine in an attempt to secure France from England.

1340: Edward III starts calling himself the "King of France".

1346: The Battle of Crécy is fought in northern France. It is an English victory.

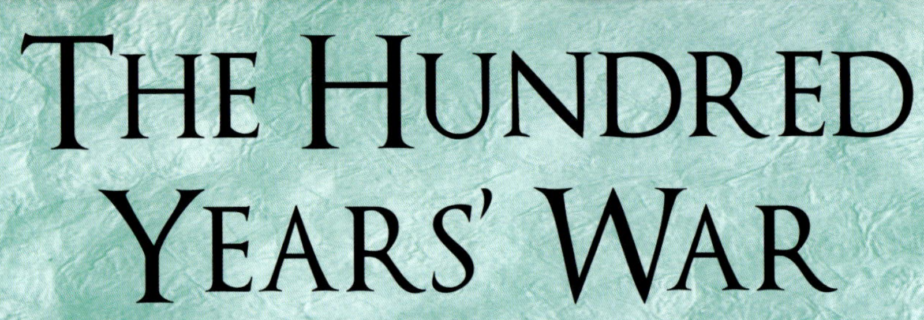

THE HUNDRED YEARS' WAR

A long series of battles between the English and French has become known as the Hundred Years' War. By the time it finished, there was nobody alive who could remember it starting.

The Battle of Crécy (1346)

HOW IT ALL BEGAN

The problems really date back to William the Conqueror, who already ruled Normandy when he invaded England. All his successors inherited parts of France, as well as England, making them very powerful – and also unpopular with the French kings.

To make things worse, French kings often sided with the Scottish during their battles with the English and supported the claim of David Bruce, son of Robert the Bruce, to the Scottish throne. There were many battles between the English and the French even before the Hundred Years' War began in earnest.

THE CONFISCATION OF AQUITAINE

Matters came to a head in 1337, when Philip IV of France confiscated Aquitaine, which Edward III (1312–1377) had inherited through Henry II. Edward responded by claiming that he was the rightful king of France himself and even started using the French royal arms.

In the early battles, it seemed that the English would be victorious, though they were often outnumbered. But because of the Black Death, neither side was able to win a clear victory, even after Edward died in 1377.

1356: The Black Prince wins the Battle of Poitiers. This is another great English triumph.

1376: Edward, the Black Prince, dies after a long illness. He is buried at Canterbury Cathedral.

1377: Edward III dies of a stroke. He is buried at Westminster Abbey in London.

SO, WHAT HAPPENED NEXT?

Edward III was succeeded by his grandson, Richard II (1367–1400), in 1377. Richard was succeeded by his cousin, Henry IV (1366–1413), in 1399. Henry spent most of his reign defending himself against various plots and rebellions in England, so had little time for fighting the French. In his later years, he had several serious illnesses.

Richard II (1367–1400, either executed or starved to death)

AWESOME FACT

Richard II was not very interested in war and, for a time, there was an uneasy peace between England and France. He may have suffered from a mental illness and was forced to give up his kingship. Historians are unsure whether he was executed or starved to death.

Henry V (1386–1482)

The Hundred Years' War actually lasted for 116 years.

THE END OF THE WAR

Henry IV's son, Henry V (1386–1482), who came to the throne in 1413, was more interested in continuing the war. He fought several successful battles and in the Treaty of Troyes was recognised as heir to the French throne. But he died in 1422, when his heir, Henry VI, was still a baby. This gave the French an opportunity to regain control. Eventually, Henry VI (1421–1471) gave up his claim to rule France in 1453 – and the war was finally over.

INTERESTING

Joan of Arc (1412–1431), sometimes called the Maid of Orleans, was a French peasant girl who had visions and heard voices. She believed that the Archangel Michael told her she would lead the French in a battle against the English.

At the **Siege of Orléans** (1428–1429), she won a great victory for the French. But she was captured in 1430, tried for heresy, and burnt at the stake in 1431. She was later made one of the patron saints of France.

1413: Henry V inherits the English throne from Henry IV.

1415: Henry V wins a famous victory against the French at Agincourt.

1422: Henry V dies suddenly, possibly from a bout of dysentery.

THREE GREAT BATTLES

Several battles that took place during the Hundred Years' War have become very famous and are still commemorated to this day. Even though the English were usually outnumbered, they still found a way to win.

The Black Prince (1330–1376)

THE BLACK PRINCE

The son of Edward III, also called Edward (1330–1376), is popularly known as the Black Prince – but the name was only given to him many years after his death. Nobody knows exactly why he was called "Black", but a possible theory is that he wore black armour and carried a black shield. He died before his father, so never became king.

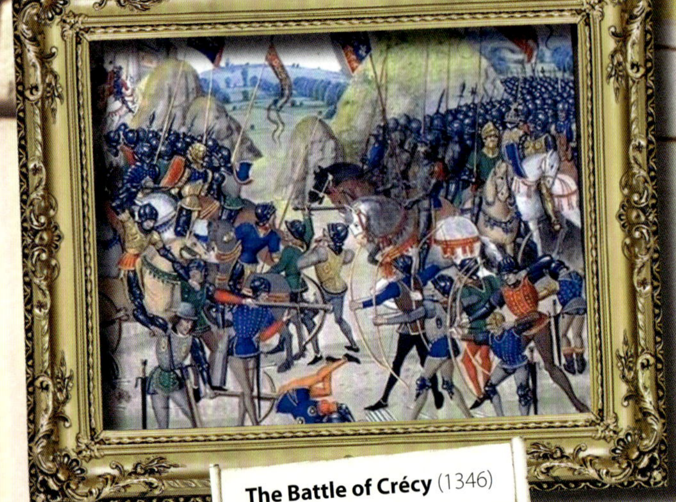

The Battle of Crécy (1346)

AWESOME FACT

During his lifetime, the Black Prince was known as Edward of Woodstock.

THE BATTLE OF CRÉCY

Crécy is a small village in northern France. In 1346 it was the site of a major victory for the English over the French. While the French army was much bigger, the English had better weapons – bows and arrows, swords and small cannons – and greater skill in using them.

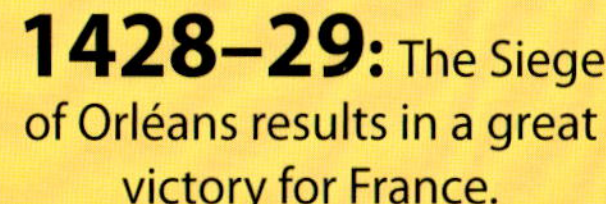

1428–29: The Siege of Orléans results in a great victory for France.

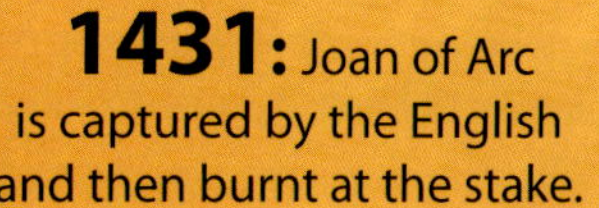

1431: Joan of Arc is captured by the English and then burnt at the stake.

1453: The Hundred Years' War finally comes to an end – after over a century of conflict.

INTERESTING

Crossbows versus Longbows
The crossbow is easier to use than the longbow, but more time is needed to load the arrows. English archers used longbows. Each archer carried 48 arrows that they fired at a rate of 10 per minute. Other soldiers would hand them a fresh supply of arrows so they could keep shooting. Their speed gave them a huge advantage.

THE BATTLE OF POITIERS

In 1356, the Black Prince won a great victory over the French King John II. Although the English had fewer men, they were able to occupy a better position on the battlefield, and the French became an easy target for the archers. When they ran out of arrows, though, it seemed the French might snatch victory. However, the English captured King John, forcing a French surrender.

The Battle of Poitiers (1356)

The Battle of Agincourt (1415)

THE BATTLE OF AGINCOURT

The Battle of Agincourt was fought in 1415 between the English king, Henry V, and the French king, Charles VI. Again, the English were heavily outnumbered but this time the weather played a major part. It had been raining heavily and the French cavalry, who were trying to charge, kept slipping and falling in the mud. The English took many prisoners. Fearing that they might be able to regroup and find lost weapons on the battlefield, Henry had most of them killed.

COOL FACTS

The Battle of Crécy:

- French forces numbered around 36,000.
- English forces numbered around 12,000.
- 7,000 of the English soldiers were archers.

The Battle of Poitiers:

- The French army numbered around 15,000–20,000.
- The English army numbered around 7,000.

1340s: Disease breaks out on the continent of Asia and is spread by rats.

1348: The Black Death arrives in England at the port of Bristol.

1349: The Scots take advantage of the disease and invade Durham.

THE BLACK DEATH

A terrible disease called the bubonic plague swept through Europe in the 14th century – it is commonly known as the Black Death. In the space of only 10 years, a third of the population was wiped out.

PLAGUE TREATMENTS

Medical science was not advanced. A frequent remedy for many illnesses was to cut a vein and allow the wound to bleed. Doctors found that when they did this to plague victims, the blood was thick, black and smelly. Patients would also be rubbed down with vinegar. Ointments were made with butter, onion and garlic, and even dried toad was used.

HOW THE PLAGUE SPREAD

The disease started in Asia in the 1340s and then rapidly spread to Africa and Europe. It was spread by rats living in the food stores on trading boats. The rats had fleas that carried the bacterium. So, if a flea bit you, you could die.

In 1348, the plague arrived in Bristol, which was an important trading port and the second largest city in England. It spread to London and East Anglia, and then found its way north.

The disease came in waves. Just as people thought it was all over, a new outbreak would occur. It was worse in towns, where people lived close together and there were no proper toilets. People just emptied their chamber pots directly into the street. Ditches full of filth and rotting meat attracted rats. The dead were buried in huge pits or piled up and burnt.

SYMPTOMS OF PLAGUE

First of all, red rings with dark central spots appeared on the arms and neck. There would be swellings in the armpits, legs, neck or groin that turned dark purple and black. People would feel feverish, then be sick and cough up blood. Death followed swiftly.

1349: The king complains to the town council about the state of London's streets.

1350: The plague breaks out in Scotland, as a result of the Durham invasion.

1361–64: The disease returns, with further outbreaks into the 1400s.

A JUDGEMENT FROM GOD

Many thought that the plague was a judgement from God. Since the priests seemed to be powerless, many people began to lose their faith in the Church. When it was all over, so many had died that there were no longer enough ordinary people to do all the work. Those in charge realised how important they were to landowners and decided that in future they should be properly paid for their work.

COOL FACTS

- In England, the plague raged from 1348–1350. Between a third and a half of the population died.
- A mass grave has been found at Spitalfields in London. It contains the remains of victims of the Black Death. The bodies were stacked in piles of five.
- *"Wretched, terrible, destructive year, the remnants of the people alone remain"* – this was carved in a church in Hertfordshire in 1349.

INTERESTING

During the Black Death, entire towns and villages were wiped out. Some were burnt down to try and contain the disease.

c.1343: Chaucer is born in London.

c.1366: Chaucer marries Philippa Roet.

1367: Chaucer becomes an esquire at the court of Edward III.

GEOFFREY CHAUCER

Much of what we know about life in medieval Britain comes from the writings of Geoffrey Chaucer, the first great poet who wrote in English. His writings are still read and studied today.

CHAUCER'S LIFE

We do not know exactly when Chaucer was born, but it was probably between 1340 and 1345, in London. He became a page to the Countess of Ulster. In 1359, he accompanied troops on an expedition to Brittany, where he was captured by the French, but was released after Edward III paid a ransom. The king later sent Chaucer to France and Italy, where he came across works by famous poets that later influenced his own writings.

Around 1366, Chaucer married Philippa Roet, a lady-in-waiting to the queen. Philippa's sister, Katherine Swynford, was the third wife of John of Gaunt, the king's fourth son, who was Chaucer's patron.

Besides writing, Chaucer was involved in many other projects and had a number of royal posts. He also worked for Edward III's successor, Richard II. Chaucer died some time after 1400.

Geoffrey Chaucer (c.1343–1400)

Canterbury Cathedral

THE CANTERBURY TALES

Chaucer's most famous work is called *The Canterbury Tales* and it is full of vivid characters. Chaucer began work on it in around 1387–1392. It is written in the form of English that was spoken at the time. For us to understand the tales today, they have to be translated into modern English.

In *The Canterbury Tales* , 29 pilgrims gather together at the Tabard Inn, in Southwark, near London, on their way to the shrine of St. Thomas Becket in Canterbury. It is decided that each pilgrim should tell two stories on the way to Canterbury and two on the way back. The best storyteller will receive a free meal, paid for by the other pilgrims.

1373: Chaucer visits Florence and Genoa in Italy.

c.1400: Chaucer dies of unknown causes.

1478: William Caxton prints the first edition of *The Canterbury Tales*.

THE CANTERBURY PILGRIMS

INTERESTING

- Knight
- Squire
- Yeoman
- Prioress
- Monk
- Friar
- Merchant
- Clerk
- Man of Law
- Franklin
- Haberdasher
- Carpenter
- Weaver
- Dyer
- Tapestry-Weaver
- Cook
- Shipman
- Physician
- Wife of Bath
- Parson
- Plowman
- Miller
- Manciple
- Reeve
- Summoner
- Pardoner
- Second Nun
- Nuns' priest
- Host (Harry Bailey)

The Wife of Bath's Story

This is one of the most famous tales. Her story is set at the time of King Arthur. As punishment for a crime, Queen Guinevere sends a knight around the world, telling him to find out what it is that every woman wants. He asks every woman he meets, but each gives a different answer. He finally meets an old woman who says she will tell him if he then grants her a wish. He agrees, and she tells him that what every woman wants is power over her husband. Guinevere says this is the correct answer. Then the knight finds out the old woman's wish – which is to marry her. Luckily, she is a magic fairy and changes into a beautiful young woman.

DID YOU KNOW?

Chaucer is buried in Westminster Abbey.

MEDIEVAL GUILDS

In towns, growing numbers of people earned their living by having a trade – such as weaving or candle-making. They organised themselves into guilds so they could all agree on a fair price for the goods they made. They also took on young people as **apprentices**, so they could pass on their skills.

Merchants made money, not by making things but by buying and selling to someone else for a higher price – called trading. They set up **merchant guilds** and they made the rules for how business was to be conducted in the towns. Many merchants became very rich.

1359: The Statute of Labourers is passed, limiting the pay and movement of peasants.

1380: The poll tax is raised to a level that provokes rioting among the peasants.

1381: In May, a tax collector is driven out of the village of Fobbing in Essex.

The Black Death affected people from every level of society. Peasants who survived had a new sense of their own value – they felt they had been spared by God and were just as good as their lords and masters.

DID YOU KNOW?

Everybody had to pay the **poll tax**, which was supposed to pay for the army. This tax was raised in 1380. Married women also had to pay, even if they did not earn money of their own.

PEASANT RIGHTS

Before the horrors of the Black Death, a peasant could only leave a village with the lord's consent. But now, lords realised how much they depended on peasants to do all the work. Lords needed the peasants to till the fields and harvest the crops. Some tried to tempt peasants from other areas to come and work for them, by offering them more money. They then refused to let them go home.

At the same time the peasants started to demand higher wages. Some even asked for their freedom. This led to the breakdown of the feudal system.

1381: In June, Wat Tyler is killed after a confrontation with the king – he becomes a national hero.

1385: Jean Froissart describes the Peasants' Revolt in Book II of his *Chronicles*.

1593: Wat and other rebels are portrayed in an anonymous play, *The Life and Death of Jack Straw*.

INTERESTING

The Statute of Labourers

In 1359, the government passed a law that stated:

- Peasants could not earn any more than they did in 1346.
- Lords should not offer peasants more pay than in 1346.
- Peasants were not allowed to leave the village they belonged to.

The Statute of Labourers did nothing to solve the problem, especially when landlords started putting up the rents that peasants had to pay. The peasants became increasingly unhappy.

"When Adam delved and Eve span, Who was then the gentleman?"

Eventually, everyone had had enough. Under the leadership of Wat Tyler (1341–1381), the peasants marched to London to present a petition to Richard II (1367–1400). As they marched, they sang a song about Adam digging and Eve spinning. What they meant was that in the early days, everybody had to work, and there were no lords and ladies doing nothing.

The young king agreed to meet the rebels but was unable to do so, as a riot broke out. The peasants stormed the Tower of London, seized the Archbishop of Canterbury and the Lord Treasurer, who had created the poll tax, and cut off their heads.

The following day, they were able to meet the king at last. At first, it seemed the rebels would get their way. But the Mayor of London suddenly lost his temper and stabbed Wat in the stomach. There was another riot and several other rebels were also killed. Some promises made by the king were suddenly withdrawn. However, the hated poll tax was abolished and Wat became a national hero.

COOL FACTS

- Wat Tyler's full name was Walter.
- The rebels numbered over 50,000.
- Richard II was only 14 years old when he met Wat.

LIFE IN A MEDIEVAL HOUSE

Life could be very tough, with few comforts for the majority of people. When peasants started to get more money after the Black Death and the Peasants' Revolt, things gradually improved for them.

PEASANT HOUSES

Many ordinary people lived in small houses that consisted of a **single room**. The house had a frame made of sticks that looked like a tent. This was plastered with straw mixed with wet mud and manure, and then left to dry in the sun. It made a strong building material. If it was available, some houses were made of stone. The **floor** inside was just beaten earth and would be strewn with straw and probably some dried herbs as well.

Most houses were very cold in winter and hot in summer. Peasants could not afford glass, so the windows were just holes cut in the wall. Some houses might not even have a proper door because of the high cost of wood. **Doors and windows** were closed with curtains. Houses that did not have chimneys would have been very smoky in winter.

There was no need to lock doors and windows, as nobody had anything worth stealing – unless they had a pig, cow or chickens. To keep these safe, and to protect them from foxes and wolves, they would be brought inside at night. This meant that the house would be quite smelly. The **animals** would also bring in fleas and flies. But at least a cow in the room would help to keep it warm.

After the Black Death, when peasants had more money, they started to build larger houses of wattle and daub with proper **thatched roofs**.

DID YOU KNOW?

In London, there were some public baths near the River Thames that were called "stews".

TOWN HOUSES

Merchants who lived in towns started to use brick for their houses, or a combination of brick and timber (which were called "half-timbered" houses). These had proper chimneys and glass in the windows. The rooms at the top of the house, sometimes in the loft, were very small. This is where the servants would sleep. Wealthy merchants had very grand houses and enjoyed a good standard of living.

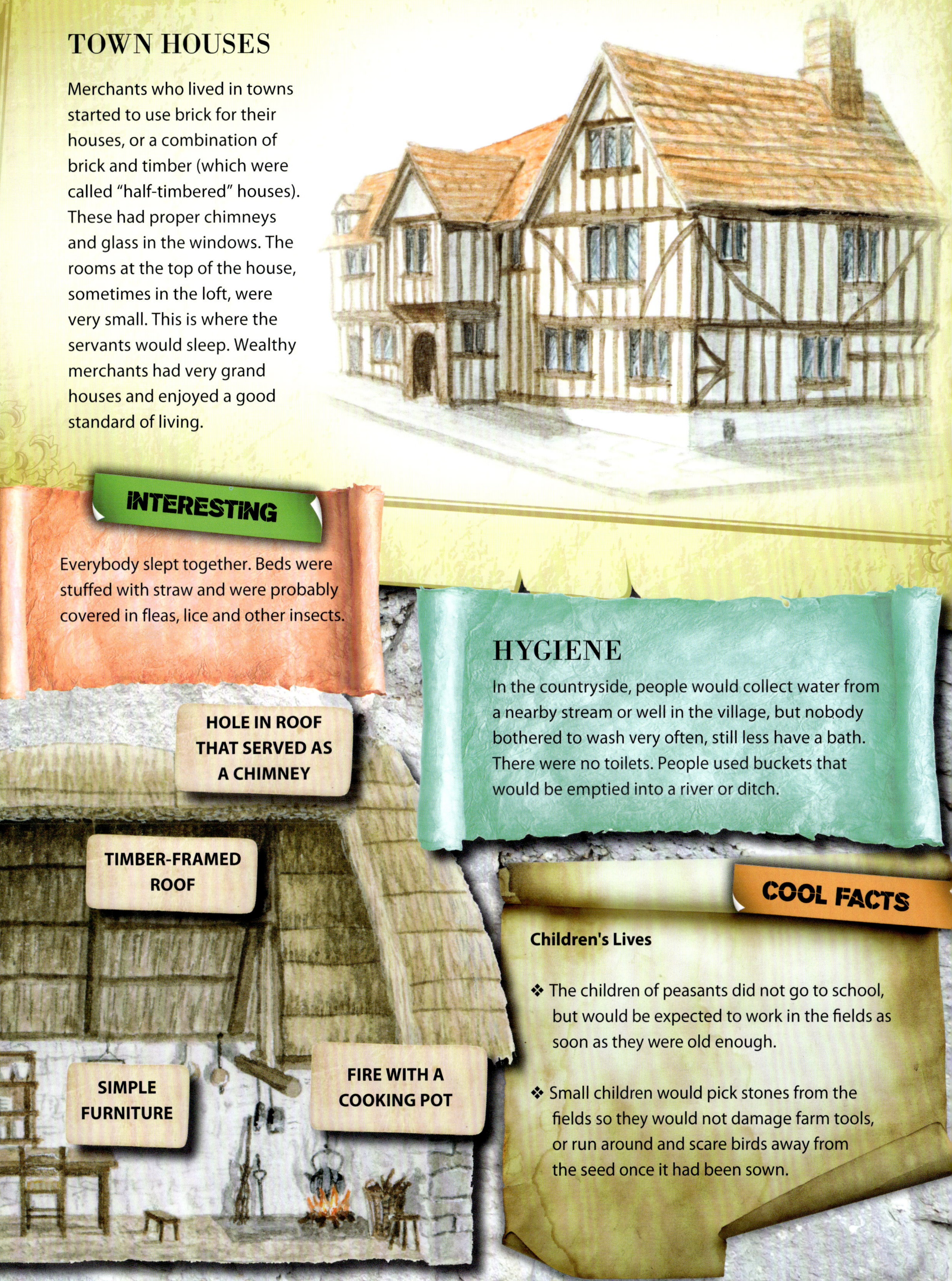

INTERESTING

Everybody slept together. Beds were stuffed with straw and were probably covered in fleas, lice and other insects.

HYGIENE

In the countryside, people would collect water from a nearby stream or well in the village, but nobody bothered to wash very often, still less have a bath. There were no toilets. People used buckets that would be emptied into a river or ditch.

COOL FACTS

Children's Lives

- ❖ The children of peasants did not go to school, but would be expected to work in the fields as soon as they were old enough.
- ❖ Small children would pick stones from the fields so they would not damage farm tools, or run around and scare birds away from the seed once it had been sown.

1421: Henry VI is born at Windsor Castle in Berkshire.

1429: Henry is finally crowned, just before his 18th birthday.

1455: The First Battle of St. Albans takes place on 22 May.

War of the Roses

1455–1485

Over a period of thirty years, one of the most turbulent periods in British history, two rival branches of the Plantagenet family fought the War of the Roses. There were many battles, but the Lancastrian Henry Tudor finally defeated the Yorkist Richard III and founded the House of Tudor, which ruled England and Wales for 117 years.

WHAT LED UP TO THE WARS?

Henry VI inherited the throne as a baby in 1422. Until he was old enough, his uncles ruled in his place. Henry was not crowned until 1429, only assuming full power in 1437 when his mother died. Henry was a gentle, kindly man who was unsuited to being king. Moreover, he suffered from periods of severe depression and his wife, Margaret of Anjou, ruled in his place when he was unwell. Many of the nobles were dissatisfied and thought that Richard, Duke of York, who also had a strong claim to the throne, would make a better king.

Henry VI (1421–1471)

AWESOME FACT

The Tudor Rose

The War of the Roses was so called because each of the rival armies used a rose as its emblem. A **white rose** symbolised the House of York, while the House of Lancaster used a **red rose**. Henry Tudor later combined both to create the Tudor rose.

1461: Edward of York is proclaimed king after the Battle of Towton.

1471: Edward of York wins a couple of important battles in the struggle for victory.

1483: Richard of Gloucester seizes the throne – to become the infamous Richard III.

INTERESTING

Richard – the Hunchback King

There are many stories about Richard III, which were probably invented after his death to exaggerate Henry VII's claim to the throne. He was said to have one shoulder higher than the other and a cruel expression. But, in his lifetime, he was said to have "a great heart".

COOL FACTS

Henry and Margaret

❖ Henry VI was the youngest person ever to inherit the throne. He was only nine months old.

❖ Margaret of Anjou was one of several powerful women during this period. She was famous for her beauty and was described as "passionate and proud and strong-willed".

Margaret of Anjou (1430–1482)

LET BATTLE COMMENCE!

Serious fighting began in 1455 at the First Battle of St. Albans. After further fighting, Richard retreated to France, but the Earl of Warwick, one of his supporters, captured Henry at the Battle of Northampton in 1460. Richard returned to England and was made Protector of England, but did not claim the throne.

Meanwhile, Margaret was building up her forces in the north. At the Battle of Wakefield in 1460, Richard was killed, and Margaret was able to move south and free Henry at the Second Battle of St. Albans. However, Richard's son, Edward, won a victory at the Battle of Towton in 1461 and was proclaimed king, as Edward IV. Skirmishes continued in the north and Henry was captured again in 1464.

However, Edward was not popular and made many enemies among his own supporters. The Earl of Warwick even tried to restore Henry to the throne. But Edward won two important battles in 1471, first at Barnet and then at Tewkesbury, during which Henry's heir, Edward of Westminster, was killed. The imprisoned Henry was murdered several days later.

RICHARD III AND THE PRINCES IN THE TOWER

This could have been the end of the conflict, as Edward was now in a position to rule unopposed. But he died suddenly in 1483 and his son, Edward V, was too young to succeed him. His brother, Richard of Gloucester (1452–1485), seized the throne to rule briefly as Richard III.

Edward V and his younger brother, Richard of Shrewsbury, were aged 12 and 9 when their father died. Richard of Gloucester was supposed to look after them until Edward was old enough to take charge of the kingdom. The two boys were housed in the Tower of London, but in around 1483, when Richard of Gloucester seized the throne, they mysteriously disappeared. According to rumour, Richard had the two boys murdered, though whether he was really responsible for their deaths has never been proved. Two children's skeletons were discovered in the tower in 1674 and reburied in Westminster Abbey.

1457: Henry Tudor is born at Pembroke Castle. He eventually becomes Henry VII.

1483: The princes in the tower, Richard III's nephews, mysteriously disappear.

1485: The Battle of Bosworth takes place in Leicestershire.

Henry Tudor and Richard III

Having seized power in 1483 Richard III was to find his kingship short-lived when a distant relative of Henry VI, Henry Tudor, who also had a claim to the throne, defeated him at the Battle of Bosworth on 22 August 1485.

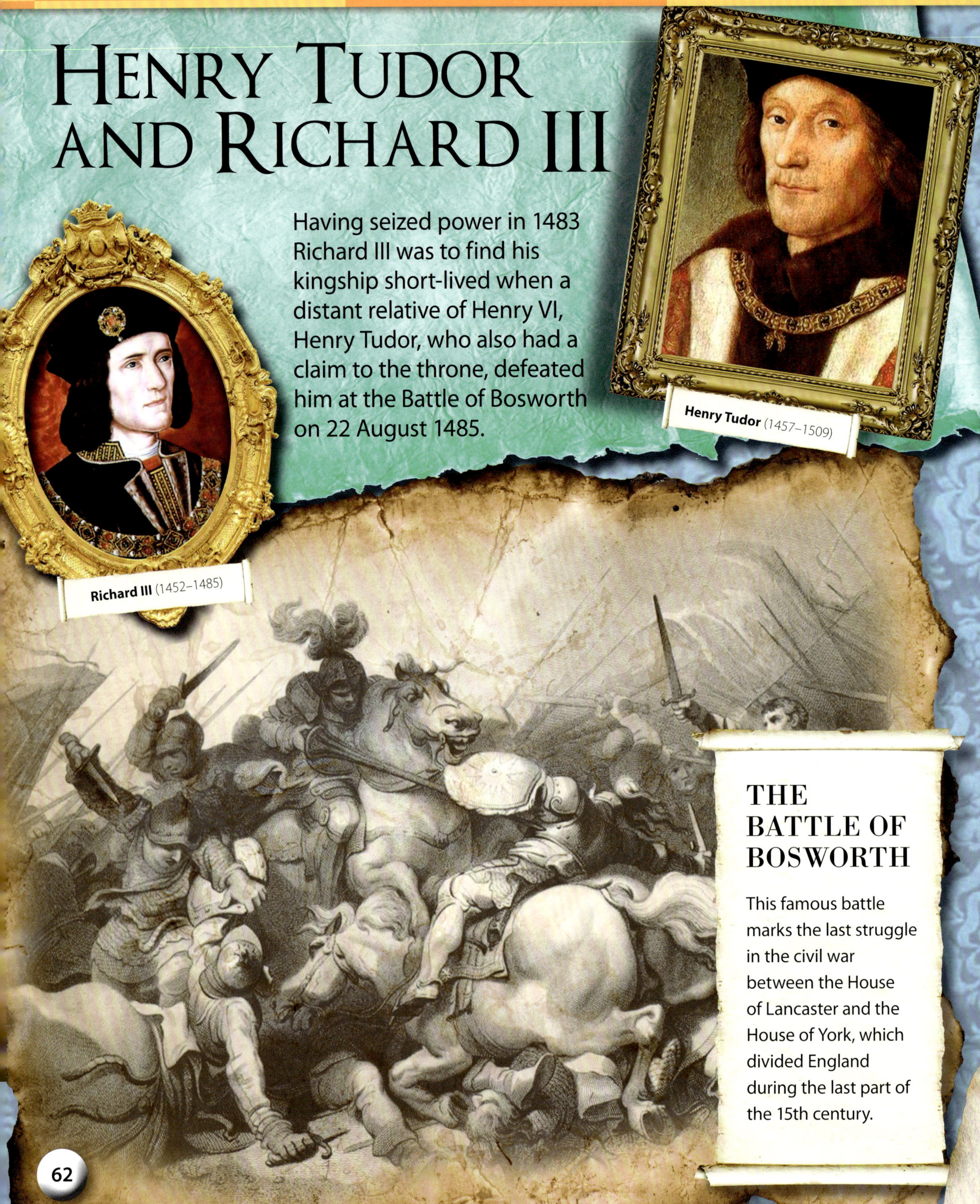

Henry Tudor (1457–1509)

Richard III (1452–1485)

The Battle of Bosworth

This famous battle marks the last struggle in the civil war between the House of Lancaster and the House of York, which divided England during the last part of the 15th century.

1509: Henry VII dies from tuberculosis at Richmond Palace.

1674: Two children's skeletons are discovered in the Tower of London.

2012: The body of Richard III is discovered under a car park in Leicester.

COOL FACTS

Henry Tudor – a Clever King

- To keep the powerful barons under control, Henry cleverly banned all private armies.
- Henry reduced the power of the barons by taxing them heavily.
- Henry enjoyed playing cards and gambling.
- Henry established the Court of Star Chamber, a group of loyal men whom he could rely on to help him control the barons.
- Henry arranged for his eldest son, Arthur, to marry the Spanish princess, Catherine of Aragon.

THE RISE OF HENRY TUDOR

Henry Tudor (1457–1509) and Richard III met to do battle on Bosworth Field in Leicestershire. Although Richard had the larger army, many changed sides during the fighting and he was betrayed when a group of men commanded by the Duke of Norfolk fled the field. Finding no support in the Duke of Northumberland, Richard risked everything by charging across the battlefield in an attempt to slay Henry Tudor, and so bring the battle to an end. Richard was surrounded and killed by Henry's men. His crown was taken and used to crown Henry later the same day.

Richard's body was laid out for a couple of days so that everyone could see he was dead. Henry Tudor was crowned Henry VII and married Elizabeth, the daughter of Edward IV, thus uniting the two families and marking the start of the Tudor dynasty – their son was the infamous Henry VIII.

A period of comparative stability ensued, though minor revolts and skirmishes continued until 1497.

THE KING IN THE CAR PARK

During an archaeological dig in a car park in Leicester in 2012, a skeleton was discovered. The bones were those of a man aged about 30 and were carbon-dated to a period around the Battle of Bosworth. DNA testing provided a match with one of Richard III's known descendants – proof that the skeleton is that of the famous king. Damage to the skull suggests Richard was most probably killed by heavy blows to the head.

A stained-glass window in St. James Church, in Sutton Cheney, in Leicestershire, commemorates the Battle of Bosworth. It shows Richard III on the left and Henry Tudor on the right.

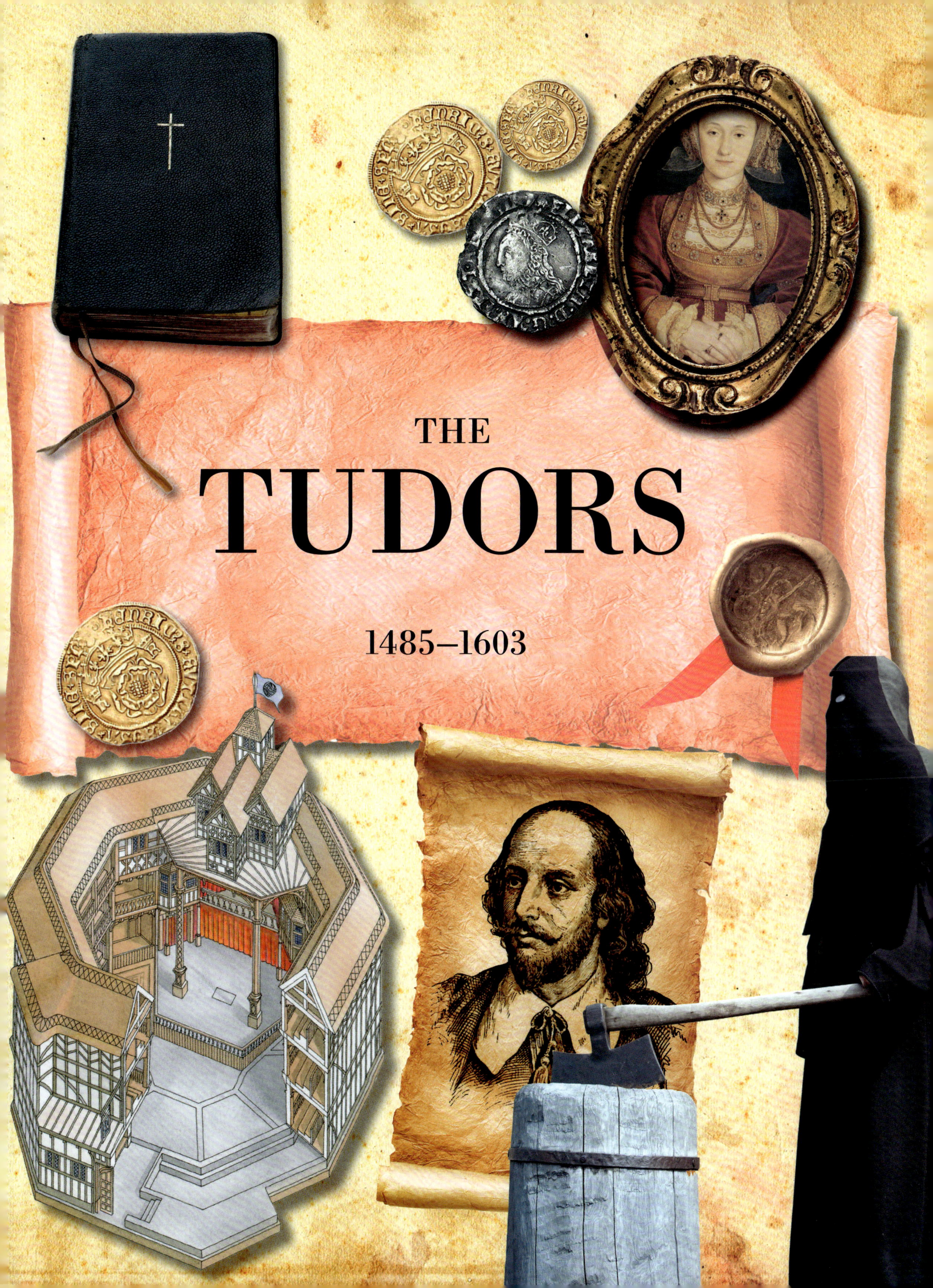

THE TUDORS

1485–1603

1491: Henry is born at Greenwich Palace, the second son of Henry VII and Elizabeth of York.

1509: Henry is crowned King of England at Westminster Abbey.

1513: James IV of Scotland is killed at the Battle of Flodden Field, in Northumberland.

HENRY VIII (1491–1547)

One of the most famous of all British kings, Henry VIII ruled England with absolute authority. Although Henry VII had brought stability to the nation by reducing the powers of the nobles, it was his son who cemented a union between England and Wales.

AWESOME FACT

As a young boy, Henry did not have to go to school. Instead, he was taught by tutors, learning French, Latin and Greek. Henry excelled at maths and writing poetry.

AN UNEXPECTED KING

Henry had an elder brother, Arthur, who was heir to the throne. Arthur was betrothed to a Spanish princess, Catherine of Aragon, as part of a treaty between England and Spain. They did not meet until she arrived in England in 1501, when Arthur was 15. They were married shortly after, while both were still children. Early the next year, Arthur suddenly died, so Henry was now heir to the throne. His parents were keen to maintain the treaty with Spain, but marriages to brothers' widows were forbidden by the Church. Luckily, the Pope authorised a marriage, which took place two days before Henry was crowned king in 1509.

Several battles took place during Henry's reign. At this time, Scotland was an independent country, ruled by James IV. In 1513, Henry invaded France, and the French king, Louis XII, persuaded James to invade England in his absence. Led by Catherine, the English defeated the Scots at the Battle of Flodden.

1520: Henry holds talks with the French king, Francis I, at the Field of the Cloth of Gold.

1536: Henry unites England and Wales to avoid a Catholic rebellion against his authority.

1547: Henry dies at the age of 55. He is buried at Windsor Castle.

The Acts of Union (1535–1542)

Parts of Wales were ruled by so-called Marcher Lords. The rest (the "principality") was governed in a similar way to England. Henry thought the Marcher Lords were not maintaining law and order. You could commit a crime in England, then escape to Wales and avoid punishment. Some of the lords supported the Pope, and Henry feared a rebellion. He passed a series of laws that united the whole of Wales.

COOL FACTS

- Henry's obesity and other medical problems may be traced back to a jousting accident in 1536 in which he suffered a leg wound. The wound festered for the rest of his life. The accident is believed to have caused Henry's frequent mood swings.
- Henry enjoyed many energetic sports, including archery, jousting and tennis. The tennis balls he used were stuffed with dog hair.

INTERESTING

Every Inch a King

Henry was very accomplished. He wrote music and poetry, and could speak several foreign languages. He also enjoyed hunting and hawking. The most famous painting of him, by Hans Holbein the Younger, shows an impressive man dressed in magnificent clothing

Cardinal Wolsey

One of Henry's most important advisers was Thomas Wolsey (1473–1530). As a young man, the king had limited interest in government, so Wolsey was able to become very powerful. He sidelined many others who might have challenged his authority.

One of the most famous Tudor palaces is **Hampton Court**. It originally belonged to Wolsey, but Henry confiscated it in 1529, after Wolsey failed to ensure the annulment of his first marriage. It became Henry's main residence.

1509: Henry marries his brother Arthur's widow, the Spanish princess Catherine of Aragon.

1533: Henry marries Anne Boleyn, formerly a lady-in-waiting to Queen Catherine.

1536: Henry takes a third wife, Jane Seymour, just 11 days after the execution of Anne Boleyn.

The Six Wives of Henry VIII

Only with a male heir could Henry VIII ensure stability for England. As each of his wives in turn failed to provide one, she was replaced – the exception being Jane Seymour.

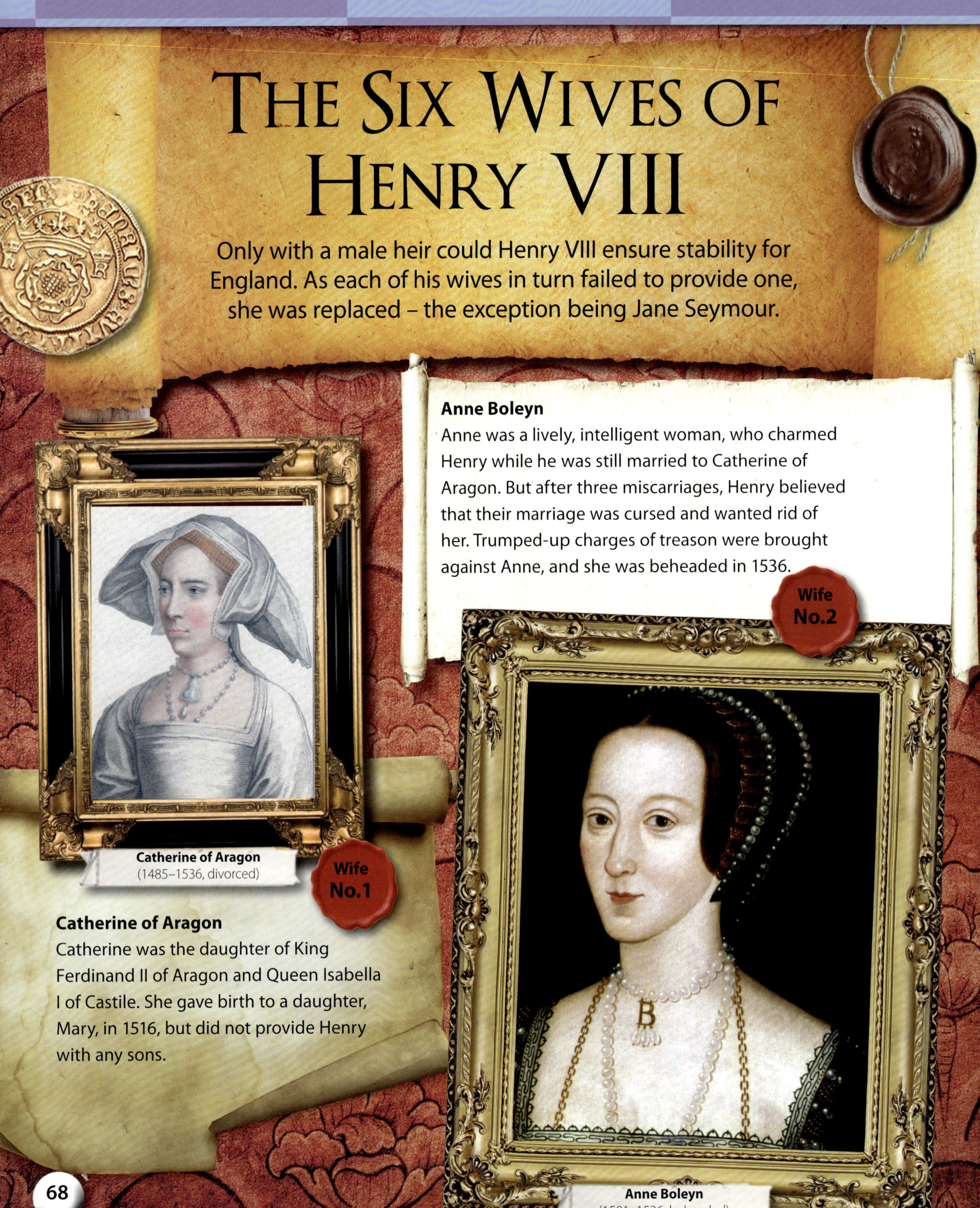

Anne Boleyn

Anne was a lively, intelligent woman, who charmed Henry while he was still married to Catherine of Aragon. But after three miscarriages, Henry believed that their marriage was cursed and wanted rid of her. Trumped-up charges of treason were brought against Anne, and she was beheaded in 1536.

Catherine of Aragon
(1485–1536, divorced)

Catherine of Aragon

Catherine was the daughter of King Ferdinand II of Aragon and Queen Isabella I of Castile. She gave birth to a daughter, Mary, in 1516, but did not provide Henry with any sons.

Anne Boleyn
(1501–1536, beheaded)

1540: Anne of Cleeves, a German princess, marries Henry but they are divorced shortly after.

1540: Henry marries his fifth wife, the young and lively Katherine Howard, a cousin of Anne Boleyn.

1543: Henry takes the twice-widowed Catherine Parr as his sixth and final wife.

Jane Seymour
(1508–1537, died)

Wife No.3

Jane Seymour

Modest and quiet Jane was probably Henry's favourite wife. He married her the day after Anne's execution. The following year, she gave birth to a son, who became Edward VI, but two weeks later she was dead. Henry was heart-broken. He is said to have called out her name as he lay dying.

Wife No.4

Anne of Cleves

It was thought that the German-born Anne would make a suitable wife for Henry. The wedding took place in 1540 but the couple soon realised they had made a mistake and the marriage was quickly annulled.

Anne of Cleves
(1515–1557, divorced)

COOL FACT

"I Like Her Not!"

Henry was sent a portrait of Anne of Cleves before he met her. On arriving in England, he found that the artist Hans Holbein had flattered her, as she was plain and lacked accomplishments. However, she was able to leave Henry on good terms and with a generous settlement – and also with her head!

Katherine Howard
(1523–1542, beheaded)

Wife No.5

Katherine Howard

Katherine was one of Anne of Cleves's ladies-in-waiting. Young and attractive, she caught the king's eye. However, their marriage was not a success. Henry was over 30 years older and very overweight. There were rumours that Katherine was in love with Thomas Culpeper, a man she had considered marrying before Henry. A love letter was found, and she was imprisoned and later beheaded.

Catherine Parr
(1512–1548, survived)

Wife No.6

Catherine Parr

Catherine had already been married twice before when she married Henry in 1543. She was an educated woman who acted as governess to Henry's three children. After Henry died in 1547, she married for a fourth time, but died shortly afterwards.

1525: Hops for making beer introduced by Dutch farmers and first grown in Kent, England.

1526: The artist Hans Holbein moves to England to become Henry VIII's painter.

1545: The *Mary Rose*, Henry VIII's spectacular flagship, sinks in the English Channel.

TUDOR LIFE

In Tudor times, most people lived in small villages in the countryside. But there were several large, prosperous cities such as London and Bristol. While most people were poor, others enjoyed considerable luxury.

FOOD

Most meals included bread. Rich people often preferred white bread, while poorer people ate coarse loaves made from grains. Vegetables were only eaten when they were in season. In winter, choice was very limited. People mainly used cabbages, which can grow in winter, and onions, which can be dried and stored. Fruits, such as apples, pears, cherries and strawberries, were sometimes preserved in syrup to be enjoyed during the year.

Poorer people often survived on pottage – a kind of porridge made with peas, milk, egg yolks and breadcrumbs.

CLOTHES

What you wore was a good indication of your station in life. Rich people could afford very elaborate clothes made of fine wool, linen and silk. Women wore long skirts, while men wore doublets (like a jacket and often padded at the shoulder) and tight-fitting trousers called hose. Both men and women wore jewels and it was usual to complete an outfit with a ruff, a kind of stiff, lacy collar that encircled the neck.

Poor people had clothes that were loose-fitting and made of much coarser fabrics. Men wore knee-length tunics over trousers, while women had long woollen dresses.

AWESOME FACT

Meat was a staple part of people's diet. As well as pork, lamb, beef and chicken, they also ate badger, wild boar, sparrows and blackbirds. With no fridges, meat could not be stored but was often preserved by rubbing salt into it.

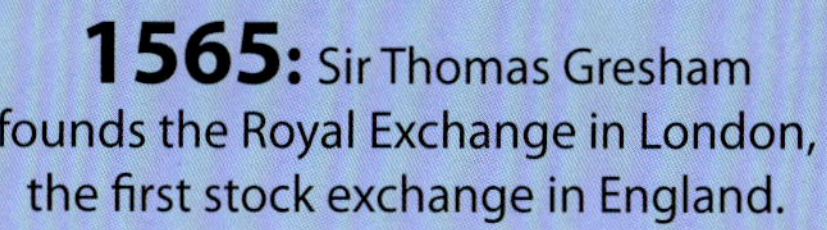

1565: Sir Thomas Gresham founds the Royal Exchange in London, the first stock exchange in England.

1596: The first flushing toilet introduced to Elizabeth I by Sir John Harington.

1599: The Globe Theatre is built by the River Thames in London.

CRIME AND PUNISHMENT

Crimes in Tudor times were punished harshly. Even stealing could result in execution. Most punishments were handed out in public, both to act as a deterrent to others – and as a form of entertainment!

Hanging was done with a length of rope tied around the neck. The criminal would be hanged until dead.

Women criminals were often **burnt at the stake**. Another barbaric death penalty was being **boiled alive** in a large tank of water.

Lesser crimes might be punished by public **flogging** or **branding** with a hot iron.

Stocks and pillories were wooden contraptions in which people could be locked for public ridicule.

Beheading with an axe was usually reserved for members of the nobility, as it was considered less degrading than hanging.

INTERESTING

Entertainment

People had to make their own entertainment. Rich people could enjoy hunting, jousting and tennis. Travelling players would perform plays or juggle outside inns in towns. Some Tudor entertainments, such as bear-baiting (where dogs would attack a bear chained to a post) and cock fighting, would be considered very cruel today. Simpler games of cards, bowls and skittles were also popular.

Life in **Tudor Britain** was **harsh:** the average life **expectancy** was only about **35 years**.

LIFE IN A TUDOR HOUSE

Most Tudor houses are easy to recognise. They had a timber frame and the bits in between were filled in with small sticks, which were then plastered with mud.

HOW WERE TUDOR HOUSES BUILT?

The **timbers** were often coated with black tar to protect them. The dried mud would then be painted white with **limewash**. The limewash could be coloured with bulls' blood, chalk, soot and charcoal.

Sometimes, the lower part of the house was built with brick. The **roof** would be thatched or sometimes it might have been covered with clay or stone tiles.

These black-and-white houses can often be seen in villages and sometimes in the middle of old towns. Many examples survive in Lavenham, in Suffolk. At the time, it was one of the 20 wealthiest towns in England.

In towns, the **upper storeys** of houses often jutted out, overhanging the ground floor. They are sometimes called **jetties**. Having a jetty meant that rooms upstairs could be bigger than the downstairs ones. In a grand house, the rooms for entertaining guests would often be upstairs.

DID YOU KNOW?

In some Tudor towns, the upper storeys jutted out so much that you could reach out of a window and shake hands with the people who lived in the house on the opposite side of the street.

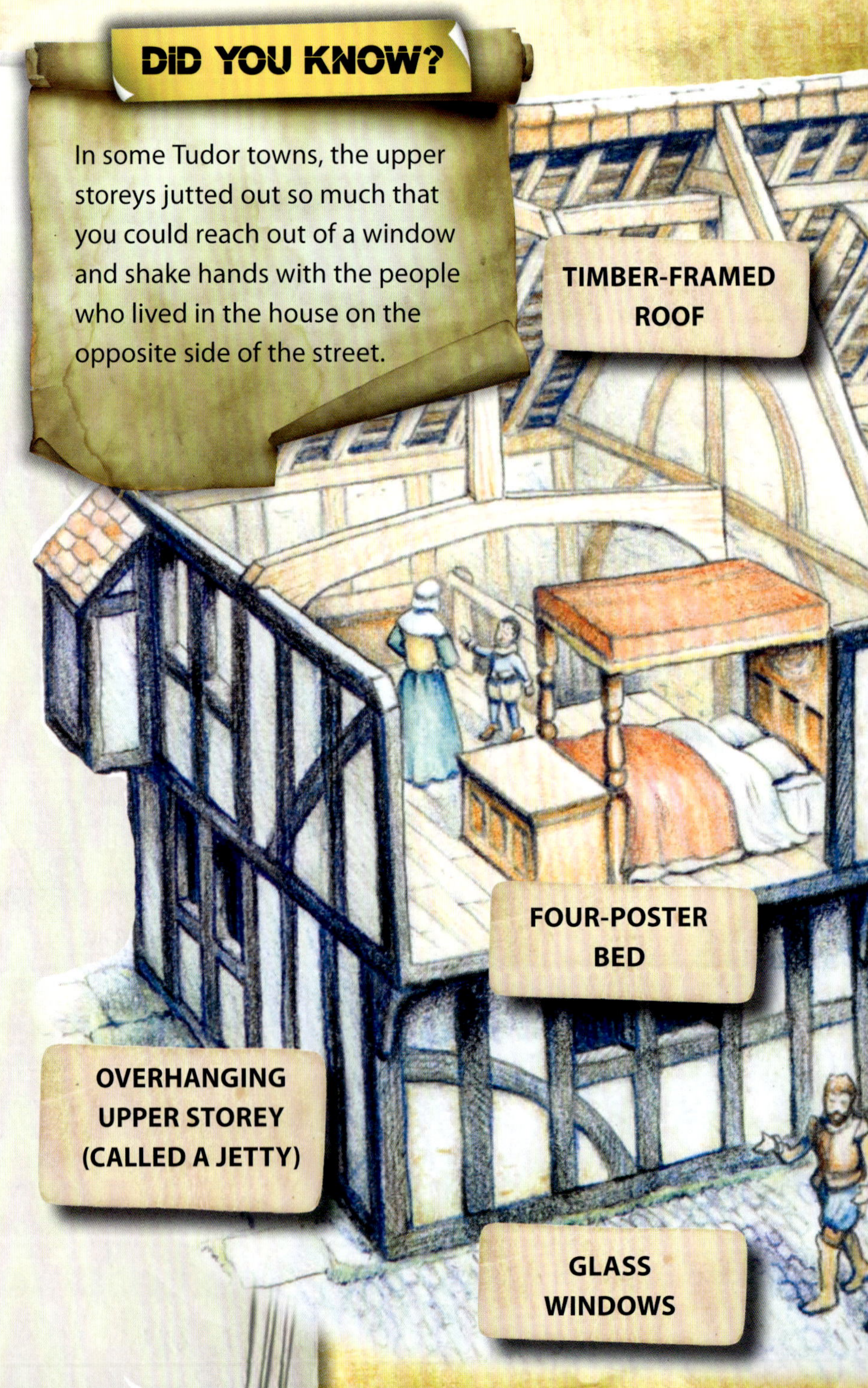

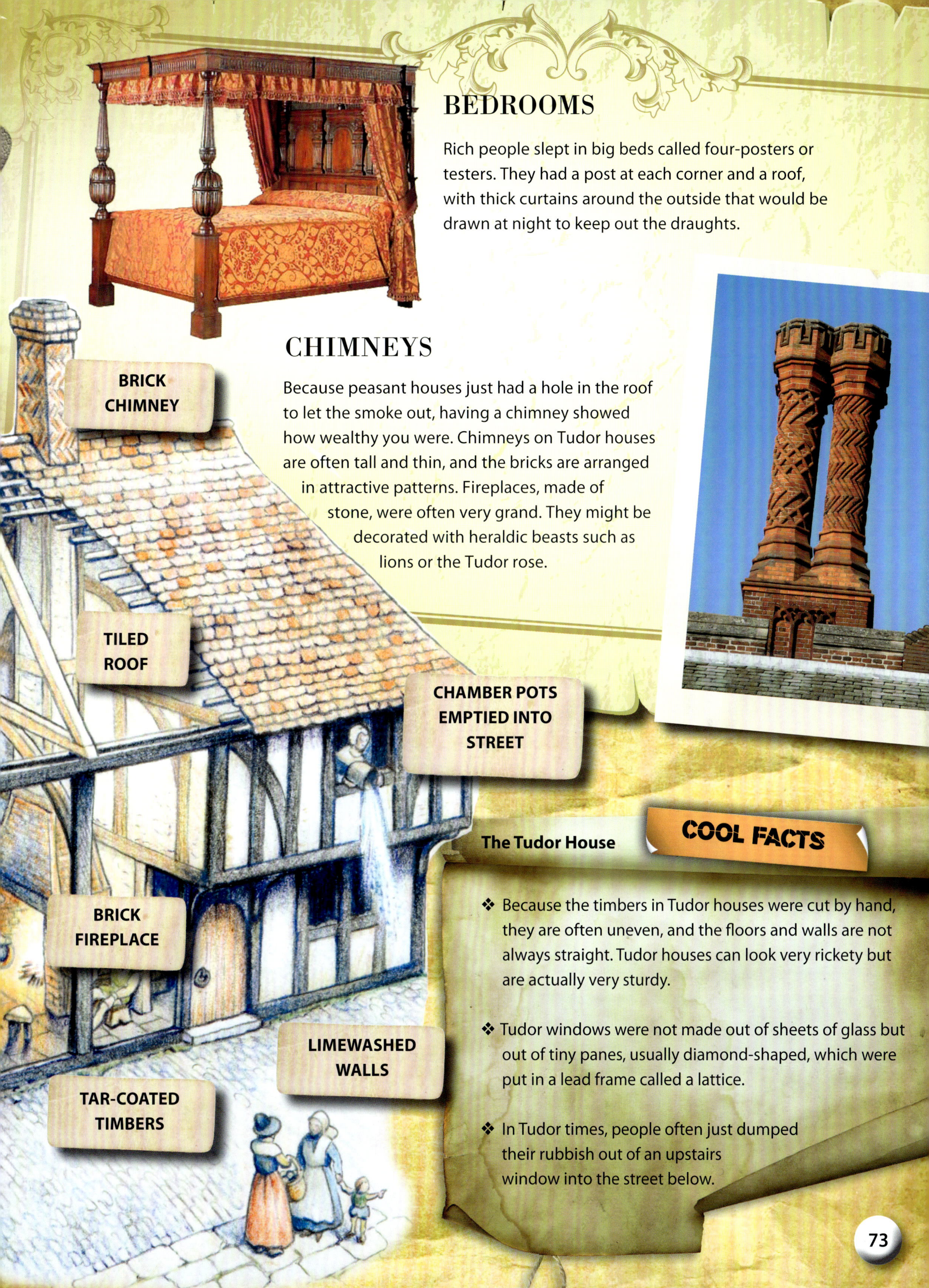

BEDROOMS

Rich people slept in big beds called four-posters or testers. They had a post at each corner and a roof, with thick curtains around the outside that would be drawn at night to keep out the draughts.

CHIMNEYS

Because peasant houses just had a hole in the roof to let the smoke out, having a chimney showed how wealthy you were. Chimneys on Tudor houses are often tall and thin, and the bricks are arranged in attractive patterns. Fireplaces, made of stone, were often very grand. They might be decorated with heraldic beasts such as lions or the Tudor rose.

The Tudor House **COOL FACTS**

- Because the timbers in Tudor houses were cut by hand, they are often uneven, and the floors and walls are not always straight. Tudor houses can look very rickety but are actually very sturdy.
- Tudor windows were not made out of sheets of glass but out of tiny panes, usually diamond-shaped, which were put in a lead frame called a lattice.
- In Tudor times, people often just dumped their rubbish out of an upstairs window into the street below.

1517: German Martin Luther's *95 Theses* marks the start of the Protestant Reformation in Europe.

1533: Protestant Thomas Cranmer becomes the Archbishop of Canterbury.

1534: The Act of Supremacy makes Henry the "Supreme Head" of the Church of England.

The English Reformation

Protestantism was a new form of Christianity, which began in Germany. Protestants at first wanted to reform the Catholic Church but ended up leaving it altogether to set up new churches.

THE BREAK FROM ROME

Henry VIII longed for a son to inherit the throne. Although he loved his daughters, he was afraid they would not be able to consolidate the Tudor dynasty, should one of them become queen after his death. He married six times, each time hoping for a baby boy. Henry began to think his marriage to Catherine was doomed because of the belief that a man should not marry his brother's widow. He hoped that the Pope would decide that the marriage had been invalid all along, freeing him to take a new wife. However, the Pope refused to allow a divorce, so Henry decided to take matters into his own hands. He declared his marriage unlawful and banished Catherine from court, at the same time creating a separate church, known as the Church of England.

Towards the end of 1532, he married Anne Boleyn in secret. The following year she gave birth to a baby – not the hoped-for son, but a daughter, Elizabeth.

The Act of Supremacy

An Act of Parliament in 1534 declared that Henry was "the only supreme head on earth of the Church in England". With this act, Henry abandoned Rome entirely, asserting the independence of the Church of England. In 1544, Parliament also conferred the title "Defender of the Faith" on Henry. Interestingly, this title had already been given to Henry by Pope Leo X in 1521 for a pamphlet he had written accusing the early Protestants of heresy. All later British monarchs have inherited both these titles.

THE DISSOLUTION OF THE MONASTERIES

Many monasteries were very wealthy and owned large areas of land. After the break with Rome, Henry VIII declared himself Supreme Head of the Church in England. Fearing that the monasteries might remain loyal to the Pope, he decided to shut them down (or "dissolve" them) and seized their assets – gold, silver and lead, as well as land. Some monasteries were allowed to continue but had to pay a large levy.

1536: The dissolution of the monasteries begins. There is an uprising against the reforms.

1554: Catholic Mary I, Henry VIII's eldest daughter, restores Roman Catholicism in England.

1558: Protestant Elizabeth I becomes Queen and makes a final break with the Catholic Church.

DID YOU KNOW?

Mary I

Mary I (1516–1558) was the only surviving child of Henry VIII and Catherine of Aragon. After becoming Queen of England in 1553, she attempted to restore Catholicism in England, burning over 275 Protestants at the stake. This earned her the nickname "Bloody Mary".

Mary I
(1516–1558)

The Great Bible

In 1538, Henry ordered the clergy to install "one book of the whole Bible of the largest volume in English" in every parish church. This was to be a revision of the bible then in use, usually known as the Tyndale bible, which was incomplete and contained some mistakes in the translation. The new bible was called "The Great Bible" because it was very large. Its production was overseen by Thomas Cromwell.

Thomas Cromwell

Thomas Cromwell (c.1485–1540) was Henry VIII's chief minister and a key player in the break with Rome. Cromwell made many enemies at court and fell from favour after arranging the unsuccessful marriage to Anne of Cleves. He was executed in 1540.

Thomas Cromwell
(c.1485–1540, executed)

1533: Anne Boleyn gives birth to Elizabeth at Greenwich Palace in London.

1558: Elizabeth is crowned Queen of England at Westminster Abbey.

1568: Mary Queen of Scots is imprisoned by Elizabeth in Fotheringay Castle in Scotland.

ELIZABETH I (1533–1603)

Poets called her "the fairy queen of the shepherds", but to most ordinary people she was just "Good Queen Bess". Though she was a popular queen, her reign had its own share of troubles and conflicts.

Half a Groat

The groat or fuppence is the name of an old English silver coin which is worth four English pence. Here you can see Elizabeth's head on the coin in the same way that Queen Elizabeth II's head appears on coins today.

ASCENT TO THE THRONE

Elizabeth had to wait her turn before becoming queen. Her half-brother, Edward VI, was only nine when he became king on the death of Henry VIII in 1547.

However, his reign was brief. He fell ill in 1553, naming his cousin, Lady Jane Grey, as his heir, rather than either of his older half-sisters, Mary and Elizabeth. It was feared that if Mary, Henry's daughter with Catherine of Aragon, came to the throne, she might attempt to restore Catholicism to England.

After his death, Jane was proclaimed queen. But supporters of Mary had her deposed nine days later. Jane was found guilty of treason and beheaded in February 1554, becoming known as the Nine-Day Queen.

When Mary I became queen, she did restore Catholicism to England. Followers of Protestantism, established when Henry VIII broke from Rome, were persecuted and often killed. She married Philip of Spain in 1554 but died in 1558 without producing an heir. Elizabeth was now queen, reigning for the next 45 years.

Although she refused to marry, Elizabeth had no shortage of suitors. Robert Dudley was a favourite and at one time it seemed that she would marry him. But her advisors thought she should marry a member of a foreign ruling family. In later life, Elizabeth became very fond of the dashing Robert Devereux, the Earl of Essex.

Queen Elizabeth refused to say who should succeed her after her death. Shortly before she died in 1603, she named James VI of Scotland as her heir.

INTERESTING

Elizabeth was the only child of Henry VIII and Anne Boleyn. Anne failed to produce a male heir and was executed when Elizabeth was only three years old.

COOL FACT

Elizabeth I's Coat of Arms

Here you can see the coat of arms of Queen Elizabeth I, with her personal motto: *Semper eadem*, which means "always the same".

1586: The Babington Plot to assassinate Elizabeth I is uncovered by Sir Francis Walsingham.

1588: Elizabeth makes her famous speech rallying the troops on the eve of the Spanish Armada.

1603: Queen Elizabeth I dies on 24 March. James VI of Scotland is proclaimed King of England.

AWESOME FACT

Elizabeth was often known as the **Virgin Queen** because she never married.

The Royal Progress
Elizabeth made frequent appearances in public and often toured England, staying at various castles and country houses. She was always very conscious of her image. Most paintings of the time depict her wearing elaborate dresses and with carefully styled hair. In later life, she wore wigs and heavy make-up. She was always a dazzling figure.

DID YOU KNOW?

Tudor Beauty
The Tudors believed a beautiful woman should have light hair, a pale complexion, and red cheeks and lips. Rich Tudor women used a mixture of white lead and vinegar on their faces as a sign of their wealth and status. Wigs were also popular: Queen Elizabeth had over 80 wigs and hair-pieces!

1564: William Shakespeare, considered to be the greatest playwright of all time, is born.

1567: Building work starts on Longleat House, in Wiltshire, taking 12 years to complete.

1577: Sir Francis Drake embarks on his circumnavigation of the globe. He returns in 1580.

The Elizabethan Golden Age

Elizabeth's reign is often considered a golden age in British history. Sea-going explorers opened up previously unknown parts of the globe, bringing great prosperity, the arts flourished, and many stately homes were built.

An Age of Exploration

Despite the difficulties and dangers of travel, the Elizabethans were keen to establish new territories overseas and to find new routes to other countries. International trade, especially in spices found in the Americas, became important.

Sir Francis Drake
(1540–1596)

Great Elizabethan Explorers

- **Sir Francis Drake** is the first known person to have completed a journey around the globe. Setting sail from Plymouth in 1577, he first went south to Africa, then headed west towards South America. He then crossed the Pacific before returning to Plymouth, arriving back home in 1580.

- **Sir Walter Raleigh** made several trips to North America from where he introduced the potato and the smoking of tobacco. He also named the state of Virginia in honour of Elizabeth I, the Virgin Queen.

Sir Walter Raleigh
(1552–1618)

Great Elizabethan Houses

Several palaces built during Elizabeth's reign are still standing, attracting many visitors from all over the world.

- **Hardwick Hall**, in Derbyshire, was built for Bess of Hardwick, who was the richest woman in England after Elizabeth. It is famous for its large windows.

- **Longleat House** is in Somerset. Its Great Hall contains a gallery where musicians would have played to entertain guests.

- **Montacute House**, which is also in Somerset, is one of the finest examples of an Elizabethan mansion. The Long Gallery is the longest in England.

1578: Sir Walter Raleigh sets sail for the Americas, returning to introduce potatoes and tobacco.

1590: The first half of poet Edmund Spenser's *The Faerie Queen* is published.

1599: Shakespeare's theatre company builds the Globe Theatre in London.

AWESOME FACT

William Shakespeare

Sometimes called the "Bard of Avon", William Shakespeare (1564–1616) is probably the most famous playwright who ever lived. He wrote history plays (some based on the Wars of the Roses), as well as tragedies and comedies, nearly all of which are still read and performed today. These and his poems are considered some of the finest works in the English language.

GREAT WRITERS AND MUSICIANS

Apart from Shakespeare, there were many other writers and musicians who contributed to Elizabethan culture. Sir Philip Sidney wrote lots of poems, many of which appeared in a collection called *Astrophel and Stella*. Edmund Spenser wrote *The Faerie Queene*, a long poem in praise of Elizabeth I. John Dowland wrote songs to be accompanied by the lute. Several refer to the queen.

THE GLOBE THEATRE

Many theatres were built during Elizabeth's reign. One of the largest was the Globe Theatre, which was built by Shakespeare's company in 1599. The circular, open-air building could accommodate an audience of around 3,000. Poor people would pay a penny to stand in the pit – the central area in front of the stage. Wealthier people would sit in the covered galleries that surrounded it, from where they could look down at the performance.

INTERESTING

A modern reconstruction of The Globe Theatre, built close to its original site, was opened in 1997.

1558: A fifteen-year-old Mary marries Francis, the young son of the King and Queen of Spain.

1565: On the death of Francis, Mary returns to Scotland and marries Lord Darnley.

1566: Mary gives birth to a son who later becomes King James I of England.

MARY QUEEN OF SCOTS

(1542–1587)

In the eyes of many Catholics, Elizabeth I was not the rightful queen. They thought that Queen Mary should have been succeeded by the granddaughter of Henry VIII's elder sister, Margaret Tudor, who had married James IV, King of the Scots.

MARY'S EARLY LIFE

This granddaughter, Mary Stuart, was born in Scotland but at a young age she was sent to live in France, where she later married the heir to the French throne, Francis. She became the darling of the French court. Francis became king at the age of 15, after his father, Henry II of France, was killed in a jousting accident, but he died the following year of an ear infection, leaving the eighteen-year-old Mary a widow.

Mary returned to Scotland, where she married Lord Darnley in 1565. Early in 1567, Darnley was found murdered, many thought by the Earl of Bothwell, who also wished to marry Mary.

INTERESTING

The Babington Plot

Mary was implicated in many plots to assassinate Elizabeth I and put her on the throne instead. The most famous was the Babington Plot of 1586, masterminded by Sir Anthony Babington, a leading Catholic nobleman. Letters revealing plans of a Spanish invasion were found, and the conspirators were arrested and executed.

1567: Lord Darnley is murdered, possibly by the Earl of Bothwell who Mary later marries.

1586: Mary is implicated among others in the Babington Plot to assassinate Elizabeth I.

1587: Mary Queen of Scots is beheaded at Fotheringay Castle in Scotland.

ELIZABETH MAKES A STAND

Elizabeth I was constantly in fear that troops would rally behind Mary Stuart and place her on the English throne. To prevent this, she had Mary imprisoned in Fotheringay Castle in Scotland. But because of the many plots against Elizabeth, Mary was sentenced to death.

Elizabeth knew that life would be simpler if she could get rid of Mary, but she was extremely reluctant to sign her death warrant. Henry VIII had beheaded two of his wives, but Mary was a queen in her own right, and her execution would cause an outcry abroad, as well as in Scotland. Elizabeth was eventually persuaded to sign. The execution was carried out almost immediately, against Elizabeth's wishes – she had hoped to delay it for as long as possible.

COOL FACT

When **Mary Queen of Scots'** head was cut off, it is said that her pet Skye terrier ran out from under her skirt where it had been hiding, refusing to be parted from its mistress.

MARY – A TRULY TRAGIC QUEEN

Mary was a tragic figure and her life was full of sadness and disappointment. Expecting to become the queen of France, she was widowed before she had a chance to enjoy the throne. Both of her later marriages brought only limited happiness.

A famous painting shows her wearing a white veil of mourning, after which she was sometimes known as "the white queen".

AWESOME FACT

Mary's Final Words

On the day of her beheading, Mary Queen of Scots showed great courage when facing her executioner. Her last words were, *"In manus tuas, Domine, commendo spiritum meum"* – which translates as *"Into thy hands, O Lord, I commend my spirit"*.

1527: Philip of Spain is born to Isabella of Portugal and the Holy Roman Emperor Charles V.

1554: Philip marries Queen Mary I (Mary Tudor) and is crowned King of Spain in 1556.

1558: On the death of Mary I Philip tries to persuade Elizabeth I to marry him – she declines.

THE SPANISH ARMADA

Philip II of Spain decided to invade England in 1588 to overthrow Elizabeth I. He sent a great fleet of ships, which became known as The Spanish Armada, across the English Channel.

A SPANISH INVASION

Philip II wanted to invade England for several reasons. He was angry that Francis Drake and other British seamen had attacked Spanish ships while on their voyages. At this time, Spain controlled the Netherlands, and Elizabeth was helping Dutch Protestants who were persecuted under Spanish rule. And, as a devout Catholic, Philip wanted to see the Catholic faith restored in England. With a much larger navy than Elizabeth, he felt sure of success.

As it turned out, the much smaller English ships had the advantage of being easier to manoeuvre. Philip's plan was to send his ships towards the English coast in a crescent formation, so that they would be able to fire their guns simultaneously, completely overwhelming the enemy. This had proved very successful in earlier sea battles.

Philip II
(1527–1598)

AN ENGLISH TRIUMPH

The English had a very cunning strategy to defeat the Spanish, however. While the Spanish ships were moored at Calais in northern France, they filled 80 ships with flammable material, set fire to them, and then sent them aflame directly into the crescent. Although no Spanish ships were burnt, they had to cut anchor and scatter in order to escape the flames – straight into the firing range of the English. With the Spanish fleet confused, the English now had a definite advantage.

The weather also played a decisive part. Strong winds blew the Spanish vessels off course, pushing them northwards. Many ran into rocks, while those that survived had to make their way around the coast and down the west coast of Ireland. Half of them never reached home.

INTERESTING

A Great English Victory
Spanish casualties far outnumbered English ones and Francis Drake became even more of a national hero than he was before.

1567: Philip II sends the Spanish army to quell a Protestant uprising in the Netherlands.

1587: Philip II gains the Pope's support for invading England – it becomes a Catholic crusade.

1588: The Spanish Armada is defeated by the English fleet, but the war continues until 1603.

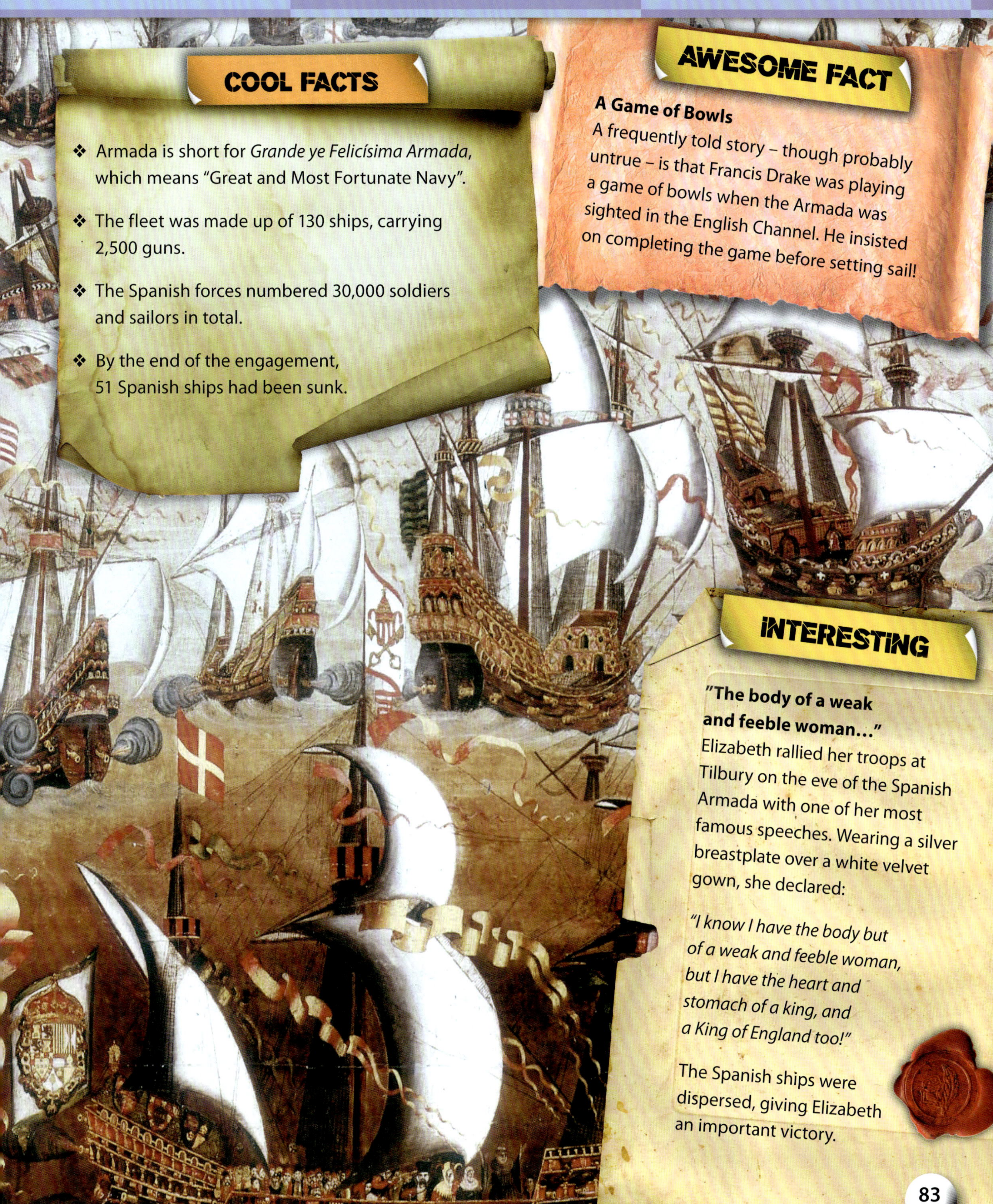

COOL FACTS

- Armada is short for *Grande ye Felicísima Armada*, which means "Great and Most Fortunate Navy".
- The fleet was made up of 130 ships, carrying 2,500 guns.
- The Spanish forces numbered 30,000 soldiers and sailors in total.
- By the end of the engagement, 51 Spanish ships had been sunk.

AWESOME FACT

A Game of Bowls

A frequently told story – though probably untrue – is that Francis Drake was playing a game of bowls when the Armada was sighted in the English Channel. He insisted on completing the game before setting sail!

INTERESTING

"The body of a weak and feeble woman..."

Elizabeth rallied her troops at Tilbury on the eve of the Spanish Armada with one of her most famous speeches. Wearing a silver breastplate over a white velvet gown, she declared:

"I know I have the body but of a weak and feeble woman, but I have the heart and stomach of a king, and a King of England too!"

The Spanish ships were dispersed, giving Elizabeth an important victory.

CHARLES 2nd
RESTORATION
1660
ESKI
XXX
GUN POWDER

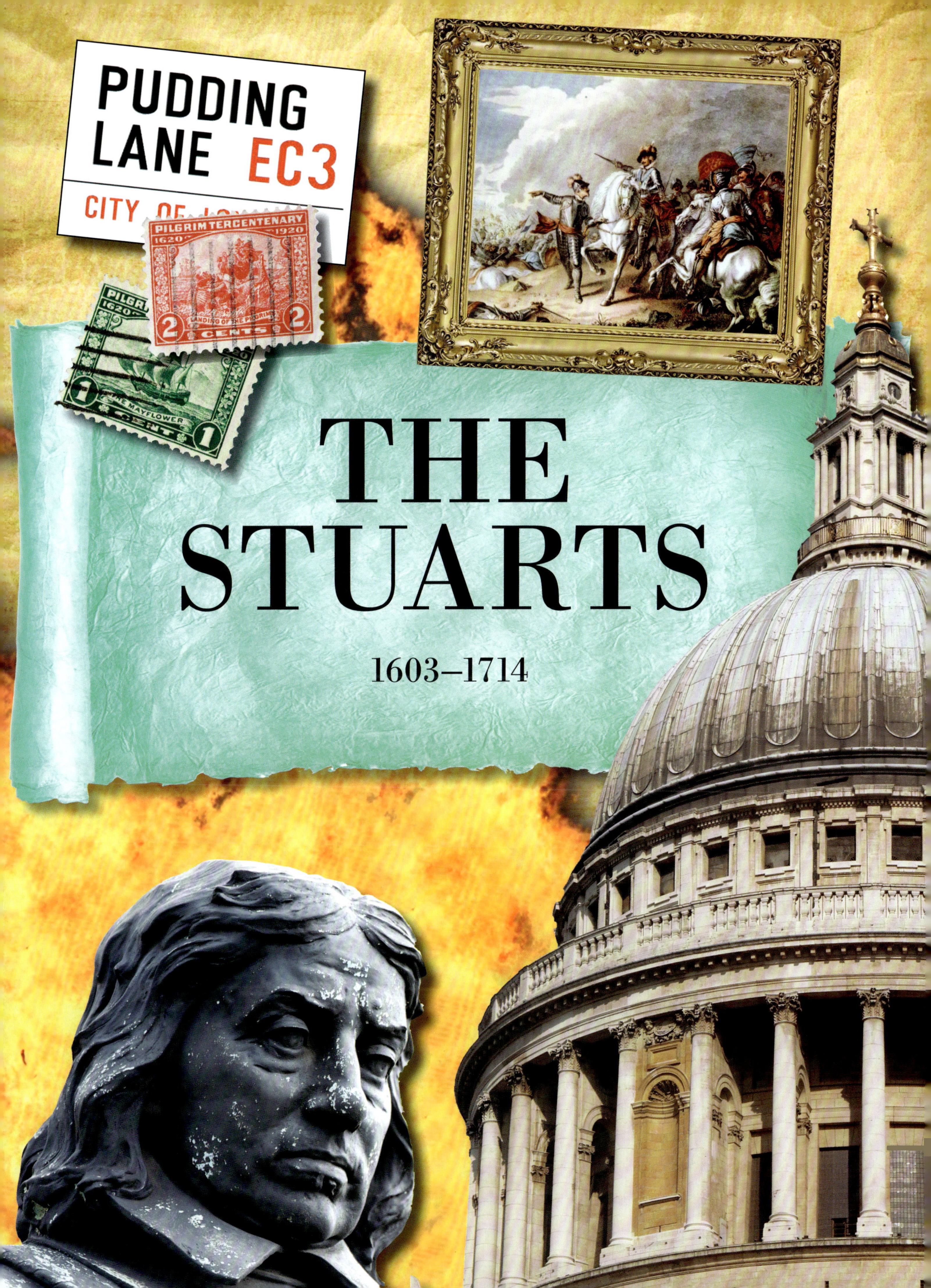
PUDDING
LANE EC3
CITY OF LO
PILGRIM TERCENTENARY
1620 1920
LANDING OF THE PILGRIMS
2 CENTS
THE MAYFLOWER
1 CENT
THE
STUARTS
1603–1714

1566: James Stuart is born in Scotland, the only son of Mary Queen of Scots.

1603: James I is crowned King of England and Ireland in London.

1604: King James commissions a new translation of the bible to be made.

THE GUNPOWDER PLOT AND THE AGE OF PURITANISM

James VI of Scotland inherited the crown from Elizabeth I, becoming James I of England. As he was the son of Mary Queen of Scots, many people thought that he might restore Catholicism.

TROUBLED TIMES

After the Spanish Armada, Catholics were considered traitors and had to practise their religion in secret. They hoped James I (1566–1625) would change the law. But, if anything, life became more difficult for Catholics, as many Protestants had very extreme beliefs which they wanted imposed everywhere. Some English people also did not like the idea of a Scottish king.

THE GUNPOWDER PLOT

In 1605, a group of Catholics decided to assassinate James I by blowing up the House of Lords during the opening of Parliament. They hid barrels filled with gunpowder in the cellars under the chamber where the king and the government would be gathering. A conspirator named Guy Fawkes was given the job of lighting the fuse. However, the king received an anonymous letter warning him about the plot. He ordered the House of Lords to be searched, and Guy Fawkes was discovered. Guy Fawkes was sentenced to death. But, instead of being hanged, he jumped from the gallows and broke his neck in the fall.

36 barrels of gunpowder were used in the plot.

1605: A group of Catholics attempts to blow up the king and his government.

1606: Guy Fawkes is tried for treason, along with other conspirators, and executed.

1625: Following a stroke, James I dies and is buried in Westminster Abbey.

AWESOME FACTS

"Remember, Remember, the Fifth November"
The Gunpowder Plot is remembered every year on 5 November or "Bonfire Night" – a night when big fires are lit, a "Guy" is burnt, and people let off fireworks.

The Gunpowder Plot Conspirators
Although Guy Fawkes is the most famous of the conspirators, the plot was actually led by Robert Catesby.

From left to right: Thomas Bates, Robert Winter, Christopher Wright, John Wright, Thomas Percy, Guy Fawkes, Robert Catesby and Thomas Winter.

THE PURITANS

Some Protestants, called the Puritans, had very extreme religious views. They wore plain clothes and lived a simple life. They believed in hard work and prayer. Sundays and other holy days were devoted to God. The Puritans also thought that churches should not be decorated. They disapproved of drunkenness, swearing and frivolous entertainments such as theatre-going, dancing and singing.

Puritans liked to give their children what were known as "virtue" names. Some, such as Joy, Hope and Faith, are still popular today. More unusual ones included:

- Justice
- Lovewell
- Pardon
- Silence
- Tolerance
- Wrestling

COOL FACTS

The King James Bible
The Puritans thought that there were many mistakes in Henry VIII's translation of the bible. James I ordered a new translation, begun in 1604 and completed in 1611, which could be read aloud in all the churches. Although there have been later translations into modern English, many phrases found in this translation are still commonly used. Here are a few of them:

- The salt of the earth, meaning "honest, ordinary people".
- By the skin of one's teeth, meaning "only just".
- The land of the living meaning "people who are alive today".

1620: A group of Puritans leaves for America in order to establish a new colony.

1621: William Bradford is made governor of the Plymouth Colony.

1629: A second *Mayflower* ship transports more Pilgrims to America.

THE PILGRIM FATHERS

In 1620, a group of Puritans set sail for America. They planned to create a new settlement where they could start a new way of life and practise their religion in peace.

PURITANS FLEE ENGLAND

Some of the Puritans were not satisfied with the state of the Church in England. They thought that the reforms made after the break with Rome did not go far enough and that Church of England services were too similar to Roman Catholic ones. They wanted them to be much simpler.

The Puritans were persecuted for their beliefs. Their services were outlawed, just as the Catholic ones were. Everybody was supposed to go to Church of England services instead. But Puritans still continued to gather together, even though they could be sent to prison or even executed for doing so. Eventually, things got so bad that they had to flee the country. Many went to Leiden in the Netherlands, where their beliefs were tolerated.

However, there was also the threat of a Spanish Catholic invasion of the Netherlands, so they decided to set sail for North America where they would be safe.

The Pilgrim Fathers board the *Mayflower*.

A Pilgrim settlement in New England, in the Americas.

1649: The Society for Propagation of the Gospel in New England is founded.

1691: The Plymouth Colony becomes a part of the province of Massachusetts.

1820: The name "Pilgrim Fathers" is given to the early settlers by Daniel Webster.

THE MAYFLOWER

In 1620, the Puritans left the Netherlands and returned to England where they boarded the *Mayflower*, which was sailing for America. Because they believed they were on a kind of pilgrimage, they later became known as the "Pilgrim Fathers". They are also called the "Plymouth Brethren" because, when they got to America, they founded what they called the "Plimoth Plantation".

DID YOU KNOW?

The *Mayflower* departed from London and picked up the Puritans from Southampton, not Plymouth, as is often assumed. However, the ship had to stop at Plymouth for repairs before setting off into the Atlantic.

COOL FACTS

The Puritan Exodus

- There were 102 passengers on the *Mayflower*, about half of whom were Puritans.
- The Atlantic crossing was very stormy and lasted 66 days.
- The *Mayflower* landed at Cape Cod, in Massachusetts, on 11 November 1620.
- The first winter the Puritans spent in America was so cold that many of the Brethren perished.
- Between 1629 and 1640, around 80,000 Puritans fled from England to America in order to avoid religious persecution.

PURITAN CHURCHES

Puritan churches were very simple, plain buildings. Men sat on one side and women sat on the other. Usually, there was no music at the services. People would pray and the minister would preach long sermons about sin and punishment. Children had to be quiet.

AWESOME FACT

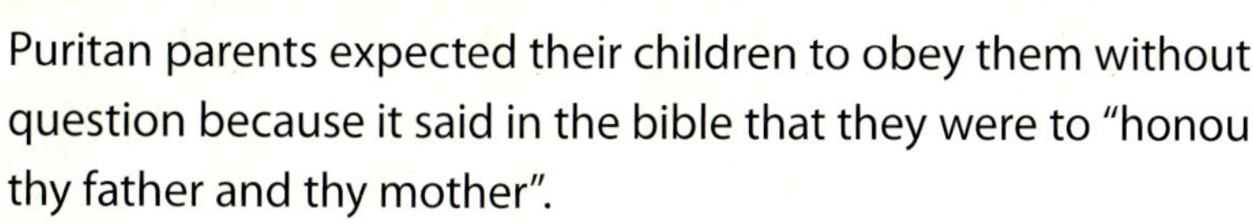

Puritan parents expected their children to obey them without question because it said in the bible that they were to "honour thy father and thy mother".

1600: Charles, King James's second son, is born in Dunfermline Palace in Scotland.

1612: Henry – Charles's older brother – dies. Charles is now heir to the throne.

1626: Charles I is crowned following his father's death the previous year.

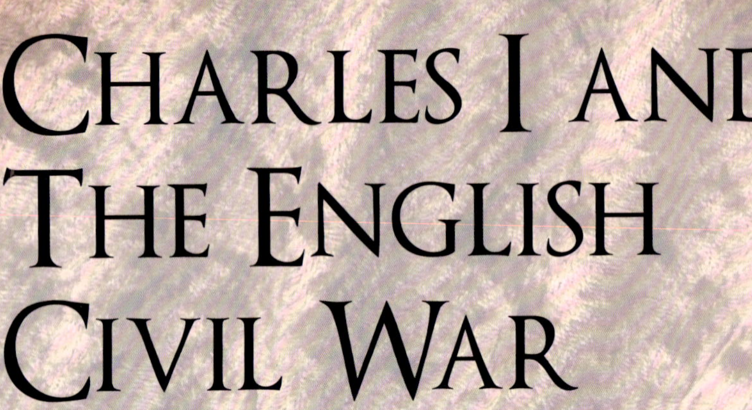

Charles I and the English Civil War

Charles was the second son of James I. His elder brother Henry was heir to the throne. But Henry died in 1612, and so Charles inherited the throne instead in 1625.

DID YOU KNOW?

Charles I was a weak child, who may have had rickets. He only grew to a height of 163cm (5ft 4in).

Charles I (1600–1649, executed)

PARLIAMENTARIANS VERSUS ROYALISTS

Charles I (1600–1649) thought he should be allowed to rule without Parliament and imposed many taxes to raise money. As he was married to a Catholic, Henrietta Maria of France, many thought he might try to reintroduce the Roman Catholic faith in England.

In 1641, Catholics in Ireland rose up against Protestants who had settled there. This caused people to panic in England. Some members of Parliament were Puritans, and they wanted even more religious reforms. Many Protestants thought there was a royal plot to restore the Catholic faith and reduce people's liberties. Soon, Charles found himself in open disagreement with Parliament. Two armed camps set up. The northern parts of England supported the king and were known as Royalists. People in Cornwall and Wales also supported Charles.

The Parliamentarians were ranged in the south and had the advantage of controlling London. They were able to make an alliance with the Scots and, after the defeat of the king's army at the Battle of Marston Moor in 1644, Charles lost control of the north of Britain.

1645: The king's army is defeated at the Battle of Naseby.

1649: Charles is beheaded in front of London's Banqueting House.

1894: The Society of Charles King and Martyr is founded to honour Charles I.

A KING IS BEHEADED

The following year, Charles was defeated at the Battle of Naseby. Charles was unwilling to surrender and gave himself up to the Scots instead, but, when they finally left England, they handed Charles over to Parliament.

Even then, the king was determined not to give up. He stirred up more violence known as the Second Civil War.

Realising that there would be no peace while Charles I remained alive, a number of MPs and soldiers decided that he had to be charged with high treason. Charles was tried, found guilty, and beheaded in January 1649.

AWESOME FACT

At the Battle of Naseby, around 1,000 Royalist s oldiers were killed and around 4,500 taken prisoner.

The Battle of Naseby (1645)

Execution of Charles I

COOL FACT

Cavaliers versus Roundheads
The Parliamentarians became known as Roundheads because they cut their hair very short or combed it close to their heads. The Royalists were called Cavaliers from the French *chevalier* – a knight who rode on horseback. They often had long, flowing hair.

INTERESTING

King and Martyr
After his beheading, some of the king's supporters started honouring him as a saint, and gave him the title Charles, King and Martyr.

THE NEW MODEL ARMY

After the Battle of Marston Moor, Parliament decided to create a new professional army called the New Model Army. Unlike the king's army, anybody could become an officer. Many of the soldiers were Puritans, and they often sang psalms before going into battle.

1599: Oliver Cromwell is born in Huntingdon in Cambridgeshire.

1653: Oliver Cromwell is named Lord Protector of the Commonwealth.

1658: Cromwell dies at Whitehall, possibly as a result of malaria.

OLIVER CROMWELL AND THE COMMONWEALTH

Following Charles I's execution, a republic – sometimes called the Commonwealth – was established in England. But many people still remained loyal to the Royalists.

OLIVER CROMWELL

Cromwell (1599–1658) was the Member of Parliament for Huntingdon in 1628–1629. In the 1630s, Cromwell became a Puritan and was convinced that he had been called on by God to lead the country. After the Second Civil War, Cromwell wanted to bring the king to justice. Once Charles had been executed, he created a new republic and became army commander and Lord Lieutenant of Ireland. He crushed Irish rebellions in 1649 at Drogheda and Wexford.

Oliver Cromwell (1599–1658)

Some Royalist supporters still thought that Charles's son should become king. There were further battles at Dunbar (1650) and Worcester (1651), where Cromwell was victorious. The civil war was over once and for all and Cromwell made himself Lord Protector. Some people thought he should be made king, but he refused.

After he died, his son Richard was named as his successor as Lord Protector. Richard was not nearly as successful as his father at running the country and soon there was the danger of a new war breaking out. He was forced to abdicate in 1659. When the monarchy was restored the next year, he fled to Paris.

Richard returned to England in 1680 and lived quietly under an assumed name until his death in 1712.

1659: Richard Cromwell, Oliver Cromwell's son, is made to abdicate as Lord Protector.

1661: Oliver Cromwell's body is dug up from Westminster Abbey and beheaded.

1712: Having lived under an assumed name, Richard Cromwell dies in Hertfordshire aged 85.

"Warts and All"

A portrait of Cromwell was commissioned by the artist Sir Peter Lely. He usually liked to flatter the people he was painting, but Cromwell wanted a more truthful picture. He is supposed to have told Lely to paint him "warts and all", so that everybody would know what he really looked like.

DID YOU KNOW?

One of Cromwell's nicknames was "Old Ironsides".

Oliver Cromwell at the Battle of Marston Moor, 2 July 1644

THE RUMP PARLIAMENT AND THE BAREBONES PARLIAMENT

From 1649 to 1651, there was no one in charge of running the country. There were many arguments in Parliament and it was difficult to pass new laws. This became known as the "Rump Parliament". When Cromwell returned from battle, he became very angry and dissolved the Parliament in 1653.

To replace it, he created a new Parliament made up of people that he had chosen himself. This was often called the "Barebones Parliament" after one of its members whose name was "Praise-God Barebone".

COOL FACTS

A Time of Austerity

As a Puritan, Cromwell passed laws banning festivals that many people enjoyed because he thought they were pagan.

- Cromwell banned working on Sundays and football.
- All theatres were closed during the Commonwealth.
- Cromwell also banned Christmas, as we know it. Instead of being a time of celebration and feasting, he wanted it to be just a quiet time for praying.

1630: Charles II is born at St. James's Palace and is baptised shortly after.

1646: To escape the Civil War, the young Charles leaves England, settling in Holland.

1660: Charles returns to England from Holland in order to reclaim the throne.

THE RESTORATION

The reign of King Charles II is often called the Restoration because when he was crowned it was the restoration of the British monarchy that had been overthrown when his father, Charles I, was beheaded in 1649.

DID YOU KNOW?

King Charles II was a very tall king, reaching over 180cm (6ft).

CHARLES II – A RESTORED MONARCH

Charles II (1630–1685), then almost 30 years old, had been staying in the Netherlands after his father had been beheaded. He was invited to come back to London as king. The Restoration Settlement was a series of laws passed between 1660 and 1664. Charles II was given money in return for the royal lands that were taken from his family.

A new Parliament was elected on 25 April 1660 and Charles was declared the new King of England and Ireland. In return, he offered to pardon everybody except the people that killed his father and from now on everyone would be allowed to worship however they wanted to.

He came back to England on 25 May 1660. There was general rejoicing. People could celebrate Christmas again and the theatres reopened. The body of Oliver Cromwell was dug up and his head was cut off and stuck on a pike at London Bridge. Then it was paraded through the streets.

In 1662, Charles married Catherine of Braganza, who was a princess from Portugal. They never had any children, so, when Charles died in 1685, his younger brother James became king.

Charles II
(1630–1685)

Charles II was very fond of King Charles spaniels and kept a lot of them as pets.

1661: Charles is crowned king in Westminster Abbey. He becomes Charles II.

1685: Charles II has a fit and dies four days later at Whitehall Palace in London.

1687: Nell Gwyn, a favourite of Charles II, has a stroke and dies shortly afterwards.

Charles II entering London after the Restoration of the monarchy in 1660.

THE PLAGUE

In 1665, there was another outbreak of the plague in London. The summer was very hot. Many people lived in squalid slums. The disease spread rapidly, as the numbers of rats and fleas increased alarmingly. Though not as bad as the outbreak in the 14th century, many people died. In the Great Fire of London in 1666 most of the slums burnt down and the disease was wiped out.

RESTORATION PLAYS

Many new plays were written when Charles returned to England. Many are very funny, and continue to amuse audiences whenever they are performed. This was also the first time that women were allowed to appear on stage – before this, female roles had always been played by boys.

INTERESTING

The Story of Nell Gwyn

Nell was a poor girl who earned money by selling oranges outside theatres. She became an actress and attracted the attention of the king. Charles fell in love with her and gave her a big mansion to live in. As he lay dying, he is supposed to have said, "Let not poor Nelly starve".

AWESOME FACT

The Comet of 1664

In the winter of 1664, a bright comet appeared in the sky. As nobody really knew where it had come from, many people thought that some catastrophe was about to happen, as indeed it did – the Great Fire of London!

1642: The scientist Isaac Newton is born prematurely in Lincolnshire.

1661: Newton is admitted to Trinity College, Cambridge, where he studies philosophy.

1662: Charles II grants a royal charter to the Royal Society, a scientific academy.

Science and Philosophy

Many scientific discoveries were made during this period, although the term "scientist" was not used at the time. Scientists were called "natural philosophers".

John Locke (1632–1704)

JOHN LOCKE

Locke (1632–1704) studied medicine, but became an important philosopher. He was elected a fellow of the Royal Society in 1668. Locke thought that everybody should have equal rights, which he wrote about in *Two Treatises of Government*, and this made him unpopular with the ruling classes. In 1683, there was an assassination attempt on Charles II, known as the Rye House Plot. Though Locke probably had nothing to do with this, he had to leave England. However, he returned after the Glorious Revolution.

SIR ISAAC NEWTON

Newton (1642–1727) is often considered to be the greatest scientist who ever lived. He thought that everything could be explained in a few simple laws which should be obvious to everybody. He also discovered that white light is actually composed of several colours, the ones that can be seen in a rainbow.

Sir Isaac Newton (1642–1727)

1675: A new observatory is commissioned at Greenwich for studying the stars.

1687: Newton publishes his *Principia Mathematica*, giving details of his three laws of motion.

1703: Isaac Newton is elected to the post of President of the Royal Society.

COOL FACTS

Newton's Ideas and Discoveries

- ***Philosophae Naturalis Principia Mathematica*** Newton's most important book – sometimes just called the *Principia* – outlines the three laws of motion and describes how gravity works. Using these laws, Newton was able to work out how the planets moved around the sun, as well as why a pea rolls around a plate. Scientists still rely on these laws today. The *Principia* was written in Latin, which all scientists around the world would have understood.

- **Calculus** Newton also invented a new form of mathematics called calculus. Calculus enabled mathematicians to study curved shapes and acceleration.

- **Newton's Theory of Gravitation** Everybody knows that things fall to the ground when you drop them. But, until Newton, nobody could really explain why this happened. Newton said he came up with his theory when he saw an apple fall from a tree at his childhood home in Grantham in Lincolnshire.

DID YOU KNOW?

Although he became very famous and respected, Newton was a difficult man who often suffered from depression.

INTERESTING

The Royal Society is the oldest scientific academy in continuous existence.

THE ROYAL SOCIETY

Scientists met regularly to share their ideas and do experiments. In 1662, Charles II granted them a royal charter. Important scientists were elected to the society as "fellows". Isaac Newton was President of the society from 1703 until his death in 1727. The society met at various locations and nowadays continues to support science and give money to important projects.

AWESOME FACT

The Royal Observatory

In 1675, Charles II commissioned a new observatory to be built at Greenwich for studying the stars. It was realised that accurate maps of the stars would help sailors navigate their way around the seas. He also created the post of Astronomer Royal.

1666: Fire breaks out in Pudding Lane in London and spreads rapidly.

1669: Christopher Wren is commissioned to build a new cathedral and other churches.

1671: The City Council approves Wren's design for a monument commemorating the fire.

THE GREAT FIRE OF LONDON

One of the most well-known disasters in British history occurred just after the plague of 1665. In a huge fire, which became known as the Great Fire of London, one third of the city of London was destroyed.

PUDDING LANE EC3
CITY OF LONDON

LONDON ENGULFED IN FLAMES

The summer of 1666 was very hot. Early one Sunday morning, on 2 September, a fire started at Thomas Farriner's bakery in Pudding Lane. Because everything was dry and it was very windy, the fire spread very quickly. The surrounding area was full of warehouses containing wood, rope and oil, which easily caught alight. In the narrow streets, the fire blew from house to house.

The fire was soon out of control and, rather than try and put it out, most people just fled, jumping from roof to roof to escape the flames. They either headed to the river or to open fields outside the city walls. The fire lasted nearly five days.

PUTTING OUT THE FLAMES

In those days, there was no fire brigade. People tried to put out the fire with buckets of water and water squirts. The best method was actually to pull down buildings to prevent the flames spreading. On the third day of the fire, they even tried blowing up buildings with gunpowder. Then the wind dropped and firefighters were able to put the fire out.

COOL FACTS

The Great Fire

- 100,000 people were made homeless.
- The fire reached a temperature of 1,700°C (3,092°F).
- Over 13,000 houses and 87 churches were burnt down.
- It took 50 years to rebuild the city.

1675: Work begins on Christopher Wren's St. Paul's, London's new cathedral.

1723: Wren dies and is buried in the south-east corner of the crypt of St. Paul's Cathedral.

1825: Samuel Pepys's *Diary*, which describes the great fire in detail, is finally published.

A NEW LONDON

After the fire, it was realised that new houses should be built much further apart from each other. Brick was to be used in place of wood, and there were new broad pavements.

Sir Christopher Wren (1632–1723) completed a plan for a new city. It was to have long straight streets with magnificent views. But London had to be rebuilt very quickly, so the plan was shelved.

However, he designed 51 churches that did get built, as well as the Royal Naval College and Royal Observatory in Greenwich.

Sir Christopher Wren (1632–1723)

INTERESTING

Sir Christopher Wren
Wren was a famous architect and scientist. In 1622, he was one of the founder members of the Royal Society, along with other famous scientists. He visited Paris, and its buildings had a great influence on his designs.

ST. PAUL'S CATHEDRAL

One of the buildings ruined in the fire was St. Paul's Cathedral, so Wren was asked to design a new one. Building began in 1675 and was finished in 1710. Wren's cathedral is the second largest in the world. Not everybody liked it at first, as they thought it looked too much like a Catholic cathedral. But it soon became one of London's best-loved landmarks.

1633: James II, the son of Charles I, is born in St. James's Palace in London.

1673: James marries the Catholic Mary of Modena who is 25 years younger than him.

1685: James comes to the throne following the death of his brother, Charles II.

James II and the Glorious Revolution

After Charles II's death, his younger brother inherited the crown and ruled as James II. But he was not a popular king, and was soon forced to give up the throne.

James II (1633–1701)

The Duke of Monmouth's Rebellion

During the time of the civil war, James had lived abroad. When his brother Charles II was restored to the throne in 1660, he came back to England and was put in charge of the Royal Navy. In 1669, he converted to Catholicism but this did not prevent him becoming king.

Although Charles II did not have any children with his wife (which is why his brother was his heir), he was the father of the Duke of Monmouth. The duke thought he should be king and raised an army against James. But the duke was easily defeated at the Battle of Sedgemoor in 1685.

The Bloody Assizes

The Lord Chief Justice, Judge Jeffreys, imposed cruel punishments on the Duke of Monmouth's supporters because the king wanted to make sure that no one else would dare rebel against him. The trials became notorious. Many convicted people were hanged, their heads cut off, and their bodies cut up into quarters. The body parts were then dipped in salt and sent around the villages to be displayed on poles. The best you could hope for was to be sent to the colonies to a life of slavery.

James II thought that Roman Catholics and Protestant sects should all have the same rights. Parliament disagreed with him, so he decided to rule on his own. He gave several Catholics important jobs and in 1687 issued a Declaration of Indulgence aimed at establishing complete religious toleration. But he remained deeply unpopular.

1688: Increasingly unpopular, James flees England in order to live abroad.

1701: James dies in Paris and is laid to rest in the Church of the English Benedictines.

1718: Mary of Modena, wife of James II, dies in poverty in a convent in France.

THE GLORIOUS REVOLUTION

In 1660, James married Anne Hyde, daughter of Charles II's chief minister, and they had two children, Mary and Anne, who survived to adulthood. Both daughters became queen later on. James then married Mary of Modena, who in 1688 gave birth to a son called James Edward Stuart.

Since James and Mary of Modena were both Catholics, many people were concerned that Catholicism would now be restored to England. However, his daughter Mary, who was a Protestant, had married the Protestant William of Orange, who ruled parts of the Netherlands. William and Mary were invited to come to England to rule as king and queen in place of James.

Late in 1688, William landed in Devon. Finding that he had few supporters, James fled abroad. In 1689, Parliament decided that James had abdicated, so William and Mary were crowned as joint monarchs.

Mary II and William III

DID YOU KNOW?

The **Glorious Revolution** that brought William and Mary to the throne is so called because there were no battles and nobody was killed.

Mary of Modena
(1658–1718)

A Catholic Threat

- Although the Test and Corporation Acts prevented James II from doing so, he appointed Catholics to senior positions in the army and government.
- When James faced objections from the Archbishop of Canterbury and six other bishops to his granting of religious freedom to Catholics, he had them arrested and sent to the Tower of London.

The Duke of Monmouth
(1649–1685)

INTERESTING

A King in a Fishing Boat
James II attempted to escape to France on 11 December 1688. He was captured by fishermen near Sheerness in Kent.

1662: Mary, the daughter of the future James II, is born at St. James's Palace in London.

1688: The Glorious Revolution puts William and Mary on the throne instead of James II.

1689: Parliament passes the Bill of Rights which limits the powers of the monarchy.

WILLIAM AND MARY

The Glorious Revolution completed the long and difficult process by which England changed itself from a Roman Catholic nation into a Protestant one.

MATRIMONY AND MONARCHY

On the face of it, William and Mary were an odd couple. He was 12 years older and, when they first met, she thought he was repulsive. Although she grew to love him, they never had any children.

After getting rid of James II, Parliament wanted Mary to rule England as queen in her own right, with William just as consort. But Mary wanted them to be joint monarchs. As it turned out, William spent much of his time out of England, and Mary ruled on her own during his absences, as Parliament had intended.

THE BATTLE OF THE BOYNE

Although exiled, James II made an attempt to regain his lost throne. The Battle of the Boyne took place near Drogheda, in Ireland, in 1690. It resulted in a resounding victory for William, and James returned to France where he spent the rest of his life.

Mary II
(1662–1694)

A POPULAR QUEEN

Mary II was greatly loved by everybody, not just by William. But she died of smallpox in 1694. There was a huge public outpouring of grief. Her funeral was a major event, and people lined the streets to pay tribute. Her coffin was accompanied by 300 women dressed in black capes with boys carrying their trains.

1690: James II makes an attempt to regain his crown at the Battle of the Boyne.

1694: Mary falls ill with smallpox and dies shortly after at Kensington Palace.

1702: William dies of pneumonia after falling from his horse and breaking his collarbone.

AWESOME FACT

HAMPTON COURT

Soon after coming to the throne, William III asked Christopher Wren to rebuild Hampton Court, Henry VIII's palace on the River Thames. At first, Wren wanted to demolish the entire palace apart from the Great Hall, but there was not enough time or money to do this. Instead, he rebuilt the east and south façades.

At first, work on Hampton Court was done too quickly, and a large section collapsed. Two workmen were killed and 11 injured. When work resumed, they took more time and care.

The Massacre at Glencoe

Some Scottish clans remained loyal to James II. William III wanted them all to sign an oath of allegiance to him. However, the MacDonalds of Glencoe (also called the Maclains) were late in signing the oath and in 1692 many were killed by the Campbells, who were their enemies. Even women and children were killed. Many people in Scotland were horrified at this outcome.

COOL FACTS

Acts of Parliament

After many years of monarchs acting like dictators, Parliament decided the rights of kings and queens should be strictly limited. Here are two important laws:

- **1689 Bill of Rights** set out basic rights for Englishmen, stating there was to be no royal interference in elections to Parliament and no cruel or unusual punishments. Citizens should also be able to petition the monarch without fear of punishment.
- **1701 Settlement Act** finally established the supremacy of Parliament over the monarch.
- Parliament also had the right to decide who would inherit the throne. James's Catholic children with Mary of Modena were barred from the succession. From now on, the king or queen had to be a Protestant.

1665: Anne is born at St. James's Palace with small chance of ever becoming queen.

1700: Anne's son William dies shortly after his eleventh birthday.

1702: Anne becomes queen on the death of William and is immediately popular.

QUEEN ANNE (1665–1714)

Anne was Mary's younger sister. Although their father was a Catholic, both sisters were raised as Protestants so there was no objection to Anne inheriting the throne.

EARLY LIFE

Anne spent her childhood in France. In 1683, she married Prince George of Denmark. Although the marriage was a happy one, Anne suffered much tragedy. Many of her babies were born dead and the ones that survived didn't live very long. Only one – William, Duke of Gloucester – survived infancy, but he died in 1700 at the age of 11.

Anne came to the throne in 1702 after the death of William, her sister Mary's husband. As she grew older, she put on weight and had to be carried around in a sedan chair.

Her friend Sarah Churchill said, "There was something of majesty in her look, but mixed with a gloominess of soul". She died in 1714.

THE ACT OF UNION

In 1707, England and Scotland agreed to combine themselves into a single kingdom, so there would no longer be any argument about who should be king or queen. There would be one Parliament that would meet at Westminster, as well as a common flag and coinage. However, Scotland could keep its own established Church and its systems of law and education. With this in place, Anne became Queen of Great Britain.

1704: John Churchill defeats the French at the Battle of Blenheim.

1707: The Act of Union finally unites England and Scotland as a single nation.

1714: Anne dies after suffering a stroke and is buried in Westminster Abbey.

WAR OF THE SPANISH SUCCESSION

Although this war was fought abroad, it was very important to England. The Spanish king had no heir, and both the French and the Austrians thought they had a claim to the throne. England and Holland realised that this would make either France or Austria extremely powerful, and were drawn into the conflict.

A famous battle took place at Blenheim in 1704. John Churchill, the Duke of Marlborough, succeeded in defeating the French and was hailed as a national hero. Under the Treaty of Utrecht in 1713, France finally recognised Anne as Queen of England. Previously, they had supported James II's Roman Catholic son.

COOL FACTS

Whigs and Tories

Anne's reign saw the development of two political parties in England:

- **The Tories** supported the monarchy and royal authority.
- **The Whigs** were more concerned with ordinary people's freedom and property.

Anne favoured the Tories, but the Whigs became increasingly powerful during her reign.

DID YOU KNOW?

The Duke of Marlborough was an ancestor of Winston Churchill.

Blenheim Palace

Anne was very friendly with the Duke of Marlborough's wife, Sarah Churchill. After the duke's successes abroad, the Churchills were given money to build a magnificent house near Oxford.

But Sarah and the queen began to argue, because Sarah was always trying to persuade Anne to support the Whigs in Parliament. Eventually, Sarah was dismissed from court and no more money was given to her for the house.

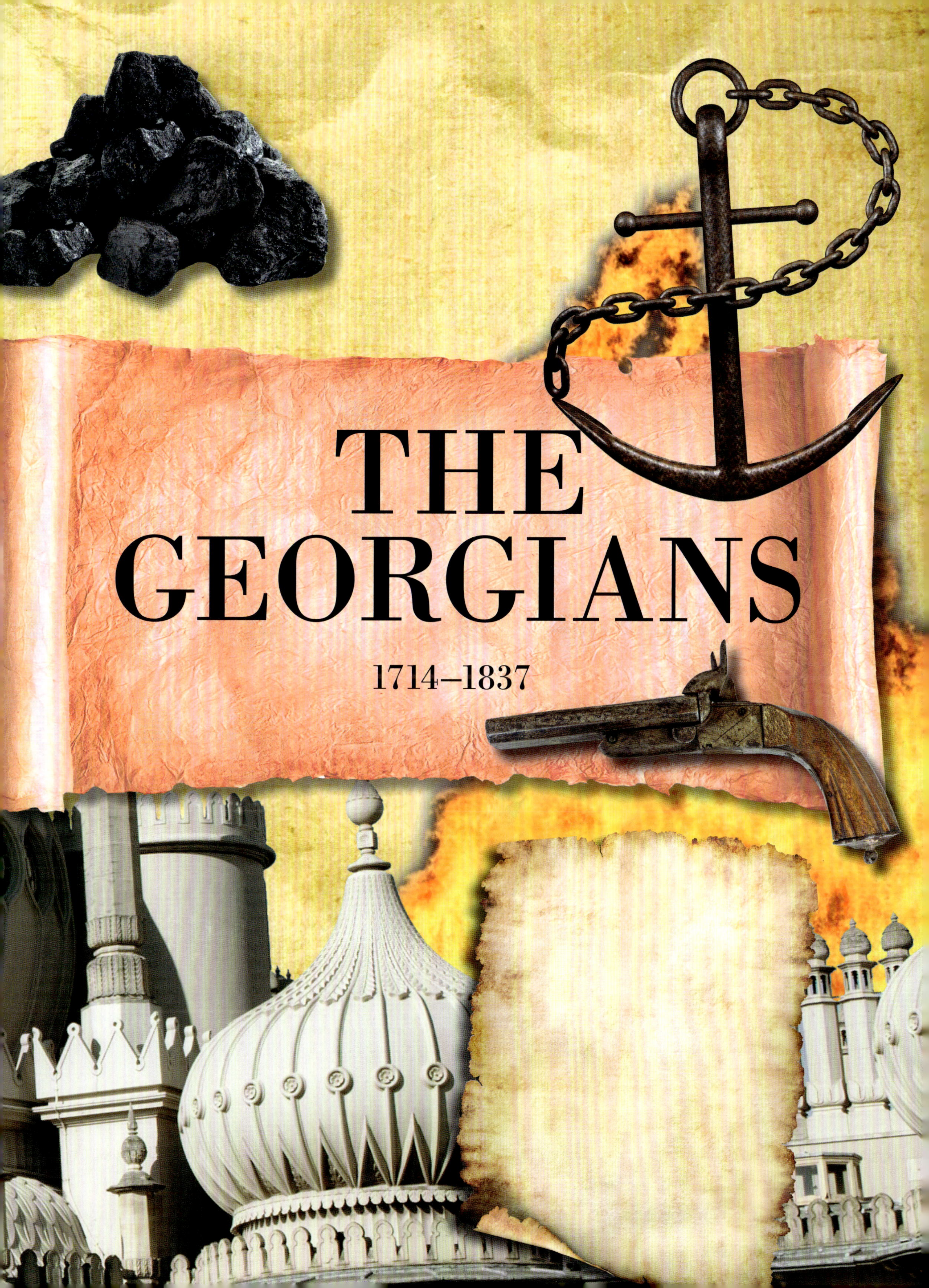
THE GEORGIANS
1714–1837

1660: George is born in Hanover, the eldest son of the Duke of Brunswick-Lüneburg.

1711: The South Sea Company is founded for trading with South America.

1714: George I inherits the throne of Great Britain on the death of Queen Anne.

GEORGE I

(1660-1727)

When Queen Anne died in 1714, the throne passed to the German House of Hanover because Parliament had stipulated that the monarch could not be a Catholic. Some people – the Jacobites – tried to replace George with Anne's half brother, James Stuart, who was a Catholic, but their attempts failed.

George I (1660–1727)

THE GEORGIAN PERIOD

This period in history is sometimes called "Georgian" because each king in succession was named George. George I inherited the throne through his mother, Sophia of Hamburg, who was a granddaughter of James I. He became king in 1714. George died in 1727 at the age of 67.

COOL FACTS

George I

- George was 54 when he came to the throne – the oldest monarch to inherit the throne up until this point.
- The new king did not speak English and made little attempt to learn it. He spent most of his time in Germany and spoke to his ministers in French.

1721: Robert Walpole becomes the first Prime Minister of Great Britain.

1727: George I dies following a stroke during a visit to Hanover, in Germany.

1745: Robert Walpole, who is now the Earl of Orford, dies at his estate in Norfolk.

SIR ROBERT WALPOLE – THE FIRST PRIME MINISTER

Robert Walpole (1676–1745) was elected as a Member of Parliament in 1701. Although he was a Whig, George I supported him because he thought the Tories did not like him, as he was a foreigner. Since the king was absent for most of the time, Walpole became very powerful. He came to lead the government and was the first Prime Minister. It was during this period that the influence of the monarch declined. Walpole kept taxes low. He built up the navy and tried to maintain peace with neighbouring countries. After the death of George I, Walpole fell from favour for a short time but was able to regain control.

Sir Robert Walpole (1676–1745)

INTERESTING

Prime Minister Moves to Number 10
Robert Walpole was not actually called the Prime Minister at the time. He was known as First Lord of the Treasury and the Chancellor of the Exchequer. But he led the government in the same way that a Prime Minister does today. In 1735, George II gave 10 Downing Street to Walpole to live in, and this has been the London home of all Prime Ministers ever since.

DID YOU KNOW?

Robert Walpole sent settlers to North America. There, they founded Georgia, which was named after the king.

THE SOUTH SEA BUBBLE

The South Sea Company traded in South America and the South Sea, which is what the South Pacific Ocean was then called. The War of the Spanish Succession had been very expensive for the government. The Company offered to pay for the cost of this, if people would invest in the company by buying shares. Since there was a lot of gold and silver in South America, many people thought they would be able to become rich very quickly.

People started buying and selling the shares, which became increasingly expensive. Then it was discovered that they were worthless. The bubble had burst. Many people lost all their money. Some politicians were imprisoned for fraud.

1683: George is born in Hanover, the last monarch to be born outside Britain.

1705: George marries German Caroline of Brandenburg-Ansbach.

1727: George inherits the British throne following the death of his father George I.

GEORGE II (1683–1760)

George II was the only son of George I. He was Prince of Wales before he inherited the throne in 1727 on the death of his father. In 1705, he married Princess Caroline of Brandenburg-Ansbach. They had nine children together.

George II (1683–1760)

THE DIFFICULT GEORGES

George argued often with his father, and Robert Walpole had to sort things out between them. The Prince of Wales was very friendly with Walpole until he became a part of his father's government. So when he inherited the throne as George II, he would have got rid of Walpole altogether, but Queen Caroline persuaded him to keep him in the government.

Walpole was extremely good to the new king. He got Parliament to give him a yearly allowance of £800,000. He also won round the Tories – some of them still wanted James Stuart as king. When there was a later Jacobite uprising, hardly any Members of Parliament would support it.

Just like his father, George II had a bad relationship with his own son, Frederick Louis, Prince of Wales. But Frederick died in 1751, while George lived on to 1760. So his grandson, also named George, became his successor.

INTERESTING

BONNIE PRINCE CHARLIE AND THE JACOBITE RISING

James Stuart, who some people still thought should be king, was sometimes called "The Old Pretender". He had a son called Charles who was known as "The Young Pretender". Charles was brought up in Rome but had many supporters in Scotland, who gave him the name Bonnie Prince Charlie. He arrived in Scotland in 1745 and set about raising an army. But when he marched on England, he found hardly anybody wanted to fight, as they were happy with the Hanoverians.

1745: Bonnie Prince Charlie arrives in Scotland and succeeds in raising an army.

1746: The Battle of Culloden takes place in Scotland and Bonnie Prince Charlie is defeated.

1760: George II dies and is buried in Westminster Abbey in London.

THE BATTLE OF CULLODEN

In 1746, a battle was fought between the Duke of Cumberland, George II's son, and Bonnie Prince Charlie at Culloden, in Scotland. But Charles was a very inexperienced soldier, and many of his men were killed. However, Charles was able to escape. According to legend, Flora MacDonald helped him sail to the Isle of Skye, disguised as her maid. Eventually, he made his way to France, then to Italy, where he died in 1807.

At the Battle of Culloden 1,500–2,000 Jacobites were either killed or wounded.

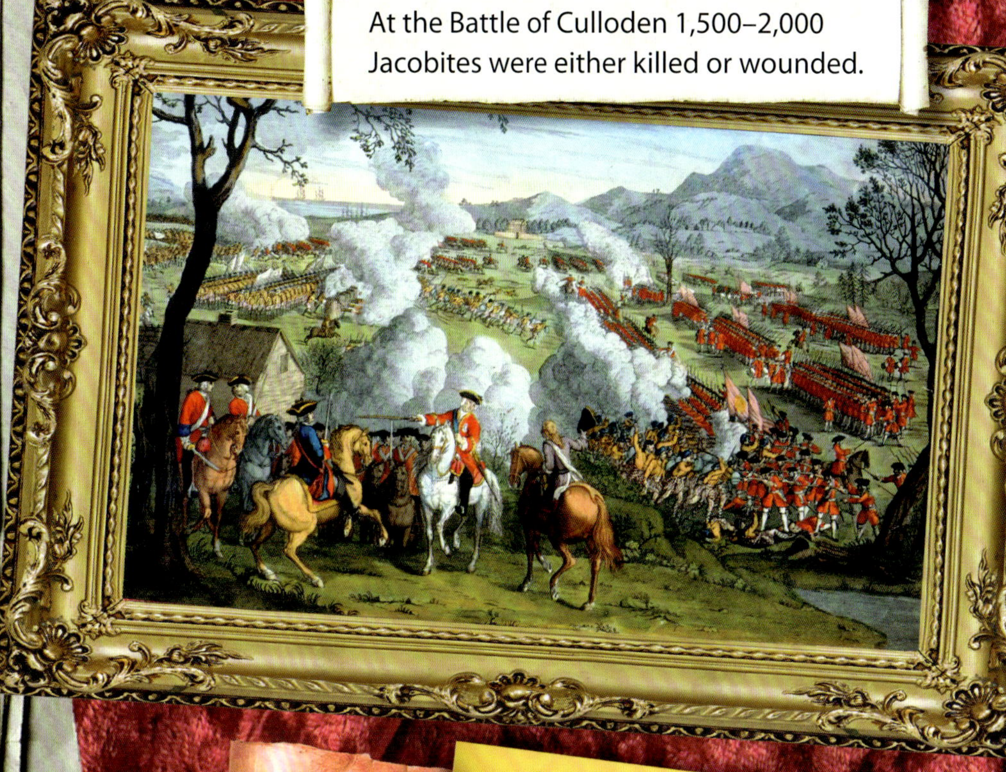

COOL FACT

The Bloody Duke

Because of the bloodshed at the Battle of Culloden (1746), the Duke of Cumberland became known as "Butcher Cumberland".

Queen Caroline (1683–1737)

QUEEN CAROLINE

Although she had little formal schooling, Queen Caroline (1683–1737) was a very intelligent woman. Her friend,Lady Montagu, had seen children in Turkey being inoculated against smallpox with an early form of vaccination. Many children died of this terrible disease, so Caroline had her own children inoculated, although most British doctors thought this a strange thing to do. Edward Jenner, a doctor from Gloucestershire, finally developed a reliable vaccine against smallpox in 1796. Nowadays, children are routinely inoculated against this terrible disease.

1600: The East India Company is founded in order to manage trade with India.

1711: The Emperor of China allows the East India Company to trade in tea and silver.

1857: After the Indian Rebellion, Britain takes control of India and expands her empire.

The Start of the British Empire

In the Age of Discovery in the 16th and 17th centuries, Britain started to establish colonies overseas. Trade began with America and Asia, and the country became increasingly wealthy.

THE BUILDING OF AN EMPIRE

After a series of wars in the 17th and 18th centuries, Britain became the dominant power in North America and India. The British either made new settlements or took over French, Spanish or Dutch territories, which they won in battle.

Once they were in control of a country or island, British companies were able to trade with them without any fear of competition. Trading ships brought back goods that were not available in Britain. Many people grew very rich during this period.

Territories in North America were lost after the American War of Independence. So Britain turned her attention to Asia, Africa and the Pacific. By 1815, Britain had become one of the world's most powerful nations.

India

Up to about 1750, Britain traded at various ports along the coast of India. In the 1750s, the British started to move inland and took over most of Bengal. By the end of the century, Britain had control of most of southern India. Major-General Robert Clive (1725–1774) – who was also known as Clive of India – was an army officer who was key to establishing Britain's supremacy in India.

The East India Company

The East India Company was founded in 1600. No other English company was allowed to trade with India. The company sent 20 to 30 ships to India each year, bringing back cotton, silk, salt and other spices, and tea.

1869: The Suez Canal is opened, linking the Mediterranean with the Indian Ocean.

1874: The East India Company is closed down after nearly 300 years in operation.

1904: Children in Britain start celebrating "Empire Day", with fireworks and bonfires.

The Caribbean

Jamaica, Barbados and other islands in the Caribbean were very important to Britain, as this was where sugar was grown. Towards the end of the 18th century, Britain also gained control of Trinidad and parts of South America.

Africa

Following wars with France, Britain took possession of a number of their territories, including Mauritius and Sri Lanka, which was then called Ceylon. They also made settlements on the continent of Africa itself – in Sierra Leone, the Gambia and the Gold Coast.

INTERESTING

Saltpetre, which was imported from India, was an important commodity. It could be used to preserve meat and make gunpowder.

COOL FACTS

A Nation of Tea Drinkers

- Tea was introduced to England in the middle of the 17th century. At that time, it was very expensive because it was imported from China.
- Only very rich people could afford to drink tea, and they kept it in fancy boxes called caddies. These were locked, so that the servants could not help themselves. Only the lady of the house was allowed to make tea.
- Traders took tea plants to India and gradually the price fell. By around 1800, most British people enjoyed drinking tea regularly.
- Nowadays, tea is cheap enough to be drunk by everybody.

DID YOU KNOW?

Today, **the British** drink about **165 million** cups of tea **a day.**

1728: James Cook, who will discover Australia, is born in Yorkshire.

1743: The botanist Joseph Banks is born in London.

1768: HMS *Endeavour* sets sail on an expedition to the Pacific Ocean.

SOUTH SEAS EXPLORATION

Our knowledge of the world and of geography greatly increased during the reigns of all of the Georges. There were many expeditions to new lands such as Australia and New Zealand.

TRANSIT OF VENUS

Astronomers predicted that Venus would pass in front of the sun in 1769. This would allow them to work out the distance between the sun and the earth. But the transit of Venus would not be visible from Britain. So, it would be necessary to sail much further south to see it. It was also hoped that some new lands might be discovered at the same time. Many geographers thought that there must be another huge continent, like America, waiting to be discovered.

INTERESTING

What is a Transit of Venus?
Transits of Venus occur in pairs, eight years apart. The most recent transits were in 2004 and 2012. The next ones are due in 2117 and 2125.

JAMES COOK AND HMS ENDEAVOUR

The government decided to send an expedition. James Cook was put in command of a ship called the *Endeavour* – on board were the astronomer Charles Green and the botanist Joseph Banks.

In 1769, they reached Tahiti, where they were able to observe the Transit of Venus. Then they went on to New Zealand and sailed along Australia's east coast, which had never been seen by Europeans. Cook claimed it for Britain and named it New South Wales. The expedition returned home in 1771.

1769: Cook arrives in Tahiti to observe the Transit of Venus.

1779: Following an argument, Cook is stabbed to death in Hawaii.

1787: The first ship carrying convicts sets sail for Australia.

COOL FACTS

Key Figures Aboard HMS *Endeavour*

- **James Cook** (1728–1779) was the son of a farm worker. In 1775, he enlisted in the Navy and was sent to North America. He learnt how to make maps of the seas.
- **Joseph Banks** (1743–1820) was a fellow of the Royal Society. He collected many new plants in Australia and thought that British people should be sent to live there. Later, he was made director of the Royal Botanic Gardens at Kew.

James Cook (1728–1779)

AWESOME FACT

Cook is the first known person to have sailed around New Zealand.

CAPTAIN COOK'S LATER TRAVELS

Cook made two further expeditions and discovered the Sandwich Islands. His third voyage in 1779 was supposed to find the Northwest Passage, which was believed to link the Atlantic and Pacific Oceans. Unable to find this, he went to Hawaii instead. One of his boats was stolen by the islanders, however, and Cook took the local leader hostage. The islanders then stabbed Cook to death.

CONVICT SHIPS

From 1787, instead of being hanged or imprisoned, many prisoners were sent to Australia in convict ships. They were treated harshly on board. Once there, they were not free, but had to work. Many died or suffered horrible diseases. From around 1840, conditions improved. Both men and women were sent, and set up colonies just as the Pilgrim Fathers had done in America. Over a period of 80 years, over 165,000 convicts were sent to Australia. Convicts were also sent to Norfolk Island and Tasmania.

1701: Jethro Tull makes a drill for sowing seeds that can be pulled by a horse.

1730: Joseph Foljambe makes a cast-iron plough based on a Dutch design.

1784: A threshing machine for separating grain is invented by Andrew Meikle.

The Agricultural Revolution

Between 1750 and 1850, farming practices changed and became much more efficient. The population of Britain grew from 5.7 million to 16.6 million because there was much less risk of starvation.

THE GROWTH OF FARMING

In eastern England, areas of wet ground were drained. Before that, people caught fish and birds to eat in this area, but now they were able to grow crops instead. In other parts of the country, trees in areas of woodland were cut down so that more crops could be grown.

Not only was land now more productive, but people were more efficient as well. Fewer farmers were needed to work the land, so people could now move to towns and cities to look for different kinds of employment.

A new system of land management was devised. The landowners would rent out large areas of land to tenant farmers, who then employed labourers to do all the digging.

BETTER CROPS

Farmers started to grow plants that produced more grain, so a bigger quantity of food would result from the same area of land. They stopped growing rye and replaced it with wheat and barley.

Previously, crops were just intended to feed people. Cows and sheep were allowed to graze in open fields. Now it was realised that crops could be grown just to feed the animals – these were called fodder crops. This meant that the animals would need less space to roam around and more land would be available for growing crops.

1801: The General Enclosure Act is passed to tidy up all the enclosure acts so far.

1830: Some farm labourers riot because their jobs are being done by machines.

1834: Improvements are made to the threshing machine to make it much faster.

Turnips and Clover

Turnips and clover were grown as fodder crops. Farmers realised that the two crops could be grown on the same patch of land but at different times. Clover was grown in the spring and summer. It could then be dug up and turnips planted instead for the winter. This system provided food throughout the year and also meant that the ground was never empty.

LAND ENCLOSURE

A process known as "enclosure" changed farming in Britain forever. Previously, individual peasant farmers farmed their own piece or strip of land in open fields. Increasingly, large areas were "enclosed", with a fence or hedge around them to prevent others from using them. This created large farms that could be put under the control of tenant farmers who ran them like businesses. These farmers employed peasants to do all the hard work and then sold the crops to merchants.

Whereas before everybody owned a bit of land that they regarded as their own, now there were a lot of people who did not own anything at all – even though they still had to work.

DID YOU KNOW?

Parliament passed many Enclosure Acts between 1750 and 1860.

AWESOME FACT

A Changing Way of Life

By 1850, only 22 per cent of the British people worked in agriculture, the smallest proportion for any country in the world.

1563: William Lee invents a stocking frame, a device for knitting stockings.

1733: John Kay develops the flying shuttle for weaving fabric in broader widths.

1775: James Watt and Matthew Boulton set up a firm to improve steam engines.

The Industrial Revolution

Towards the end of the 18th century, changes began to take place in the lives of ordinary people. Instead of working in the fields, they moved to towns and found jobs in factories.

NEW FACTORIES

Many people found jobs making clothing, pottery and other household goods in factories. The people who owned the factories paid them wages for the work they did. It was necessary to bring important raw materials, such as wool to make yarn, to the factories. Once the goods had been made, they then had to be transported to other towns to be sold.

IMPROVED ROADS

Up until this time, the old Roman roads were still in use. Now existing roads were improved and new ones were built. Thomas Telford (1757–1854) built many new roads and bridges. He was known as "the Colossus of Roads". In about 1820, John Loudon McAdam (1756–1836) found a way of mixing small stones with cement. This made a much better road surface.

1779: Richard Crompton invents a spinning mule that can spin thread.

1786: Richard Arkwright puts a Watt engine in a London cotton mill.

1812: The steamboat *Comet* starts operating on the Firth of Clyde.

THE CANAL NETWORK

Canals are channels of water that link lakes, rivers and the sea. Canals had been used for transport since ancient times, but there was now a new interest in them, and many new canals were dug.

Canals linked important cities and towns. Before cars were invented in the 20th century, canals were the best way of moving things around the country. Whatever needed to be transported was loaded onto a barge that was pulled along by a horse. The horse walked along a towpath next to the canal.

On roads, a horse could only pull a wagon. But a barge is bigger than a wagon and can hold much more. The barge is also easy for the horse to pull along because it is floating in the water. If the factory made fragile goods, such as pottery, the objects would be less likely to get broken, as going by barge was a gentle method of transport. Wagons often tipped over, especially if the road was uneven.

COOL FACTS

Disadvantages of the Canals

- A horse pulling a barge cannot walk very fast, so canal travel was quite slow. It is also difficult to turn a barge round.
- As water is always level, it is difficult for barges to go up and down hills. Systems of locks were devised to make this possible.

THE TURNPIKE TRUSTS

The sections of road that were owned by the Turnpike Trusts were called turnpikes. If you wanted to use the road, you had to pay a fee – called a toll. The companies used this money to repair roads and sometimes build new ones. Before the turnpikes, roads were very stony and uneven.

To use the road, you had to pay to pass through a toll gate. The person who collected the toll lived in a toll house next to the gate. But some people were angry about the Turnpike Trusts because they now had to pay to use roads that used to be free.

DID YOU KNOW?

The first Turnpike Trusts were set up after an Act of Parliament in 1707.

The toll gate at Hyde Park Corner in London.

1678: Abraham Darby is born in Woodsetton, in Staffordshire, into a Quaker family.

1707: Abraham Darby patents his new method of casting brass and iron.

1709: Abraham Darby buys premises in Shropshire where he sets up a factory.

New Industries

Hand in hand with improved transport systems, new industries started to spring up throughout Britain. New inventions meant that things could be made both quickly and cheaply.

The Coal Industry

Coal mining became very important. Previously, coal had mainly been used for burning in houses for warmth. Now it was used to drive powerful machinery and in large furnaces for working with metals. Coal is found in many areas of Britain, particularly in Wales, Scotland, Northumberland, Yorkshire, Lancashire, parts of the Midlands, and Kent. Many new towns were built where coal could be mined. The coal was sent round the country on the canals.

1717: Abraham Darby dies in Shropshire following a long illness. He was only 38 years old.

1779: The first iron bridge is built in Shropshire by Abraham Darby's descendants.

1967: The Ironbridge Gorge Museum Trust is established to honour the Industrial Revolution.

ABRAHAM DARBY AND THE IRON INDUSTRY

Abraham Darby (1678–1717) played an important role in the Industrial Revolution. He was born in the West Midlands and trained as a metal worker. Around 1700, he moved to Bristol, where set up his own business. In 1709, he bought some premises in Coalbrookdale, in Shropshire, where he set up a brass and iron works. This became the most important iron-producing area in the world.

Darby perfected a new way of smelting iron called coke smelting. Coke is made by heating coal. In iron smelting, iron is extracted from the iron ore by heating and melting it. Before, people had used charcoal, which is made by heating wood. By 1700, there was a shortage of charcoal and, anyway, it was much more expensive than coke.

COOL FACTS

Abraham Darby

- Abraham Darby was a Quaker. Quakers were groups of Christians who believed in living v ery simply. They disapproved of making images of people, so there are no portraits of Darby or his family.
- Descendants of Abraham Darby built the world's first iron bridge in Coalbrookdale, in Shropshire, in 1779.

AWESOME FACT

In 1712, one of Abraham Darby's Bristol factories was using 250 tonnes of coal (the equivalent of 400 horseloads) a week.

Using Darby's method, it was also possible to make things out of brass or iron much more cheaply than before. These items could now be mass-produced, too. Darby was able to make goods of greater smoothness and with more detail than had been possible before. This included making intricate parts for steam engines.

THE COTTON INDUSTRY

Cotton production now became a major industry. Previously, cotton was imported from India already woven into fabric. But raw cotton was now being grown in America. The raw, unspun cotton was brought to England by boat where it arrived at the port of Liverpool. Liverpool now became a very important trading city.

The cotton was taken to many factories throughout northern Britain to be spun and woven, and then made into clothes. Many factories were either built next to fast-flowing rivers that powered the machinery or they used steam engines powered by coal.

1759: William Wilberforce, a leading campaigner, is born in Kingston-upon-Hull.

1787: Quakers and others set up a society to abolish the slave trade.

1807: The slave trade is officially abolished by an Act of Parliament.

THE SLAVE TRADE

Between the 16th and the 19th centuries many European nations, including Britain, became rich through the slave trade. People were taken from Africa to the Americas where they faced a life of hard labour.

SLAVES IN AMERICA

Europeans who settled in America seized vast areas of land. Native Americans were driven from their settlements and many died from the diseases that the Europeans brought with them. The ones who were left refused to work for the new settlers. But the Europeans need people to work for them and slaves were the cheapest form of labour.

The majority of slaves were taken from the coast of West Africa and sent directly to the Americas. Men, women and children were all sold as slaves.

From the 1600s onwards, Britain did more trade in slaves than any other country. They traded guns and other weapons with African kings in exchange for prisoners that had been captured in battle. The kings used the weapons to win more battles so that they would have more prisoners to trade. However, they had no idea that the prisoners would be sold into a life of slavery.

DID YOU KNOW?

The slaves were often brought to the ports of Bristol or Liverpool on their way to America. Both cities became very rich through the trade in slaves.

1833: Wilberforce dies and is honoured with a burial in Westminster Abbey.

1840: A statue of William Wilberforce is unveiled in Westminster Abbey.

1903: Wilberforce House in Hull is opened as Britain's first slavery museum.

CROSSING THE ATLANTIC OCEAN

Conditions on board the slave ships were very poor. The slaves were packed together like sardines in a tin and many died on the crossing. When they finally got to America, the slaves were sold to plantation and mine owners. They would be oiled to make them look healthier.

COOL FACTS

The Life of an American Slave

- Slaves worked down mines or in the fields, picking cotton and sugar cane.
- Some slaves worked as unpaid servants in the master's house.
- Slaves were not treated like other human beings. They were often worked to death, as it was cheaper to buy a new slave than to keep an older one alive.
- Slaves all lived together in large huts and were only given enough food to keep them alive.
- Slaves had no rights and were not allowed to marry. Children were separated from their parents and often sold separately.

ABOLITION OF THE SLAVE TRADE

In the 1770s, many churchgoers in Britain began to question the use of slaves. They thought that slavery was a sin. In 1807, the slave trade was abolished, but this did not free those who were already slaves. In 1833 an act was passed that gave freedom to all the slaves in the British Empire. However, the new law was difficult to enforce, and the buying and selling of slaves continued for many years.

William Wilberforce (1759–1833) campaigned for an end to the trafficking of slaves. Over a period of nearly 20 years he made many speeches and wrote books to try and persuade Parliament to change the law.

1698: Thomas Newcomen invents a steam engine that can pump water.

1736: James Watt, who will develop the steam engine, is born.

1764: James Hargreaves invents the spinning jenny to speed up spinning.

New Machines

New machinery revolutionised the world of work. Machines could work much faster than people, which meant that work was now often a matter of operating the machines and keeping them in good order.

HAND-MADE VERSUS MACHINE-MADE

Making things by hand usually takes a long time. Also, no two pieces can ever be exactly the same. The use of machines guaranteed that every item made in factories could be identical.

Some items could be made by machine and then finished by hand. China crockery would be mass-produced and then individual pieces could be hand-painted. Clothes could be machine-made, and then hand-embroidered.

AWESOME FACT

James Hargreaves had no formal education and never learnt how to read or write.

DID YOU KNOW?

James Hargreaves is said to have got the idea for the spinning jenny when his daughter Jenny knocked over a spinning wheel and he saw the spindle roll across the floor.

THE SPINNING JENNY

It was only possible to spin one thread at a time if you were using a spinning wheel. James Hargreaves (1720–1778) invented the spinning jenny in 1764. The jenny could produce several threads at once, thus speeding up the spinning process. The first spinning jennies were difficult to operate, so various improvements were made to the original machine until a spinning jenny could produce 50 threads. Using the jenny, along with the flying shuttle, spinning frame and cotton gin, meant that large quantities of harvested cotton could be handled at once.

1771: Richard Arkwright builds the first cotton factory in Derbyshire. He becomes very wealthy.

1792: Richard Arkwright dies at his home in Derbyshire. He is remembered as a great industrialist.

2001: Cromford Mill, in Derbyshire, is named as a World Heritage Site.

SIR RICHARD ARKWRIGHT

Richard Arkwright (1732–1792) started his career as a hairdresser. He improved James Hargreaves' invention, so that it was easier to use and could produce stronger yarn. Arkwright was also the first industrialist to use steam engines to power machinery in the production of textiles. Using the steam engine together with machinery led to the development of the power loom. Arkwright was knighted in 1786 and died a wealthy man.

Sir Richard Arkwright (1732–1792)

INTERESTING

The First Cotton Factory

Sir Richard Arkwright built the first cotton factory at Cromford, in Derbyshire, in 1771. The mill buildings still exist.

THE STEAM ENGINE

The steam engine was a very important invention. Thomas Newcomen (1664–1729) invented the steam engine in 1698. In a steam engine, water is heated by a fire and turned into steam. The steam can then be used to power machinery. An early use of the steam engine was to pump underground water out of coal mines, so that the miners could reach the coal. Steam engines were also used in paper, flour, cotton and iron mills, as well as distilleries, canals and waterworks. The use of the steam engine increased the demand for iron to make them.

An engineer called James Watt (1736–1819) realised that the design could be improved further. With Matthew Boulton, he began making steam engines and their factory became the most important engineering firm in the country. In 1785, they were elected fellows of the Royal Society.

The Luddites

With new machines to do a lot of the work, employers thought they could pay workers less money. In 1811, some workers in Nottingham decided to attack the factories. The protest spread to other towns. The protesters were called Luddites, after Ned Ludd, who in 1779 was whipped for laziness. He got his own back by smashing some knitting frames.

1738: George, the grandson of George II, is born at Norfolk House in London.

1756: The Seven Years' War breaks out involving several countries.

1761: George III is crowned king at Westminster Abbey in London.

GEORGE III

(1738–1820)

George III had a long reign but it was not continuous. Unfortunately, George suffered from severe mental health problems and eventually his son had to rule in his place.

In 1761, George III married Charlotte of Mecklenburg-Strelitz. They had 15 children.

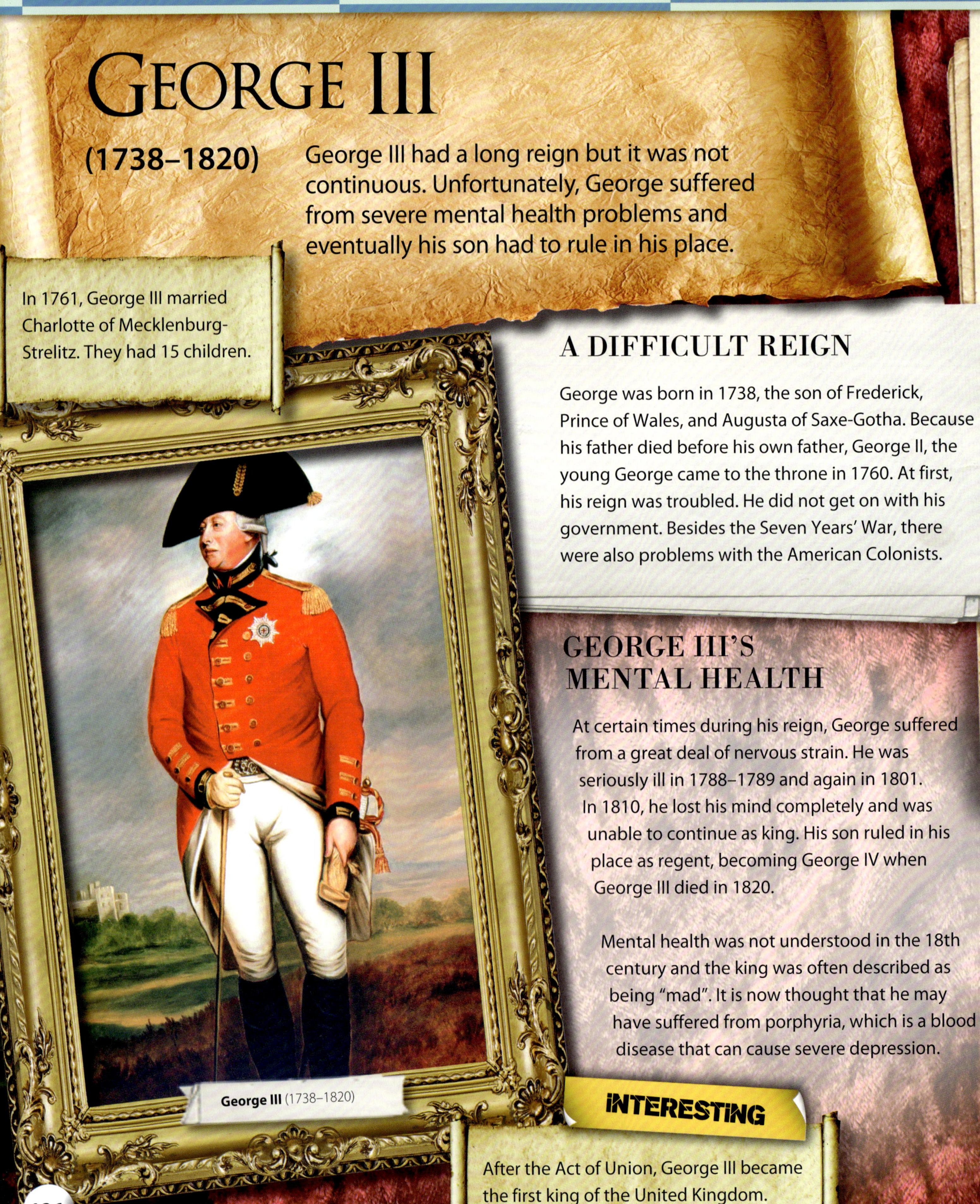

George III (1738–1820)

A DIFFICULT REIGN

George was born in 1738, the son of Frederick, Prince of Wales, and Augusta of Saxe-Gotha. Because his father died before his own father, George II, the young George came to the throne in 1760. At first, his reign was troubled. He did not get on with his government. Besides the Seven Years' War, there were also problems with the American Colonists.

GEORGE III'S MENTAL HEALTH

At certain times during his reign, George suffered from a great deal of nervous strain. He was seriously ill in 1788–1789 and again in 1801. In 1810, he lost his mind completely and was unable to continue as king. His son ruled in his place as regent, becoming George IV when George III died in 1820.

Mental health was not understood in the 18th century and the king was often described as being "mad". It is now thought that he may have suffered from porphyria, which is a blood disease that can cause severe depression.

INTERESTING

After the Act of Union, George III became the first king of the United Kingdom.

1783: William Pitt the Younger becomes the youngest ever Prime Minister.

1819: The Peterloo Massacre takes place in Manchester. There is a national outcry.

1820: George III dies after a long period of poor health. He is succeeded by his son, George.

THE SEVEN YEARS' WAR (1756–1763)

This was a long period of conflict involving most European nations, America and India. Austria was at war with Prussia, a powerful north German state. Britain sided with the Germans because the British king was German. France, supported by Spain, came into the war, opposing Britain. France and Britain were also fighting over territories in North America and were rivals for trade in India. A key figure in the British war against France in the Americas was General James Wolfe (1727–1759) who defeated the French at the Battle of Quebec in Canada in 1759, although he died on the battlefield. Britain was eventually victorious over France and became the most powerful nation in the world.

Austria defeats Prussia at the Battle of Kolin (1757).

William Pitt the Younger
(1759–1806)

THE PITT PRIME MINISTERS

William Pitt (1708–1778) was an important politician. He helped win the Seven Years' War and became Prime Minister himself from 1766 to 1768. After several unsuccessful governments, George III appointed William Pitt the Younger (1759–1806) as his Prime Minister in 1783. The Seven Years' War and the American War of Independence were very expensive for Britain, and Pitt the Younger worked hard to build up Britain's finances again.

In 1798, there was a rebellion in Ireland. In 1801, Pitt introduced an Act of Union with Ireland, uniting Britain and Ireland into one kingdom. But he wanted the Irish to be free to be Catholics. George III was opposed to this, so Pitt resigned.

AWESOME FACT

William Pitt the Younger was the youngest ever British Prime Minister. He was only 24.

1732: George Washington, later the first President, is born in Virginia.

1773: At the Boston Tea Party, tea is dumped into the sea.

1775: British troops try to seize weapons from the Colonists.

THE AMERICAN WAR OF INDEPENDENCE

What is usually called The American War of Independence was more like a world war, as several nations were involved in the conflict and not just Britain and the American Colonies.

THIRTEEN COLONIES

Before gaining independence, America was made up of 13 British colonies. There were also French, Spanish and Dutch settlements, but these were not as important as the British ones. At first, most people who lived in the British colonies, called the Colonists, were loyal to Britain. But they had to pay British taxes and even ordinary things like tea were taxed.

Eventually, many began to think this was unfair and started to argue for their rights. However, some aristocrats remained loyal to Britain, which they still considered their home country.

In 1775, British troops in Boston tried to seize weapons owned by the Colonists. As they were outnumbered, the British were quickly defeated, but this was really only the start of the troubles.

The Battle of Bennington (1777)

1776: A group of Colonists declare Independence in Philadelphia.

1781: The British are defeated at the Battle of the Chesapeake.

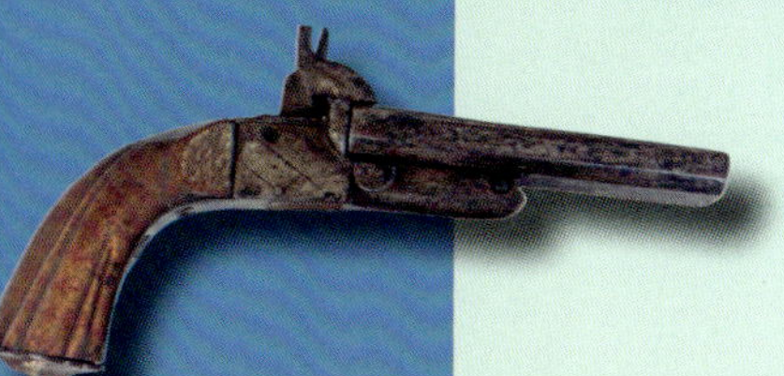

1783: The War of Independence ends with the Treaty of Paris.

COOL FACTS

The Boston Tea Party

- In 1773, some of the Colonists dumped three shiploads of tea into the sea at Boston Harbour. This became the famous incident that led up to the war.
- The group of men that dumped the tea into Boston Harbour called themselves the "Sons of Liberty".

Thomas Paine

Thomas Paine (1737–1809) was an English writer who went to America. He wrote a pamphlet called *Common Sense* in which he rejected the idea of a monarchy. His writings were later read to American soldiers before they went into battle.

THE DECLARATION OF INDEPENDENCE

In 1776, 75,000 British troops arrived to put a stop to the American rebellion. On 4 July 1776, the Colonists met in Philadelphia and declared their independence. But with a superior army, the British soon gained the upper hand. However, France intervened in support of the Colonists. For a while, both sides held various territories without being able to win a convincing victory over the other.

At the Battle of the Chesapeake, the French navy defeated the British. George Washington was able to take advantage of this and won the Battle of Yorktown in 1781. In 1782, the House of Commons in London voted to end the war.

A peace agreement was reached and, the following year, Britain declared that it would stop fighting. The war ended formally when the Treaty of Paris was signed in 1783.

George Washington

George Washington (1732–1799) grew up in Virginia. In 1775, he was made general of the Colonist army. Most of the soldiers were just farmers, and had not had the training of the British.

After losing many battles, Washington was finally able to lead his army to victory when the British surrendered at Yorktown.

Washington became the first president of the newly created United States of America. He established many traditions that continue to this day.

1758: Admiral Lord Nelson is born in Burnham Thorpe in Norfolk.

1769: Napoleon Bonaparte is born in Ajaccio on the island of Corsica.

1805: The Battle of Trafalgar takes place and Lord Nelson is killed.

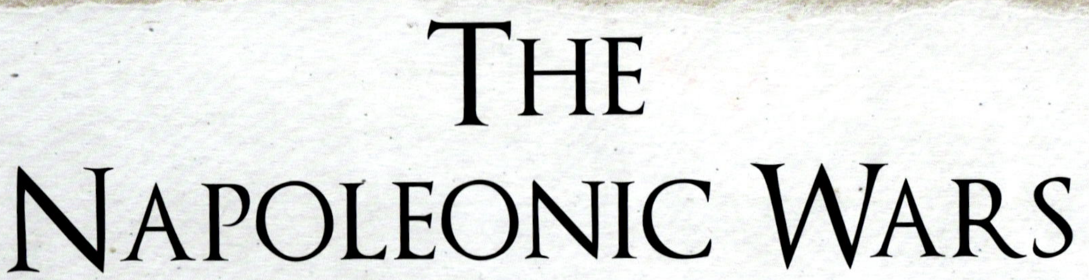

The Napoleonic Wars

Around the turn of the century, after the French Revolution of 1789 had deposed the monarchy, France was led by the Emperor Napoleon Bonaparte. He wanted to create a large French empire, and so Britain faced the threat of a French invasion.

NAPOLEON BONAPARTE

Napoleon (1769–1821) was a French army leader who was so successful that he was able to take over the running of France. He declared himself Emperor of France in 1804. Napoleon wanted to take over Europe and fought many wars. In 1814, he was defeated and forced to go and live on Elba, an island in the Mediterranean. But he escaped and returned to power.

However, Napoleon's second reign did not last long. He was defeated at the Battle of Waterloo in 1815. After this, the British locked him up for good on the island of St. Helena in the Atlantic Ocean.

Napoleon Bonaparte (1769–1821)

AWESOME FACT

You can see Napoleon Bonaparte's death mask on display in the British Museum in London.

1815: At the Battle of Waterloo, Napoleon Bonaparte is finally defeated.

1821: Napoleon dies while still in exile on the island of St. Helena in the Atlantic.

1840: Work begins on Nelson's Column in Trafalgar Square in London.

WAR WITH FRANCE

In 1797, Napoleon announced that he intended to invade Britain. To do this, he would have to defeat the British navy. He attempted to land in Ireland and attack Britain from there, but this was unsuccessful. In 1802, a truce was called, but it didn't last. War began in earnest in 1803.

THE BATTLE OF TRAFALGAR

Cape Trafalgar is on the Spanish coast. A great sea battle was fought there in 1805. The French had help from Spain and had a slightly larger fleet. But the British, led by Lord Nelson, captured most of the enemy ships. Sadly, Nelson was shot and killed during the battle.

The Battle of Waterloo (1815)

THE BATTLE OF WATERLOO

Nowadays, Waterloo is in Belgium, but it was a part of the Netherlands during the Napoleonic Wars. The British had combined their forces with the Prussians. Napoleon was afraid that they would try and invade France. The Battle of Waterloo took place in 1815. It had been pouring with rain and Napoleon's army had difficulties in the mud. The allied British and Prussian troops were able to capture Napoleon and win the battle. The war with France was over.

Admiral Lord Nelson

Nelson (1758–1805) is one of Britain's great military heroes. He fought many battles, in which he was blinded in one eye and lost an arm. After he was killed at the Battle of Trafalgar in 1805 during the Napoleonic Wars, he was brought back to England and given a state funeral. He is commemorated by Nelson's Column in Trafalgar Square, which is one of London's best-known landmarks.

After he was killed, Nelson's body was preserved in brandy.

The Duke of Wellington

Wellington (1769–1852) joined the army in 1787. He won many battles, and then became a Member of Parliament. But he was needed to lead the army against Napoleon. His victory at Waterloo in 1815 meant that the threat of invasion was at an end. Wellington became Prime Minister in 1828. However, he was so used to telling people what to do on the battlefield that he was unpopular in Parliament. He was called "The Iron Duke".

1762: George IV is born at St. James's Palace in London.

1787: Work begins on a pavilion for George at Brighton by the sea.

1795: The marriage takes place between George and Caroline of Brunswick.

THE REGENCY

The time when the Prince of Wales ruled in place of his father is known as The Regency. The Prince Regent was a very flamboyant ruler who was fond of parties and parades.

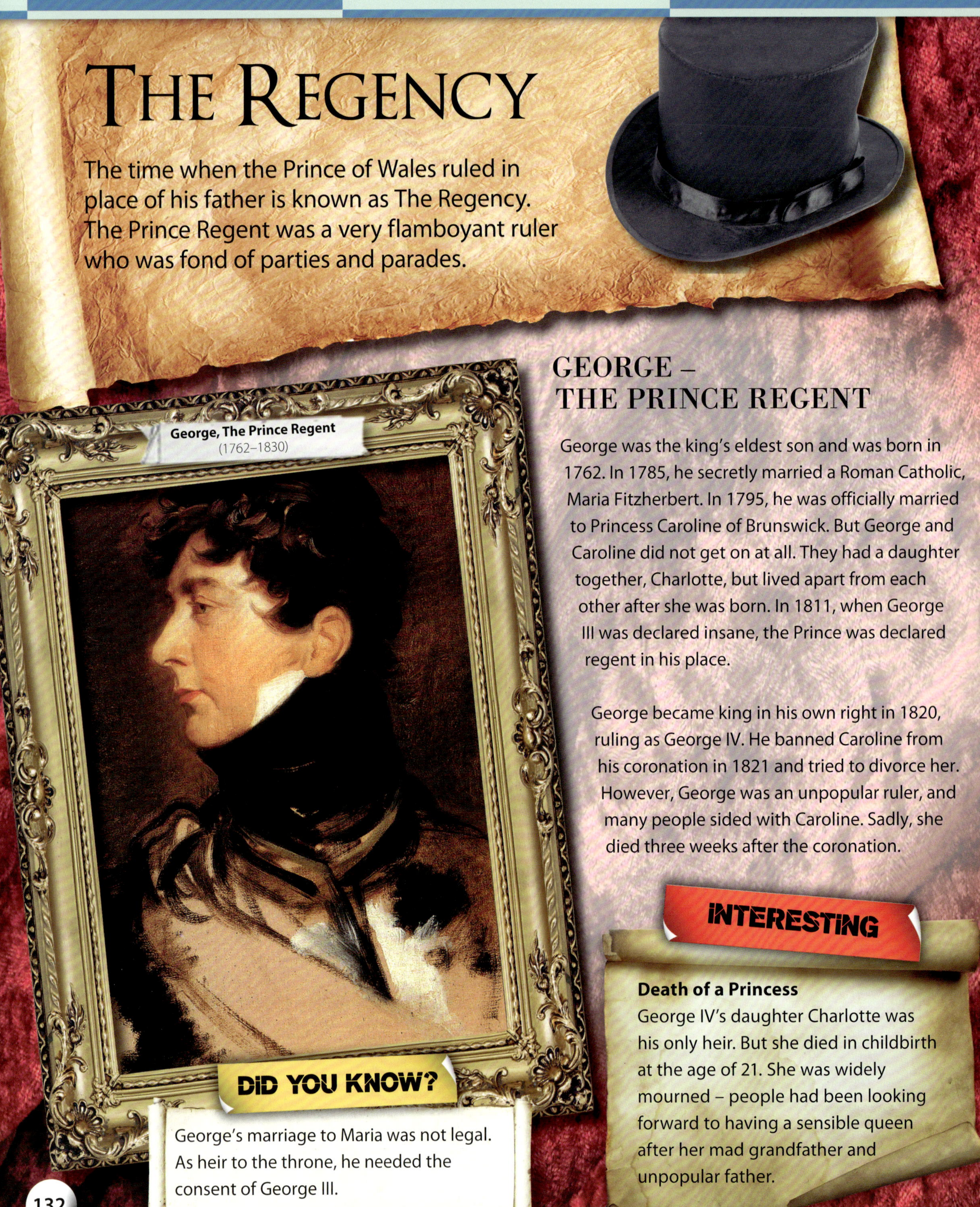

George, The Prince Regent
(1762–1830)

GEORGE – THE PRINCE REGENT

George was the king's eldest son and was born in 1762. In 1785, he secretly married a Roman Catholic, Maria Fitzherbert. In 1795, he was officially married to Princess Caroline of Brunswick. But George and Caroline did not get on at all. They had a daughter together, Charlotte, but lived apart from each other after she was born. In 1811, when George III was declared insane, the Prince was declared regent in his place.

George became king in his own right in 1820, ruling as George IV. He banned Caroline from his coronation in 1821 and tried to divorce her. However, George was an unpopular ruler, and many people sided with Caroline. Sadly, she died three weeks after the coronation.

DID YOU KNOW?

George's marriage to Maria was not legal. As heir to the throne, he needed the consent of George III.

INTERESTING

Death of a Princess
George IV's daughter Charlotte was his only heir. But she died in childbirth at the age of 21. She was widely mourned – people had been looking forward to having a sensible queen after her mad grandfather and unpopular father.

1811: George is named Prince Regent in place of his father, George III, who is ill.

1820: George becomes monarch in his own right and is crowned the next year.

1830: George IV dies and is buried in St. George's Chapel, Windsor Castle.

BEAU BRUMMEL

The Prince Regent had a friend called George Brummel (1778–1840) who was always known as "Beau", meaning "handsome". Beau was a style icon for men, rather like David Beckham today, and was the first dandy. He spent up to five hours a day getting dressed. He wore fitted trousers and jackets, and always cleaned his teeth very carefully.

COOL FACTS

A Day in the Life of a Dandy

Rich people with lots of leisure time led very self-indulgent lives. This is how a dandy such as Beau Brummel would spend his days:

- **Morning** Beau would spend the morning getting dressed and going shopping.
- **Afternoon** Beau would go to his club or ride his horse around Hyde Park.
- **Evening** Beau would either visit the theatre or go to a party.

The Peterloo Massacre

Many people lived in great poverty and could not even afford bread. In 1819, ordinary people met up in the middle of Manchester to protest. They did not want to cause trouble, but soldiers and police were called in to drive them away. People were trampled on by horses and some were even killed. This event was named the Peterloo Massacre after the Battle of Waterloo of 1815.

Jane Austen (1775–1817) is one of Britain's most famous writers. Her novels include *Pride and Prejudice*, which is sometimes considered to be the first rom-com. In this novel, the rich and handsome Mr. Darcy meets sparky Elizabeth Bennet. She hates him at first, but they finally fall in love. Jane Austen's books are very funny and give us a good idea of what life was like for many people in those days.

Brighton Pavilion

George first visited Brighton in 1783. He liked it so much that he had a palace built there, called the Pavilion. It was meant to look like an Indian palace by the sea. Inside, a lot of the furniture and decoration is in the Indian and Chinese style. Because of George's interest, Brighton became a very fashionable place to live.

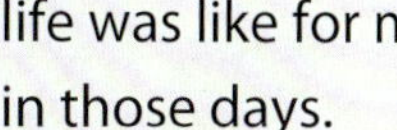

1781: George Stephenson – "The Father of the Railways" – is born near Newcastle upon Tyne.

1814: William Hedley builds an engine called "Puffing Billy" to pull coal wagons.

1823: Robert Stephenson and Company is set up to build railway engines.

The Coming of the Railways

The railways transformed Britain. Before trains, people travelled around the country either in wagons or coaches pulled by horses or by canal. These forms of transport were often slow and uncomfortable.

AWESOME FACT

"Puffing Billy"
We remember the steam locomotive Puffing Billy when we say things like "running out of puff" or "running like Billy-o".

THE FIRST LOCOMOTIVE

The first steam locomotive was made by Richard Trevithick (1771–1883) for his iron works at Penydarren in Wales. It was not a reliable machine, but it did inspire others to improve it. In 1814, an engine called "Puffing Billy" was built by William Hedley to pull coal wagons at a colliery in Northumberland. It was so good that it was used for 50 years.

GEORGE STEPHENSON

George Stephenson (1781–1848) was born near Newcastle upon Tyne. His father worked at a coal mine, where he looked after steam engines. George was fascinated by machinery. At that time, steam engines were mainly used to drive machinery in factories, but sometimes they were made to run on wheels along roads. But these engines were slow and could not go up hills. George realised that they would go faster on rails.

In 1819, he built a small railway at Hetton colliery, which had an 13-km (8-mile) track. The first passenger railway was opened in 1825. George made the track and the locomotive, and drove the first train.

1825: Trains that carry passengers run for the first time on the Stockton to Darlington railway.

1830: A new railway that links Liverpool and Manchester is opened.

1862: Stephenson's *Rocket* is donated to what is now the Science Museum in London.

STEPHENSON'S ROCKET

In 1829, Stephenson made another railway to link Liverpool and Manchester. A competition was held to see which locomotive should be used on the new railway. There were three contenders, one of which was made by Stephenson himself. It was called the *Rocket*. The two rival locomotives kept breaking down. Stephenson's went faster than the others and was much more reliable. The *Rocket* won the competition hands down.

On 15 September 1830, the new railway was opened. But a tragedy occurred. William Huskisson, a government minister, was knocked down and killed by the *Rocket*, which had a speed of 58 km/h (36 mph). This was much faster than any horse and was the fastest anyone had ever travelled.

COOL FACTS

George Stephenson

- George Stephenson is sometimes called "The Father of the Railway".
- Stephenson's first locomotive could only travel at 6.4 km/h (4 mph).
- The first proper train could carry 450 passengers at a speed of 24 km/h (15 mph).

ROBERT STEPHENSON

Together with his son, Robert, George built many more railways. Robert Stephenson (1803–1859) made the first railway from London to Birmingham, which was finished in 1838. He went on to make railways all over the world and also built the Menai Bridge in North Wales. He was a friend of the engineer Isambard Kingdom Brunel.

1765: William, younger brother of George IV, is born at Buckingham House.

1818: William marries Adelaide of Saxe-Meiningen, who is half his age.

1830: William comes to the throne as his brother has no surviving children.

William IV

(1765–1837)

William IV was the last of the Hanoverian kings. He is often forgotten because his reign was so short, but several important reforms were made during this time.

WILLIAM'S BRIEF REIGN

Born in 1765, William was the younger brother of George IV. He inherited the throne in 1830. In 1818, William married Adelaide of Saxe-Meiningen. Their marriage was happy, but their two daughters died while still very young.

William IV (1765–1837)

PARISH RELIEF

Then, as now, there were people who were unable to work, usually through illness or because they had had an accident. People who could not pay their rent were made to leave their own home. Some children became orphans because their parents died and there was no relative available to take care of them.

Homeless people could apply for parish relief, which was a sort of charity. In villages, the system worked well because everybody knew everyone else and would understand the difficulties of being without work. In towns and cities, it was more difficult to decide if strangers were in real need of help or were just being lazy and unwilling to work.

1832: The Reform Act, passed following riots, allows more people to vote in elections.

1834: A Poor Law is passed that is designed to keep poor people off the streets.

1837: William IV dies at Windsor Castle, tended by his wife during his last days.

THE POOR LAW

In towns, people who were unable to work often took to the streets as beggars if they had no relatives to help them. Even children went onto the streets. In 1834, a new Poor Law was passed that was intended to solve this problem. Homeless people would be sent to workhouses, where they would be clothed and fed. Children would also receive some education. In return, they would all have to work. However, the workhouse was more like a prison and people dreaded being sent there.

LIFE IN A WORKHOUSE

COOL FACTS

When you entered a workhouse, you would be stripped, searched and washed. Your hair would be cut short and then you would have to put on a rough uniform. If, for any reason, you went out of the workhouse, everyone would know where you had just come from.

- ❖ Inmates were made to get up a 5 o' clock in the morning. Prayers were read before breakfast and after supper. Bed-time was at 8pm.
- ❖ Food consisted of bread and gruel, which was a kind of thin soup made from boiling oatmeal in water.
- ❖ Children up to the age of seven had half a pint of milk a day (which is just over a quarter of a litre).
- ❖ Men were made to break up stones or work in the fields. Women would work in the fields or do washing and scrubbing, though sometimes they did needlework as well.
- ❖ If anybody broke the workhouse rules, they were either sent to prison, which was even worse, or shut up in a room on their own.
- ❖ Men, women and children all lived separately, so families were split up.

WOOLLEN & MIXED FAB

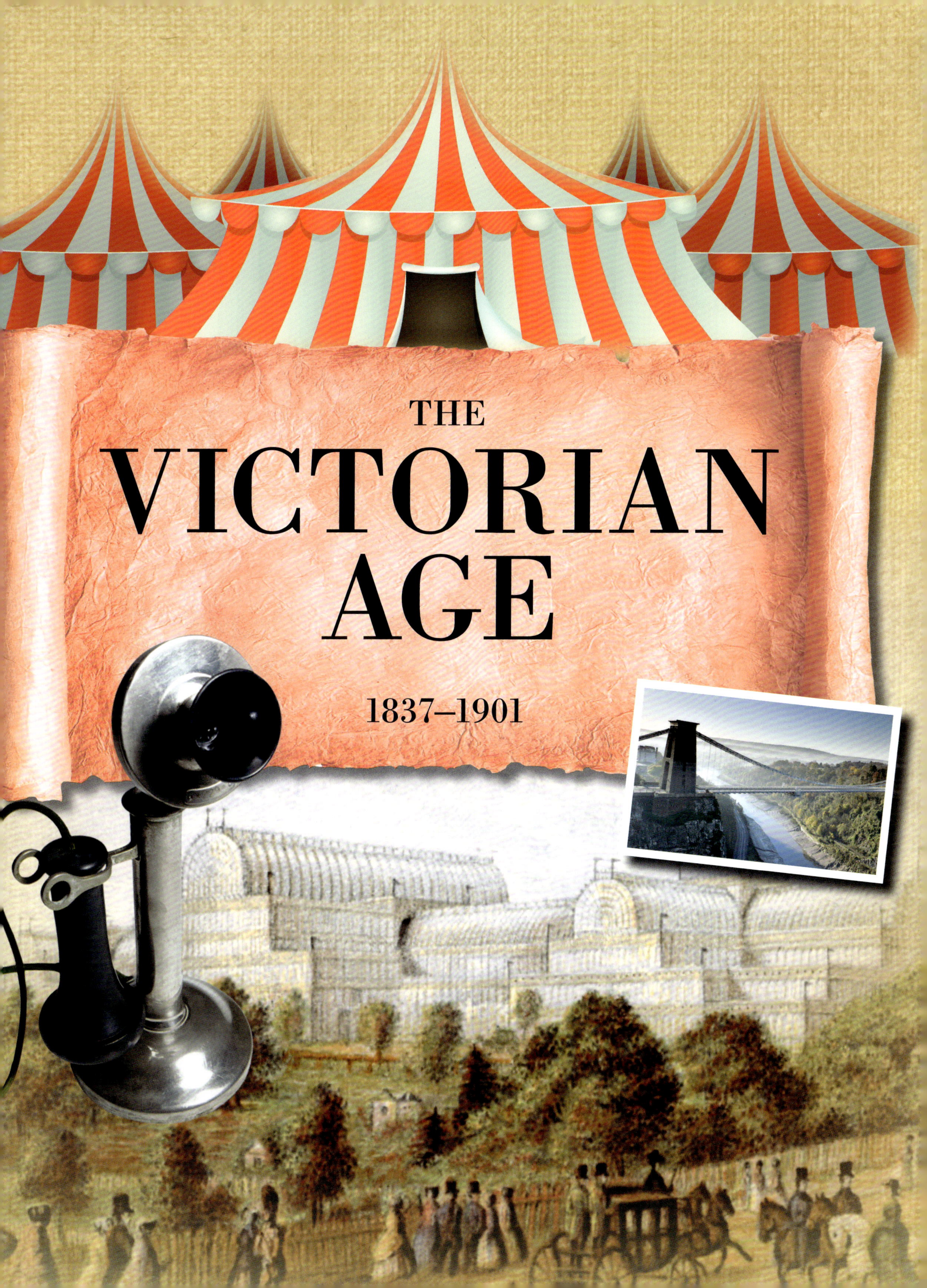
THE
VICTORIAN
AGE
1837–1901

1819: Victoria is born at Kensington Palace and becomes fifth in line to the throne.

1837: At the young age of 18, Victoria inherits the British throne.

1840: Queen Victoria marries her cousin, Albert of Saxe-Coburg-Gotha.

QUEEN VICTORIA (1819-1901)

On his death William IV was succeeded by Victoria who was the daughter of George III's fourth son Edward. Victoria's reign saw a great deal of change to life in Britain, as well as the expansion of the British Empire.

DID YOU KNOW?

Victoria was the last of the Hanoverians. When she got married, she took the name Saxe-Coburg-Gotha.

A PROTECTED PRINCESS

Victoria's father died when she was only eight months old. It looked as if she would inherit the throne when she grew up and her mother, Princess Victoria of Saxe-Coburg-Saalfeld, was afraid that someone might attempt to kill her. So, just as in a fairy story, she kept Victoria locked up. She had to sleep in her mother's room every night until she became queen. Victoria was not allowed to play with other children and all her food was tasted before she ate it in case it was poisoned.

A HAPPY MARRIAGE

In 1840, when Victoria was 21, she married her cousin, Albert of Saxe-Coburg-Gotha. They were very happy together and had nine children. They built Osborne House on the Isle of Wight as a summer home. Albert designed the house himself. It is meant to look like an Italian palace. Victoria and Albert were also very fond of Scotland and, in fact, many Victorian paintings show Scottish scenes. In 1848, they bought Balmoral Castle. Today's royal family also spend some of their holidays there.

When Albert died in 1861 from typhoid, Victoria was very sad and wore black for the rest of her life. People called her the "Widow of Windsor". After Albert's death, Victoria spent a lot of her time at Balmoral Castle, as if she were in hiding. She became unpopular, as people could not see the point of a queen that they never saw. Some even thought that Britain should get rid of the monarchy altogether.

1861: Albert dies of typhoid and Victoria begins a long period of mourning.

1897: Victoria celebrates 60 years of being queen with her Diamond Jubilee.

1901: Victoria dies at Osborne House on the Isle of Wight.

Victoria's Jubilees

Victoria celebrated her Golden Jubilee in 1887 – after 50 years on the throne. There was a big procession and a service in Westminster Abbey in London. This made her popular again. Ten years later she had her Diamond Jubilee and this was even more lavish. There was an open-air service outside St. Paul's Cathedral. She sat in an open carriage so that everybody could see her.

INTERESTING

In 1876 Victoria was proclaimed "Empress of India" because India was a part of the British Empire.

COOL FACTS

- Victoria was queen for nearly 64 years, making her the longest-reigning British monarch so far.
- Victoria was 152cm (5ft) tall.
- Victoria was the first monarch to live at Buckingham Palace in London.
- Victoria died at Osborne House on the Isle of Wight in 1901.

John Brown

John Brown was one of Victoria's servants. After Albert's death, they became very good friends. Later on, there were even rumours that they had married in secret.

From left to right: Prince Alfred and the Prince of Wales; Queen Victoria and Prince Albert; Princesses Alice, Helena and Victoria

1844: A large exhibition is held in Paris that inspires Britain to organise one, too.

1851: The Crystal Palace is built in Knightsbridge in London.

1854: The exhibition hall is moved to a new site in south London.

THE GREAT EXHIBITION

Prince Albert had an idea for a huge exhibition to showcase the wonders of industry from around the world. It was a chance for every country to show what they could do.

A CELEBRATION FOR GREAT BRITAIN

In Knightsbridge, in London, a huge glass exhibition hall was built in 1851, which was known as The Crystal Palace. It was designed by Joseph Paxton and looked like an enormous conservatory. It was the biggest glass building ever made and took everybody's breath away. It was like going to a huge shopping mall full of amazing things.

Because Britain was the host nation, the British had the most exhibits. There was a lot of machinery on display that most people would never have seen before, including a printing machine.

There was a big opening ceremony for which you could buy tickets, just as for the Olympics in 2012. Later on, you could get in for 1 shilling – about £3 in today's money. Everybody could now afford to go and special trips were organised by travel agents.

Exhibits included models of dinosaurs, huge vases twice the height of a man from Russia, and some stuffed animals from Germany. Among these was a group of kittens taking tea. India sent a beautiful ivory throne and a coat covered with pearls, emeralds and rubies.

Everybody flocked to see the Koh-i-Noor diamond from India, which is now part of the Crown Jewels.

INTERESTING

The Crystal Palace had a special desk for lost children and umbrellas.

1877: The Koh-i-Noor diamond from India becomes part of the Crown Jewels.

1936: The Crystal Palace burns down in a huge fire that is visible from eight counties.

1979: The Crystal Palace Foundation is set up in memory of the exhibition.

Joseph Paxton

The Crystal Palace was designed by an architect called Joseph Paxton (1803–1865) who was famous for building large greenhouses and conservatories. When Albert had his idea for the exhibition, a competition was held to decide who would design the buildings. None of the entries were suitable, as they would all take too long to build.

DID YOU KNOW?

The building was moved to Sydenham in south London in 1854. It burnt down in 1936.

Joseph Paxton
(1803–1865)

Public Toilets

For the first time ever, there were "waiting rooms and conveniences". These were public toilets, with separate cubicles. But you had to pay a penny to use one. For a long time afterwards, people spoke about "spending a penny".

COOL FACTS

- 300,000 square metres (3 million square feet) of glass were used to make The Crystal Palace.
- More than six million people visited the Great Exhibition.
- Over 100,000 objects were displayed at the exhibition.

1834: The old Palace of Westminster burns down, though a few buildings survive.

1840: Work starts on the new Houses of Parliament that dominate the River Thames.

1852: The Victoria and Albert Museum is founded to showcase the decorative arts.

VICTORIAN STYLE

Many famous buildings were put up during Victoria's reign. The centres of many towns and cities are full of Victorian architecture, which is usually very grand and imposing.

GRAND ARCHITECTURE AND FLAMBOYANT INTERIORS

All the new industries had made Britain a rich country. People wanted to show off their wealth. Not only did the Victorians build some impressive civic buildings but they also decorated their own homes in a very lavish style. Thick velvets and brocades, dark polished wood, and marble were very popular. The Victorians liked richly patterned oriental carpets on the floor and used deep, warm colours on the walls. Then they would add a lot of pictures in heavy frames. Unlike today, nobody used white. A Victorian sitting room, called the parlour, was meant to look cosy and inviting, although we would think it very cluttered today.

The Houses of Parliament

The Houses of Parliament are sometimes called the Palace of Westminster. This is where Parliament meets to debate laws. There used to be a royal palace there, but most of it burnt down in 1834. Work on the buildings we see today started shortly afterwards but took several years to finish.

1857: The Science Museum is founded as part of the South Kensington Museum.

1871: Queen Victoria opens The Royal Albert Hall in memory of Prince Albert.

1881: The Natural History Museum is established to house important specimens.

Left : The Victoria and Albert Museum.

Below: The Natural History Museum

COOL FACTS

South Kensington Museums

The money made from the Great Exhibition of 1851 was used to build some museums in South Kensington.

- **The Victoria and Albert Museum** was founded in 1852 as a museum of design and fashion.
- **The Natural History Museum** is a museum of animals and plants.
- **The Science Museum** is a museum of science and technology. Stephenson's *Rocket* can be seen there.
- **The Royal Albert Hall** is a big circular hall for concerts and other live events.
- **The Albert Memorial** near the Royal Albert Hall contains a statue of Prince Albert to mark his memory. Another statue of Albert shows him holding a catalogue of the Great Exhibition.

The Royal Albert Hall

Facial Hair

Nearly all Victorian men had "whiskers". Beards and moustaches would be carefully trimmed and combed into shape. Sometimes men would shave their chins, but have long sideburns that joined up to their moustache. This would be combed and waxed so that it stuck out on either side of the face. Facial hair made you look serious and important.

CLOTHES AND FASHION

Victorian clothes were not very comfortable. Men wore long jackets with "tails" that hung down at the back, always with a waistcoat underneath. Shirts had stiff collars. Ladies had big dresses. The top half was fitted and the skirt was like a balloon. The skirt was supported on a frame made of whalebone. Many women wore a corset under their dresses. This would be pulled tight to make the waist smaller. Often, women could not breathe properly and would faint. But this was considered ladylike. Ordinary people had simpler clothing, usually in dark colours that would not show the dirt.

1825: The first passenger railway is opened between Stockton and Darlington.

1830: The Manchester and Liverpool Railway is opened and proves successful.

1841: The first train runs from London to Brighton on the south coast.

THE GREAT AGE OF THE TRAIN

Huge advances were made in transport in the Victorian age, especially to the railway network. At first, trains carried raw materials to factories around the country. But soon people wanted to travel by train as well.

DID YOU KNOW?

The first passenger railway was opened between Stockton and Darlington in 1825.

GROWTH OF THE RAIL NETWORK

The first really successful railway was the Liverpool and Manchester Railway (1830). This set a new trend in railway building that lasted for 20 years. By 1854, nearly every town in England had a station, although there were fewer trains in Wales. Because it is difficult for trains to go up and down hills, new tunnels and bridges also had to be built.

SCAN ME

Instructions on page 5

The railways were made by a number of different companies. They all used track of different widths. Trains were built to run on certain railway lines and could not run on other ones. As a result you had to keep changing trains to get round the country. When Isambard Kingdom Brunel was building the line from Bristol to London, he found that his trains would not be able to enter Euston station. So, he built a new station of his own – Paddington. The problem was not completely solved until the 1890s, however, when all tracks were laid in the same way.

To start with, travelling by train was quite expensive, so only well-off people could afford it. Some trains were very luxurious, with padded seats and velvet curtains at the windows.

1854: Brunel's Paddington Station is opening, linking Bristol and London.

1868: The Midland Railway opens a station at St. Pancras in London.

2000: A bronze statue of Paddington Bear is unveiled at Paddington Station.

GETTING TO THE SEASIDE

Now that there were trains, seaside towns became popular destinations. Small fishing villages were turned into towns with big hotels and other attractions. There would be a long, wide pavement next to the beach, which was called a promenade, and benches so that visitors could enjoy a view of the sea.

For people who lived in London, Brighton became very popular. The first train from London to Brighton ran in 1841. It only had first-class carriages, however, so only rich people could afford to go. The people who ran the railways soon realised that if they could make the fares cheaper, more people would be able to travel by train.

AWESOME FACT

Victorian Stations

Railway stations were often impressive buildings, with glass roofs, iron staircases and marble pillars. Some were almost like cathedrals. Big Victorian railway stations that are still in use are:

- Bristol Temple Meads
- Paddington
- St. Pancras
- York

INTERESTING

The Blackpool Tower

In Blackpool, a tower was built as a special attraction. The Blackpool Tower is made of iron and looks like a smaller version of the famous Eiffel Tower in Paris. The tower was finished in 1894. You paid sixpence to go in and then another sixpence to go in the lift right to the top.

INTERESTING

The Blackpool Tower caught fire in 1897 and could be seen 80km (50 miles) away.

1828: The London Zoo is established in Regent's Park in London to display wild animals.

1840: Thomas Cooke returns to England from the United States, bringing a circus with him.

1847: Queen Victoria sets a trend for sea bathing while on holiday at Osborne House on the Isle of Wight.

DAYS OUT AND HOLIDAYS

The railways made it possible for people to get around the country easily. Besides having a day out in London to visit the Great Exhibition, people started to go to the seaside.

POPULAR SEASIDE RESORTS

Popular resorts were Great Yarmouth, Blackpool and Margate. Just like today, people enjoyed eating fish and chips and ice cream. Children could go on donkey rides on the beach. Because most people could not afford to buy bathing costumes that would only be used once a year, they just rolled up their trousers and skirts and paddled in the sea.

Rich ladies would not want to be seen on the beach in their swimming costumes. So, they used bathing machines, which were like bathing huts on wheels. Servants would wheel the bathing machine into the sea and then you could get into the sea. You certainly would not go very far and most ladies probably never learnt to swim. When you had finished, you got back inside the bathing machine and came back up the beach.

INTERESTING

Sea Bathing
It was thought that bathing in the sea was good for you. Queen Victoria went for a dip while on holiday on the Isle of Wight in 1847. Then everybody wanted a go, and seaside towns became popular destinations for summer holidays for many Victorian families.

Victorian Bathing Suits
Victorian swimwear was meant to preserve your modesty. Everything had to be decently covered up. Men wore a sort of onesie or a long T-shirt over a long pair of shorts. Often these were jauntily striped. Women had loose three-quarter-length trousers worn with a top like a jacket, with a blouse underneath.

1891: Work begins on the Palace Pier in Brighton on the south coast of England.

1894: The Blackpool Tower opens to attract visitors to go to the seaside resort.

1902: An electric tramway system is opened at Great Yarmouth in Norfolk.

AWESOME FACT

Zoos

Zoos were much more popular than today, and nobody objected to seeing wild animals in cages or even doing tricks. Children could ride on elephants or camels and a highlight would be the chimps' tea party, where all the chimpanzees would sit round a table and have tea and cakes.

TRAVELLING SHOWS

Funfairs and circuses travelled around the country to entertain people who could not get out very often. They would set up in open fields near towns and villages so you could walk to them.

At the funfair, you could go for a ride on a merry-go-round or try and win a prize in a shooting gallery. There might also be a strong man lifting weights.

Circuses put up big tents (called a "big top") and everybody sat on wooden benches around a "ring". The ringmaster was in charge and wore a top hat and a tailcoat.

Horses would walk round the ring in time to a band and other acts could include a tightrope walk and an animal tamer. Seals would do tricks with balls or there might be lions in a big cage.

1806: Isambard Kingdom Brunel is born at Portsea in Portsmouth.

1822: Work begins on a tunnel under the River Thames between Rotherhithe and Wapping.

1831: Brunel wins a competition to build a suspension bridge in Bristol over the River Avon. Gorge..Darlington.

Isambard Kingdom Brunel

Isambard Kingdom Brunel was a famous Victorian engineer. He built bridges, tunnels, railways and docks. Many of these are still in use today and have become famous landmarks.

THE BUSY ENGINEER

Brunel was born in Portsmouth in 1806. He married Mary Horsley in 1836. He was always working and made himself ill through worrying about all the jobs he had to do. He collapsed in 1859 and died a week later.

One of Brunel's first jobs was to make a tunnel under the River Thames in London. The tunnel connects Rotherhithe and Wapping and was built for horse-drawn carriages. Work began in 1822, but it was very dangerous. Parts of the tunnel kept collapsing and water rushed in. Several men lost their lives and Brunel nearly drowned in 1828. Because of this, work stopped for several years and the tunnel was not finished until 1843. The tunnel is still in use today.

INTERESTING

Brunel Facts

- Brunel often worked for 18 hours a day and slept in his office.
- At just over 150cm (5ft) tall, Brunel was not very big. He often wore a top hat to make himself look taller.

1836: Brunel marries Mary Horsley and they set up home in Westminster in London.

1837: The *Great Western* steamship, built by Brunel, is launched.

1859: Brunel collapses and dies, probably as a result of overwork.

DID YOU KNOW?

THE GREAT WESTERN RAILWAY

The Great Western Railway was a very important railway because it joined London to Bristol where ships arrived from America. Brunel designed tunnels, bridges and viaducts for the line. These helped the trains travel as fast as possible, so that travellers arriving in Bristol could quickly get to London. The Box Tunnel and Bristol Temple Meads station form part of the line.

THE CLIFTON SUSPENSION BRIDGE

In 1831, Brunel won a competition to build a bridge at Bristol over the Avon Gorge. The bridge was high enough for ships to sail under it. It is a suspension bridge – there are two towers on either side of the river and the bridge hangs between them. The bridge is designed to move slightly in the wind but is perfectly safe.

To build the bridge, Brunel had to put an iron bar between the two opposite banks of the gorge. The workers were in a basket that ran along the bar. Work started in 1831, but the bridge was not finished until 1864.

Isambard Kingdom Brunel's ship, the *Great Eastern*

AWESOME FACT

Brunel's Docks
Brunel also worked on many docks, including:

- Bristol
- Cardiff
- Milford Haven
- Monkwearmouth

Ships
Brunel designed many ships. The *Great Western* was launched in 1837. It was the first steamship to go to America and back. The *Great Britain*, launched in 1843, was the world's first steam-powered passenger liner. The *Great Eastern* was launched in 1859 and was the biggest ship ever built up to that time.

1789: The benefits of cod liver oil are recorded at Manchester Infirmary.

1857: Thomas Hughes writes *Tom Brown's School Days* about life in a boarding school.

1866: The Sanitary Act requires local authorities to improve living conditions and remove health hazards.

VICTORIAN DAILY LIFE

Most people lived in terraced houses in towns and cities. People with more money had bigger houses. Sometimes, houses were built in pairs and called "semi-detached".

VICTORIAN HOUSES

Victorian houses were often called "villas" because they had gardens. Some were very big, with separate rooms in an attic for servants and a "basement" where the kitchen would be. Blocks of flats were called "mansion" flats to make them sound grand.

WELL-OFF FAMILIES

People who could afford it had a nanny to look after their children. The nanny would live with the family and have her own room. The children all slept together in the nursery. The children would see their parents in the evening, just before they went to bed. They would be washed and put into clean clothes so that their parents could inspect them. When they got older, boys were sent away to boarding school, while girls were usually taught by a governess at home.

POOR FAMILIES

Most grown-ups in towns worked in factories. Women sometimes worked in laundries washing or did sewing and made clothes. In poor families, most children did not go to school. They were expected to work from an early age.

Because their parents worked long hours, children would play together in the street. This was usually safe, as there were no cars to run them over, and the older children would look after the little ones.

They could hardly ever afford new clothes. Children would hand down clothes to the smaller ones when they grew out of them. Rips in clothes would be darned or covered with a patch.

INTERESTING

Large Families
Many people had big families. To be one of eight or nine children was not unusual. Sadly, some women died in childbirth. Husbands often remarried, so "blended" families were common.

1880s: By this time, over one million people are employed in domestic service.

1887: A sanatorium to care for tuberculosis sufferers is established in Edinburgh.

1963: A vaccine to combat measles in children is developed to help end the disease.

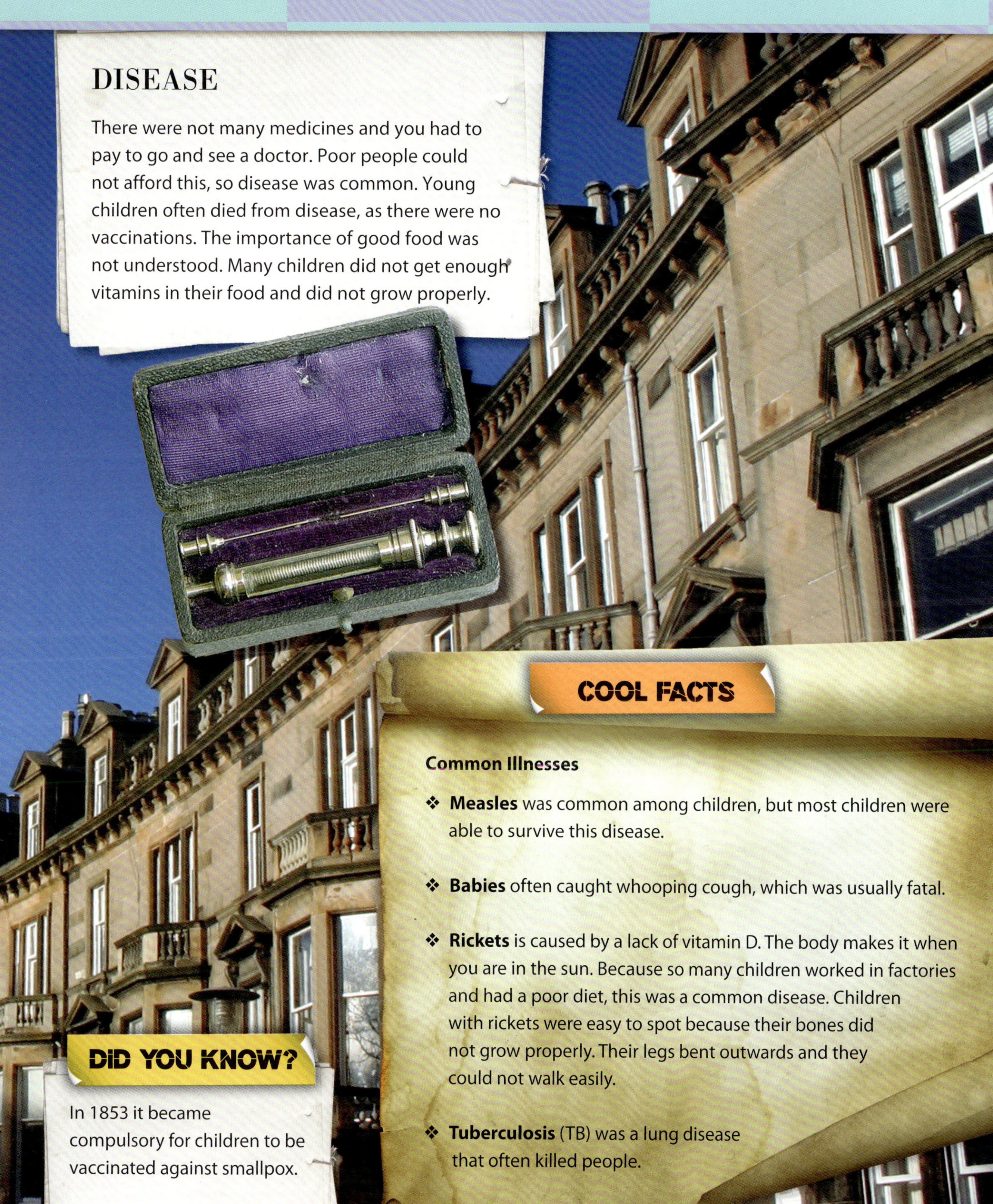

DISEASE

There were not many medicines and you had to pay to go and see a doctor. Poor people could not afford this, so disease was common. Young children often died from disease, as there were no vaccinations. The importance of good food was not understood. Many children did not get enough vitamins in their food and did not grow properly.

COOL FACTS

Common Illnesses

- **Measles** was common among children, but most children were able to survive this disease.
- **Babies** often caught whooping cough, which was usually fatal.
- **Rickets** is caused by a lack of vitamin D. The body makes it when you are in the sun. Because so many children worked in factories and had a poor diet, this was a common disease. Children with rickets were easy to spot because their bones did not grow properly. Their legs bent outwards and they could not walk easily.
- **Tuberculosis** (TB) was a lung disease that often killed people.

DID YOU KNOW?

In 1853 it became compulsory for children to be vaccinated against smallpox.

1838: Charles Dickens's *Oliver Twist*, his second novel, is published in London.

1840: Inspired by Florence Nightingale, Elizabeth Fry opens a school to train nurses.

1869: Octavia Hill is one of the founder members of the Charity Organisation Society.

SOCIAL REFORMERS

While some people became very prosperous during Victoria's reign, many did not have an easy life at all. But there were some men and women who took an interest in the poor and did a lot to improve things.

CHILD LABOUR

Many reformers were worried about the way children were treated. They often had to work, sometimes doing very unpleasant jobs in factories.

Some boys were chimney sweeps. They were small enough to climb up chimneys on the inside. This was a very dirty and dangerous job. You could fall or even get stuck! In 1862, Charles Kingsley wrote a book called *The Water Babies*, which tells the story of a young chimney sweep called Tom.

BOURNEVILLE

The Cadbury family were chocolate-makers in Birmingham. In 1895, George Cadbury (1839–1922) set about building some new housing for his workers. He wanted the houses to be comfortable and set among trees and open green spaces. He called the estate Bourneville. Other forward-thinking employers created model villages as well, including the Lever Brothers who built "Port Sunlight" in Cheshire to house their soap-workers.

ELIZABETH FRY

Elizabeth Fry (1780–1845) was appalled by the way people were treated in prison. Like George Cadbury, she was a Quaker. She visited the poor and set up a Sunday school. When she visited Newgate Prison, in London, she was horrified to see women and children sleeping on straw. She taught the women to sew and read the Bible.

Elizabeth also set up a homeless shelter, so that people with nowhere to go could find a bed for the night. Queen Victoria admired her and gave her money to help with her work.

Elizabeth Fry
(1780–1845)

1888: The Lever Brothers start work on Port Sunlight to house workers.

1895: George Cadbury creates the Bourneville housing development.

1902: Newgate Prison is closed down and demolished two years later.

Octavia Hill

Octavia Hill (1838–1912) was very concerned with how poor people had to live in towns and cities. With her friend the poet John Ruskin (1819–1900), she improved the slums that many people lived in. She thought everybody should be able to visit open fields. She also helped save Hampstead Heath in London.

Charles Dickens (1812–1870)

DID YOU KNOW?

Octavia Hill was one of the people who set up the National Trust, which preserves places of outstanding beauty for everyone to enjoy.

INTERESTING

Dickens Facts

- As a boy, Charles Dickens worked in a blacking factory, which meant he had first-hand knowledge of life for the labouring poor.
- Dickens visited the United States and gave lectures against slavery.
- While in the United States, Dickens was travelling on a train that derailed over a bridge – he helped to save friends and other people.
- Charles Dickens is buried in Westminster Abbey.

CHARLES DICKENS

In his books, the writer Charles Dickens (1812–1870) gives a vivid picture of what life was like for poor people. The books are very long and full of vivid characters. He wrote about what school was like in *Great Expectations* and *David Copperfield*. In *Oliver Twist*, he describes a workhouse where orphans are given hardly anything to eat. Oliver runs away to London, where he falls in with a band of pickpockets. Eventually, Oliver is rescued by a Mr. Brownlow and finds his lost family.

SOCIAL REFORM

Many changes were made to the law in Victorian England to improve the lives of ordinary working people. Some politicians took a great interest in children and how they were treated.

THE REFORM ACTS

Although Britain had had a Parliament for centuries, only people who owned property could vote. As most people rented their homes, this gave them no say in how the country was run. The Reform Act of 1832 extended the vote to men who rented land with a house on it. The Reform Act of 1867 further extended the vote to men who rented houses in towns.

DID YOU KNOW?

Women did not get the vote until 1918.

LORD SHAFTESBURY

Lord Shaftesbury (1801–1885) was very concerned about how children were made to work and he argued in Parliament for new laws to be passed.

Inspectors, called Commissioners, went into factories and mines to find out exactly what was going on.

Factories

Children often worked in factories. Most children did not complain and they were good at crawling under machinery. But the work was often hard and dangerous. Girls worked in cotton mills collecting stray bits of thread that could be reused. But their hair or clothing could get caught in the machinery and there were many nasty accidents.

1847: The Ten Hour Act makes it illegal for children to be made to work for more than 10 hours.

1874: The Factory Act makes it illegal to employ children younger than 10 years old.

1880: The Education Act makes education up to the age of 10 compulsory.

COOL FACTS

Factory and Mine Acts

- The **Ten Hour Act of 1847** meant that no child should work more than 10 hours a day.
- The **Factory Act of 1874** made it illegal to employ a child younger than 10 years old in a factory.
- The **Mines Act of 1842** stopped women and children under 10 working underground.
- In 1862, the age for boy-miners was raised to 12 and in 1900 to 13.

EDUCATION

Unlike today, there was no free education, so most Victorian children did not go to school. "Ragged Schools" were schools for poor children. One of the first was started in Portsmouth. Ragged Schools were often in one room of a house or in an old barn. From 1833, factory owners were supposed to provide at least two hours' education every day for children, but hardly any of them did.

Mines

Women and small children often worked in coal mines. Some just worked above ground sorting out the coal, but others had to push trucks of coal through the tunnels underground. Often, they hardly ever saw daylight. Some boys called "trappers" had to sit in the dark all day, opening and closing a door to let air in.

INTERESTING

Education for All

- The **Elementary Education Act of 1870** provided education for all children aged between the ages of five and twelve.
- The **Education Act of 1880** made it compulsory to attend school from age five to ten.
- Even with these acts in place, not all children went to school because their families needed them to work.

1829: As Home Secretary, Robert Peel founds the London Metropolitan Police.

1834: A group of protesters from Tolpuddle is arrested and sent to Australia.

1845: Potato blight arrives in Ireland, ruining the crop and causing widespread famine.

POLITICS AND POLITICIANS

With the Reform Acts in place, more people could vote, which meant that everybody took more of an interest in politics. Politicians had long arguments in Parliament over new laws.

THE IRISH POTATO FAMINE

A terrible potato disease arrived in Ireland in 1845. It was called potato blight and it destroyed the crops. Most of the potatoes rotted and were inedible. The potato famine lasted until 1852. Many people died of starvation. Some tried eating the rotten potatoes, and got ill and died anyway. This was one of the worst disasters ever to happen in Ireland. Nearly a quarter of the population died. Many young people left the country, and went to America, Canada or Australia. Some went to Scotland or England. People also died in Scotland where the famine was known as the "Great Hunger".

Many people emigrated because of the Irish Potato Famine.

THE CORN LAWS

The government passed laws concerning how food was produced and sold. At the start of the 19th century, cheap corn was brought into Britain from abroad. British farmers were worried that nobody would buy the crops they were growing. "Corn Laws" passed in 1815 reduced the amount coming in from abroad and allowed British farmers to charge what price they liked. Many of the farmers owned huge areas of land, and so the Corn Laws made them rich. But poor people found that they could no longer afford to buy the bread that was made from the corn. The laws were very unpopular.

1846: The Corn Laws, which caused problems for many poor people, are repealed.

1868: Following Disraeli, Gladstone becomes Prime Minister for the first of four times.

1874: Disraeli becomes Prime Minister for the second time, having defeated Gladstone.

Robert Peel

Robert Peel (1788–1850) became Home Secretary in 1822. He reformed the prisons and created the first police force. In 1834, he became Prime Minister. In 1846, he managed to get the Corn Laws repealed. This meant that the price of food came down and bread could now be sent to Ireland, which was struggling with the potato famine.

COOL FACTS

The police are still sometimes called "Bobbies" or "Peelers" in memory of Robert Peel.

The Tolpuddle Martyrs

A group of labourers from Tolpuddle in Dorset got together to complain about low wages. In 1834, they were arrested and sent to Australia. They were known as the Tolpuddle Martyrs and became popular heroes. They were released in 1836 and some of them returned to England.

AWESOME FACT

Around 800,000 people signed a petition asking for the Tolpuddle Martyrs to be released.

William Gladstone
(1809–1898)

Benjamin Disraeli
(1804–1881)

William Gladstone and Benjamin Disraeli

There were two very important politicians during Victoria's reign. Between 1867 and 1885, one or the other was Prime Minister. They each represented different parties – and they hated each other. Queen Victoria detested Gladstone (1809–1898), who was a Liberal, but really liked Disraeli (1804–1881), who was a Conservative. Gladstone lectured the Queen, but Disraeli was careful to flatter her. He supported her wish to be known as the Empress of India.

1833: A book of Christmas carols is published for everyone to enjoy.

1840: The postal service begins, allowing people to send Christmas greetings.

1843: Charles Dickens writes *A Christmas Carol*, a ghost story with a happy ending.

VICTORIAN CHRISTMAS

Before Victoria's reign, people did not celebrate Christmas as we do today, and some workers were not given any time off. Victoria and Albert turned it into the biggest celebration of the year.

NEW TRADITIONS

Prince Albert brought many Christmas traditions from Germany, including the Christmas tree, which was decorated with candles, sweets, fruits and small presents. Pictures were published of Victoria and Albert with their children around their Christmas tree. The idea of the family Christmas was born. Before the Victorians, people exchanged small gifts at New Year. This tradition was moved back to Christmas and bigger presents were placed under the tree.

CHRISTMAS FOOD

Turkeys became popular at Christmas because they were big enough to feed a large group of people. In Tudor times, mince pies had been made with meat. Now they were made with dried fruits and quickly became a standard Christmas treat.

The highlight – literally – would be the Christmas pudding. Brandy would be poured over this and then set alight. An alternative, but dangerous, dessert was Snap-dragon. Raisins, nuts and sweets would be put in a dish in the middle of the table and brandy poured over them. This would be set alight, and everybody would reach in and try and grab what they could without burning their fingers.

1848: Thomas Smith invents Christmas crackers that snap when pulled apart.

1861: Isabella Beeton publishes her *Book of Household Management.*

1870: A halfpenny postal rate is introduced so more people can send cards.

Mrs. Beeton

In 1861, Isabella Beeton (1836–1865) published her *Book of Household Management*. It is a huge book that tells you how to run a house and is full of recipes. Today, many cooks still follow her instructions for Christmas cake and Christmas pudding. Mrs. Beeton was not really a domestic goddess – she only collected the recipes and probably cooked hardly any of them herself.

INTERESTING

Crack!

In 1848, Thomas Smith invented Christmas crackers. The first crackers were just packets containing sweets that snapped when you pulled them open. Soon, the sweets were replaced with small novelties and paper hats.

CHRISTMAS CARDS

In 1843, Henry Cole had the idea of exchanging cards that contained a simple Christmas greeting. The first card showed a family enjoying their Christmas dinner. Children were encouraged to make their own cards.

The postal service had begun in 1840. It cost a penny to send a letter. The stamps were black, with Victoria's head on them. They were called "Penny Blacks". Then the price was reduced to half a penny and everybody could afford to send Christmas cards.

Nowadays, stingy people are often called "Scrooge" after the character in Dickens's novel *A Christmas Carol*.

AWESOME FACT

A Christmas Carol

Charles Dickens wrote *A Christmas Carol* in 1843. It tells how mean and grumpy Ebenezer Scrooge is visited by a group of ghosts on Christmas Eve who make him realise how stingy he is being. The next day, he decides to become more generous and gives a turkey to the Cratchit family who are very poor.

1809: Charles Darwin is born in Shrewsbury in Shropshire.

1831: HMS *Beagle* sets sail for South America with Darwin on board.

1836: HMS *Beagle* returns home, landing at Falmouth in Cornwall.

Charles Darwin

Charles Darwin (1809–1882) was a naturalist. He went on a long sea voyage and came up with the theory of evolution, which changed the way people think about living things and where we come from.

CHARLES'S EARLY LIFE

Charles was born in 1809 in Shrewsbury. As a boy, he loved collecting stones, plants and creepy crawlies. With his brother Erasmus he made a laboratory in the garden shed where they conducted experiments.

He went to Edinburgh to study to be a doctor, but did not like it. So, he went to Cambridge instead, where he thought he might become a vicar. But he made friends with other scientists and realised that he wanted to be involved in research.

Darwin and the Age of the Earth
Scientists could not agree how old the earth was. The most famous scientist at the time was Lord Kelvin. He thought that the Sun was 20 million years old and the Earth had to be younger. But Darwin realised that much more time was needed for evolution to take place. Now we think the Earth is 4.5 billion years old – Lord Kelvin was way out.

1843: Darwin moves to Kent where he works on his theory of evolution.

1859: *On the Origin of Species* is published, making Darwin famous.

1882: Darwin dies at his home in Kent and is buried in Westminster Abbey.

HMS BEAGLE AND THE GALAPAGOS ISLANDS

When Charles was 22, he was invited to go round the world in a boat called HMS *Beagle*. The boat was going to cross the Atlantic, and then visit New Zealand, Australia and South Africa. The mission was to map the South American coastline.

In South America, Darwin found some fossils of huge creatures that were nothing like anything living today.

The Galapagos Islands are a group of islands near the equator. While Darwin was there, he saw some amazing animals – lizards that swam in the sea, huge tortoises and some strange birds. He studied some finches that looked like ones he had seen in South America. But their beaks were different because they ate different food. He realised that they had changed over time. They had evolved.

ON THE ORIGIN OF SPECIES

Back home, when Darwin had had time to think about everything he had seen, he wrote a book called *On the Origin of Species*. In the book he explained how all living things had evolved – including people – and presented his theories on evolution and natural selection. The book was published in 1859. It made him famous, but many people were very angry, especially bishops. They thought that God had created everything all in one go.

COOL FACTS

Darwin's Travels

- Charles Darwin's journey on board HMS *Beagle* lasted for five years.
- Darwin took a copy of the Bible with him on the voyage, as well as a magnifying glass, a pair of binoculars and special jars for preserving specimens.
- While at sea, Darwin was often seasick and just lay in his cabin feeling miserable.
- After he came home, Darwin lived in Kent where he died in 1882.

Darwin's Animals

In Victorian times, scientists did not worry about protecting nature as we do today. Darwin trapped and killed some animals so he could bring them home to study them. Some of these are in The Natural History Museum in London.

1853: A war breaks out in the Crimea, involving Britain, Russia, France and Turkey.

1854: Florence Nightingale is sent to the Crimea to improve the hospital there.

1856: The Crimean War comes to an end with the signing of the Treaty of Paris.

THE CRIMEAN WAR

Between 1853 and 1856, Britain was at war with Russia. France, Turkey and the Kingdom of Sardinia also took part. The war was fought on the Crimean peninsula, which is in the Black Sea.

A BATTLE FOR CONTROL

France, Turkey and Sardinia were on the same side as Britain. They were all in it for different reasons, but having control of the Crimea was important for both sides. Reports of the war were sent to Britain. People were shocked by the description of the Barrack Hospital where wounded soldiers were sent. There were not enough beds and some soldiers had to lie on the floor. They only had one meal a day. The whole place was dirty and there were rats running everywhere. Diseases such as typhus and cholera spread rapidly and many people died. The war came to an end when the Treaty of Paris was signed.

INTERESTING

The Crimean War was the first war in which the electric telegraph was used to send messages between different parts of the army.

COOL FACTS

Crimean Facts

- More than 300,000 troops were killed during the war.
- Florence Nightingale was the first woman to be given the Order of Merit – better even than being made a dame!
- Timothy the Tortoise (who was actually a female) was the last survivor of the Crimean War, dying in 2004 at the age of 65. She had been the mascot of HMS *Queen* which was involved in the attack on Sevastopol.
- "Mother Seacole" was the nickname given by Crimean soldiers to a nurse called Mary Seacole.

1907: Florence Nightingale becomes the first woman to receive the Order of Merit.

1991: Many years after her death, Mary Seacole is given the Jamaican Order of Merit.

2010: The Florence Nightingale Museum at St. Thomas's Hospital reopens.

FLORENCE NIGHTINGALE

A nurse called Florence Nightingale (1820–1910) believed that she had been called on by God to go and look after the wounded men. She went to the Crimea with some other nurses. They cleaned up the hospital and made sure that everybody had better food and clean water to drink.

At night she used to walk round the hospital checking that everybody was alright. Because she carried a lamp, she was known as "the lady of the lamp".

When she came back to Britain, she was hailed as a hero just as much as the soldiers.

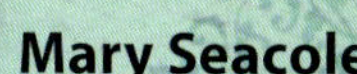

Mary Seacole

Mary Seacole (1805–1881) probably did as much as Florence to help the soldiers, but she faced racial prejudice because she was of mixed race.

She wanted to go the Crimea as a nurse but was turned down. She went anyway and set up a hotel that she ran like a hospital. She also went onto the battlefield to treat wounded men, which Florence did not do.

THE BATTLE OF BALACLAVA

In October 1854, a famous battle took place. During the battle, the British "Light Brigade" charged on the Russian army. It was all a big mistake. The cavalrymen realised they had no chance of winning, but charged anyway because that was the order. Out of 673 men, 118 were killed and 127 wounded. But the Russians were astonished by their bravery. The cavalrymen became instantly famous. The poet Lord Alfred Tennyson wrote a poem called *The Charge of the Light Brigade* six weeks after the battle.

1831: James Starley, the father of the British bicycle industry, is born in Sussex.

1845: Charles Pearson proposes building an underground railway in London.

1863: The first underground line opens, connecting Paddington and the City.

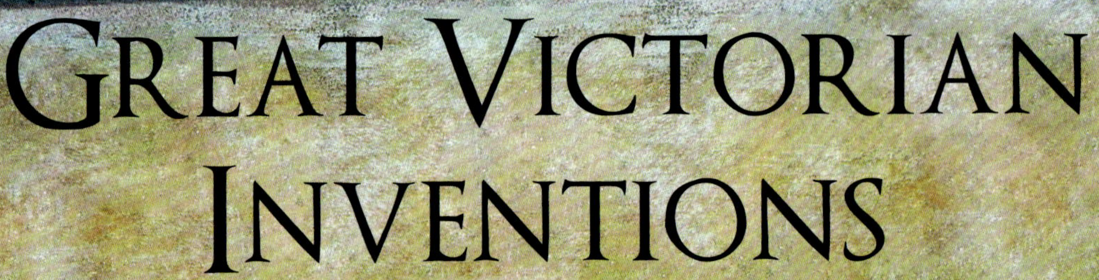

Great Victorian Inventions

Gadgets that we take for granted today had their beginnings in the Victorian era. Many inventions were made that improved everyone's comfort and lifestyle.

Early train

Early 20th-century train

Modern train

THE LONDON UNDERGROUND

It was difficult to get around London in Victorian times. The streets were busy and a railway through the city was not allowed. In 1845, Charles Pearson put forward an idea for a railway underground. The first underground line was built to connect Paddington and the City of London. It was opened in 1863. The underground meant that people could live outside the city but still get to work easily.

COOL FACTS

The Tube

- Some people thought that the idea of a railway underground was mad. In 1862, *The Times* newspaper described it as an "insult to common sense".
- 30,000 people travelled on the new underground train on the first day.
- The first underground trains were powered by steam.

1876: Alexander Graham Bell, a Scottish inventor, invents the telephone.

1878: Joseph Swan demonstrates the first electric light bulb.

1881: The first factory making electric light bulbs is set up in Newcastle.

Bicycles

If you could not afford the fare for the train and did not keep a horse, you still had to walk everywhere. The bicycle was invented in Germany but soon appeared in Britain. Some early bikes had a big wheel at the front and a small one at the back. They were called "penny-farthings" and were not very safe.

Even when the wheels were the same size, bikes were not very comfortable to ride. Before they had rubber tyres, they were known as "bone-shakers". It was like sitting on a wooden bench that jiggled you up and down.

An early bike called a "penny-farthing"

TELECOMMUNICATIONS

People have always wanted to send messages to other people a long way away. The electric telegraph was invented in America in the 1830s, but you could only send messages in code along wires. In 1876, Alexander Graham Bell, a Scottish doctor, discovered a method of sending sounds along the wires instead of a code. He had invented the telephone. Now two people could have proper conversations.

Bloomers

The bicycle had one big drawback. Ladies, with their big skirts, could not ride them. So, a new garment was invented – bloomers. These were like very loose trousers that looked like a skirt as you walked along. But because they had separate legs, you could get on and off your bike.

DID YOU KNOW?

The first private home was lit by electricity in 1880.

Electric Lighting

Houses were lit by gas or with paraffin lamps. Both of these were smelly and dangerous. In 1878 Joseph Swan demonstrated an electric light bulb that he had invented. In 1881, he set up the first light bulb factory in Newcastle. In 1883, he teamed up with Thomas Edison, who had also invented a light bulb in the United States. Electric light was much brighter and cleaner than people had known before.

POLICE

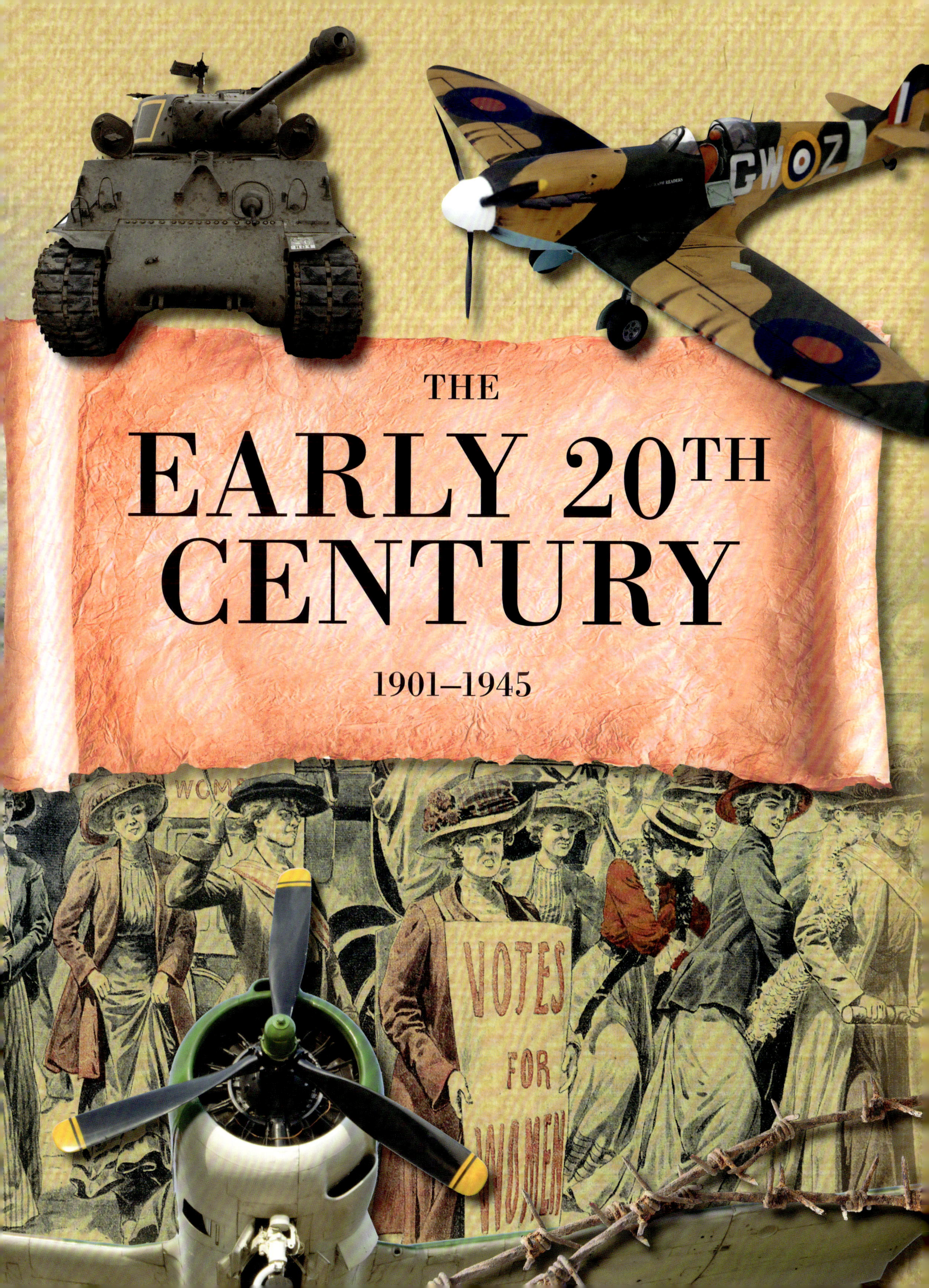
THE
EARLY 20TH
CENTURY
1901–1945
VOTES
FOR
WOMEN

1841: Edward is born at Buckingham Palace, the eldest son of Victoria and Albert.

1899: The Second Boer War, which will see many killed, begins in South Africa.

1901: On the death of Victoria, Edward inherits the throne and reigns as Edward VII.

EDWARD VII

(1841–1910)

When Queen Victoria died in 1901 she was succeeded by her eldest son, Edward. Though he was king for less than ten years, his reign saw many changes in British society.

AWESOME FACT

Lillie Langtry

Edward VII was very fond of the theatre. Lillie Langtry (1853–1929) was a famous actress who became one of the first celebrities to be written about in the media. She advertised skin products, just like modern celebrities. For a while, she was the face of Pears soap.

A NEW ROYAL ERA

In 1863, Edward married Princess Alexandra of Denmark and they had six children, five of whom survived to adulthood. While he was Prince of Wales, Edward was overshadowed by his mother, Queen Victoria. He spent a lot of time eating, drinking and gambling, and nobody thought that he would be any good as king. But when Edward finally became king in 1901, he threw himself into the role with gusto. He became immensely popular, even more so because Victoria's reign had been very gloomy after Prince Albert died. Edward VII died in 1910 and then his eldest son, George (1865–1936), reigned as George V.

1902: An education act is passed that sees the setting up of Local Education Authorities.

1908: The summer Olympic Games, an international event, are held in London.

1910: Edward VII dies at Buckingham Palace following a series of heart attacks.

THE BOER WAR

Two wars took place in South Africa between the British and the descendants of Dutch settlers. The first took place in 1880–1881 and the second in 1899–1902. Many people in South Africa were made homeless during the fighting. Women and children were put in concentration camps and many died. People in Britain were appalled by what was happening there.

INTERESTING

The 1902 Education Act

Arthur Balfour became Prime Minister in 1902. A new education act was passed in the same year. In the past schools had been run by school boards and by the Church of England and the Catholic Church. The act created Local Education Authorities to take control of the schools. The act is sometimes known as Balfour's Act.

TRADE UNIONS

Although laws passed during Queen Victoria's reign improved the lives of working people, they still did not have many rights. Trade unions protected workers' rights. Membership of the trade unions increased in the period 1910–1914, as many workers were unhappy about their working conditions.

1908 Summer Olympics

The Olympic Games took place in London in 1908. The Games were not as big an event as they are today, and only 22 countries took part. The White City Stadium was specially built for the Games. It was considered a marvel. The stadium was demolished in 1985.

Joseph Chamberlain

Chamberlain (1836–1914) was a politician who worked to improve education and trade unions. He also created parks that everybody could visit and built museums and schools. After Britain won the Boer War in 1902, he visited South Africa to improve the relationship between the two countries.

DID YOU KNOW?

Birmingham University has a clock tower named after Joseph Chamberlain.

1897: Millicent Fawcett founds the National Union of Women's Suffrage Societies (NUWSS).

1903: Emmeline Pankhurst founds the Women's Social and Political Union (WSPU).

1913: The Prisoners (Temporary Discharge for Health Act) is introduced.

THE SUFFRAGETTE MOVEMENT

Although laws passed during Victoria's reign allowed many more men to vote than before, women still could not vote. It was thought that women should be at home looking after the children.

WOMEN'S SUFFRAGE SOCIETIES

Many women thought it was unfair that they were not allowed to vote, as plenty of them had jobs just like men. Some of them formed Women's Rights groups. In 1897, Millicent Fawcett founded the National Union of Women's Suffrage Societies (NUWSS). However, she believed in peaceful protest and not much happened to improve things.

In 1903 Emmeline Pankhurst (1858–1928) founded the Women's Social and Political Union (WSPU) with her two daughters, Christabel and Sylvia. Emmeline thought that women would have to start making proper protests, so that they would be taken seriously.

DID YOU KNOW?

"Suffrage" means the right to vote in elections, and the campaigners became known as "Suffragettes".

Emmeline Pankhurst and her daughter Christabel

AWESOME FACT

Emmeline's daughter Christabel was arrested in 1905 for spitting at a policeman.

A Fatal Accident
In 1913, a Suffragette named Emily Davison was killed when she threw herself under the king's horse at the Derby as a protest.

1918: Women over the age of 30 are finally allowed to vote in elections.

1928: All women over the age of 21 are allowed to vote, the same age as men.

1970: The Equal Pay Act ensures that women earn the same as men for doing similar work.

Women Get the Vote!
Women were finally allowed to vote in 1918. But they had to be aged over 30, and it was a long time before they enjoyed the same rights as men.

THE "CAT AND MOUSE" ACT

The Prisoners (Temporary Discharge for Health) Act was introduced in 1913. When women prisoners refused food, they were released when they were too weak to do any harm. It was assumed that they would start eating again once they got home. The women were arrested again when they were strong. But it soon became known as the "Cat and Mouse" Act. The Suffragettes thought that the government was playing with them cruelly, just like a cat plays with a mouse .

Ethel Smyth
Ethel Smyth (1858–1944) was a composer who strongly supported the Suffragettes. In 1911 she wrote *The March of the Women*, which became their theme song. She was sent to prison after breaking some politicians' windows. When the conductor Thomas Beecham visited her there, he saw some women marching around the courtyard singing this song and Ethel leaning out of a window conducting them with a toothbrush!

THE SUFFRAGETTE CAMPAIGN

Suffragettes went on demonstrations and smashed windows. Some of them chained themselves to the railings outside the Houses of Parliament, so that the Members of Parliament inside would take notice of them. Some Suffragettes were even sent to prison. To continue their protest, some of them refused to eat. This was known as a hunger strike. They knew that if they starved themselves to death, then it would cause a scandal – these Suffragettes had to be force fed.

INTERESTING

Force Feeding
Feeding by force is very unpleasant. A tube was put down the prisoner's throat and liquid food poured down it.

1908: Drawings for a new ocean liner, which will be called the *Titanic*, are presented and approved.

1911: The *Titanic* is officially launched from Belfast harbour where she was built.

1912: The *Titanic* sets sail from Southampton harbour bound for New York.

THE TITANIC

The *Titanic* is the most famous ocean liner ever built. It was supposed to be unsinkable. But it hit an iceberg on its maiden voyage in 1912 and many people lost their lives.

INTERESTING

Although the *Titanic* had four chimney stacks, only three were actually necessary. The fourth one was added because the designer thought it would look better.

THE HEIGHT OF LUXURY

Everything about the *Titanic* was done on a lavish scale. It was like being in a huge floating hotel. *Titanic* was also one of the first ships to have a telephone system and electric lights in all the rooms. There were four lifts, a heated swimming pool, a gym, two libraries, a Turkish bath and two barber's shops. A notable feature was the grand staircase, which was covered with a glass dome. But only the first class passengers got to see this. Some of the richest people in the world were on board the *Titanic*. Some of them even took their pet dogs with them. Two of the dogs were saved when the boat sank.

AWESOME FACT

There were about 2,200 people on board (including the crew), though the ship could actually carry 3,547.

THE FATAL VOYAGE

The ship left Southampton on 10 April 1912, heading for New York. On the night of 15 April, it struck an iceberg. At first, it was thought the ship would stay afloat and that all the passengers and crew would be rescued. But the captain soon realised that nothing could be done to stop the ship from sinking. He sent out a distress signal, using the ship's radio. The message was picked up by another ship called the *Carpathia*, which was 93km (58 miles) away. There were not enough lifeboats to save everybody. For a ship of this size, there should have been 64. But there were only 16. Survivors were picked up by the *Carpathia*. Many later commented on how eerily calm the ocean was that night.

1997: *Titanic*, a film about the liner, receives its première in Hollywood.

2009: Millvina Dean, the last surviving passenger of the *Titanic*, dies in Hampshire.

2012: The *Titanic* Belfast Visitor Centre opens in Belfast in Northern Ireland.

DID YOU KNOW?

A first class suite cost £870 (US$ 1,350) – which is about £45,000 (US$ 70,000) in today's money. And that was just one way!

COOL FACTS

The Titanic in Numbers

- The crew numbered 900.
- The *Titanic* was 269m (882ft) long – which is almost as long as three football pitches.
- 800 tonnes of coal a day were needed to keep the ship moving. The top speed of the *Titanic* was 24 knots (27 mph).
- Of the 2,200 people on board, only 705 survived.
- The remains of the *Titanic* are still at the bottom of the sea, over 3,780m (12,400ft) beneath the surface.

The Unsinkable Molly Brown
Margaret Brown was a rich American woman. She was involved in politics and was a supporter of votes for women. When the ship sank, she worked non-stop to help other survivors. She became a legend as "the unsinkable Molly Brown" – though, in fact, nobody who knew her ever called her Molly.

1922: The British Broadcasting Company is founded for broadcasting news.

1926: John Logie Baird invents television for broadcasting moving images.

1927: The Empire Theatre in Leicester Square is demolished and replaced by a cinema.

Radio and Television

It is difficult for us to imagine life without radios and television sets. But during the first part of the 20th century, these were luxuries that most people had to do without.

EARLY PASTIMES

People entertained themselves in different ways before the advent of radio and television. At home, they would read books they had borrowed from a public library or play cards or board games. Most people just went to bed early. At the weekend, people would often go to the music hall or, later on, to the cinema.

The music hall had been a popular form of entertainment since Victorian times. Theatres would put on a "variety show", with a number of different acts, introduced by a Master of Ceremonies. There would be dancing girls, jugglers and comedians, with a "star turn" who was usually a singer. Marie Lloyd (1870–1922) was a famous singer of comic songs. Performers would tour the country, which meant that you could see a different show every week. In the 1950s and 1960s, many Saturday night TV shows followed a similar format.

RADIO

Radio was first used to send messages, which meant that it was very useful in times of war. In 1922, the British Broadcasting Company was founded and started to broadcast the news. In 1927, the name was changed to the British Broadcasting Corporation, the name that is still used today – usually referred to as the BBC.

INTERESTING

Several people were involved in inventing radio, including Italian Guglielmo Marconi.

1930: The BBC begins transmitting television programmes regularly.

1936: Alexandra Palace, in north London, becomes the headquarters of the BBC.

1976: *The Muppet Show*, based on the music hall tradition, is broadcast for the first time.

TELEVISION

Although early television sets were big and bulky, they only had a small screen. They were usually made of polished wood, and so would look like a smart piece of furniture. Early broadcasts were in black and white. In 1930, the BBC started transmitting regular programmes. They were suspended in 1939 because of the Second World War, however, and only started again in 1946. In the early days, not everybody had a television set. When Queen Elizabeth was crowned in 1953, some people bought a set specially, so that they could watch it. All the neighbours would come in to gather round.

Children's Programmes

Soon there were programmes being broadcast just for children. On radio, *Children's Hour* started in 1922. On television, children's programmes started in 1946. There were several puppet shows, including *Muffin the Mule* and *Hank the Cowboy*.

DID YOU KNOW?

Television was invented in 1926 by the Scottish inventor John Logie Baird.

CINEMA

Cinema-going also became popular at this time. Many cinemas were made to look luxurious with grand entrances and red velvet seats. Early films were in black and white, and were silent. An organist would play music while the film was showing.

Most films came from America, but there would often be "newsreels" that would be shown before the main film. These showed recent events that had happened in Britain and often featured the royal family or the Prime Minister. When sound was added to film, there was more of an appetite for British films since the American accent sounded strange at first.

AWESOME FACT

The first film to contain speech that synchronised with the action – often called a "talkie" – was an American musical called *The Jazz Singer*, starring Al Jonson, in 1927. It marked the end of the era of silent movies.

1914: The assassination of Archduke Ferdinand in Serbia leads to the outbreak of war.

1916: The Battle of the Somme, which results in many casualties, takes place in northern France.

1917: George V changes the name of the royal family from Saxe-Coburg-Gotha to Windsor.

THE FIRST WORLD WAR

The First World War (1914–1918) was a huge conflict that involved many countries. Millions lost their lives and it changed the face of Europe forever. It is often known as the Great War.

WHY DID THE WAR START?

The reasons for the war are complicated. At the beginning of the 20th century, Germany was starting to build up its army and navy. This made other countries nervous. But to many a war seemed unlikely, as most of the European monarchs were related to each other through Queen Victoria.

In 1914, Archduke Franz Ferdinand of Austria was assassinated in Serbia. This triggered an international crisis. Germany invaded Belgium and France, so Britain declared war on Germany, since the French were our allies at that time. Other countries were then drawn in.

INTERESTING

A Change of Name

The British royal family still used the family name inherited from Prince Albert – Saxe-Coburg-Gotha. George V realised that this sounded very German, so it was changed to Windsor – which is the name the Queen uses today.

THE WESTERN FRONT

A famous battleground was the Western Front. This was a series of trenches that ran from the coast of Belgium to the Swiss border. The soldiers lived in the trenches, which were protected from the enemy by barbed wire. The area between the German trenches and the Allied trenches was called "No Man's Land", and this is where most of the fighting took place. Many soldiers were killed or lost arms and legs. Some suffered from "shell shock" – they were so affected by the horror of it all that they lost their minds.

1918: Wilfred Owen, a war poet, is killed in action crossing the Sambre-Oise Canal in northern France.

1918: The war comes to an end and the Treaty of Versailles is signed.

1967: Siegfried Sassoon, a well-known war poet, dies of stomach cancer.

War Poetry

Some of the soldiers wrote poems that described the terrible conditions and the emotions they felt. Famous poets included Wilfred Owen (1893–1918), Rupert Brooke (1887–1915) and Siegfried Sassoon (1886–1967). Some of these poets died on the battlefield.

THE BATTLE OF THE SOMME

The Somme is a river in northern France. A famous battle took place there in 1916. The British had been shooting at the Germans for five days non-stop. Believing that most of the German defences were destroyed, the British generals ordered the soldiers to leave their trenches and walk over to the German ones. But they had overestimated the damage they had inflicted on the Germans. The Germans could see the British coming and were able to fire at them. By the end of the battle over 350,000 British had been hit. Other famous battles were fought at Verdun later the same year and at Passchendaele in 1917.

Rupert Brooke (1887–1915)

SCAN ME

Instructions on page 5

DID YOU KNOW?

THE END OF THE WAR

Wanting to bring peace to Europe, America entered the conflict in 1917. In November 1918, the war was brought to an end, with a victory for the Allies. The German Emperor Wilhelm II abdicated and the Treaty of Versailles was signed.

1926: The coal miners go on strike, causing other workers to strike in sympathy.

1928: Alexander Fleming discovers penicillin, which is the first antibiotic.

1929: The stock market crashes in New York, causing a global financial crisis.

THE GREAT DEPRESSION

Towards the end of the 1920s, a huge crisis occurred in banking. It started in America and then spread around the world. It had a massive impact on the lives of many ordinary people.

THE WALL STREET CRASH

The financial centre of the United States is in Wall Street, in New York. This is where many big international banks have their headquarters. In 1929, the stock market collapsed, causing a global financial crisis.

Some of the things that the British government did in the United Kingdom actually made everything worse. For example, to pay for the benefits they had to give to the unemployed, they increased the amount of tax that working people had to pay. This meant that people who had jobs had less money to spend. Then they went on to cut the amount they were paying to the unemployed.

Many industries that were based in the north of England were forced to close. At the same time, some people in the south of England did quite well. Prices fell, which meant that they were able to afford more luxuries.

THE GENERAL STRIKE

In 1926, Britain's coal miners went on strike because the people who owned the mines wanted them to work longer hours but for less money. The Trades Union Congress (TUC) supported the strike and encouraged other workers to stop working as well, which resulted in the General Strike. There were riots in the streets. The violence made the workers unpopular. The TUC leaders called off the strike and everybody went back to work.

1931: The government raises taxes and cuts unemployment pay, making things worse.

1933: Unemployment in Britain reaches 2.5 million – a quarter of the workforce.

1934: The Special Areas Act encourages the setting-up of new businesses in poor areas.

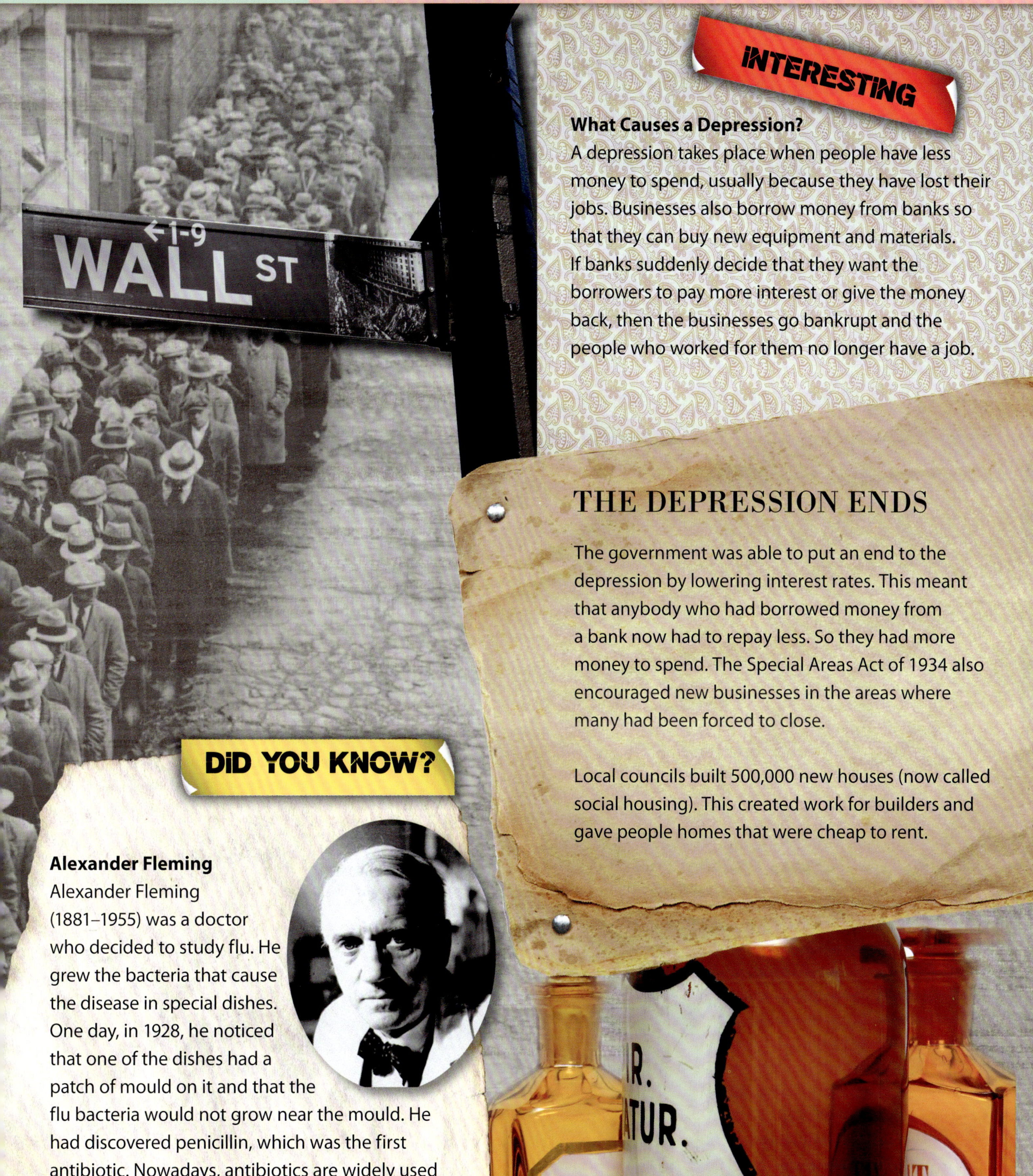

INTERESTING

What Causes a Depression?

A depression takes place when people have less money to spend, usually because they have lost their jobs. Businesses also borrow money from banks so that they can buy new equipment and materials. If banks suddenly decide that they want the borrowers to pay more interest or give the money back, then the businesses go bankrupt and the people who worked for them no longer have a job.

THE DEPRESSION ENDS

The government was able to put an end to the depression by lowering interest rates. This meant that anybody who had borrowed money from a bank now had to repay less. So they had more money to spend. The Special Areas Act of 1934 also encouraged new businesses in the areas where many had been forced to close.

Local councils built 500,000 new houses (now called social housing). This created work for builders and gave people homes that were cheap to rent.

DID YOU KNOW?

Alexander Fleming

Alexander Fleming (1881–1955) was a doctor who decided to study flu. He grew the bacteria that cause the disease in special dishes. One day, in 1928, he noticed that one of the dishes had a patch of mould on it and that the flu bacteria would not grow near the mould. He had discovered penicillin, which was the first antibiotic. Nowadays, antibiotics are widely used to treat all kinds of infections.

1894: Prince Edward is born, the eldest son of George V and Queen Mary.

1931: Lady Furness introduces Edward to her friend Wallis Simpson.

1936: George V dies and Edward inherits the throne but abdicates in December.

The Abdication Crisis

Although the 1930s were a time of austerity, people at the top of society continued to have a good time. The Prince of Wales, Edward (1894–1972), was famously fun-loving. He became Edward VIII when George V died in early 1936.

EDWARD AND MRS. SIMPSON

Edward was very dashing. He liked playing golf and going to parties. He was always well dressed and often seen in the company of glamorous women. Everybody expected Edward to marry a suitable English girl or the daughter of a foreign king. However, once he met Wallis Simpson in 1931, he felt he had found the love of his life. He was determined to marry her.

However, Wallis would have been unsuitable as queen. She was an American and had already been married twice before. In fact, she was still married when she met Prince Edward. Most people could not imagine what he saw in her. She said herself that she was not pretty, but she made up for this by wearing beautiful clothes. She was very good at parties and had a sparkling personality. The prince had never met anybody like her.

Knowing that he could not marry a divorced woman and still be king, Edward decided to abdicate in 1936. His younger brother, Albert, would now become king. When the abdication was announced, it came as a complete shock to most people. Unlike today, the private lives of the royal family were not discussed in magazines and newspapers.

Edward and Wallis were married in 1937, becoming known as the Duke and Duchess of Windsor and spending their lives abroad.

Edward VIII (1894–1972)

Wallis Simpson (1896–1986)

1937: George VI is crowned king at Westminster Abbey in London.

1937: Edward and Wallis get married at the Château de Candé in France.

1972: Edward, now the Duke of Windsor, dies at his home in Paris.

GEORGE VI AND QUEEN ELIZABETH

Albert was dismayed at becoming king, as he was extremely shy and had a stammer. But his wife, Elizabeth, was very supportive. As king, he took the name George VI, but was always known in the family as Bertie. George and Elizabeth had two children: Princess Margaret (1930–2002) and Princess Elizabeth (b. 1926) – who is now our Queen Elizabeth II.

In 1938, George VI and his wife Elizabeth made a state visit to France. But the Queen's mother had recently died, so the royal couple were in mourning. Members of the royal family always wear black when in mourning. But the Queen's dress designer had the brilliant idea of dressing her all in white instead. Her clothes created a sensation and the visit was a huge success.

George VI (1895–1952)

DID YOU KNOW?

With a reign of just 326 days, Edward was one of the shortest-reigning British monarchs. He was never crowned.

INTERESTING

"The Woman I Love"

Edward made a famous speech that was broadcast on the day after he abdicated:

"I have found it impossible to carry the heavy burden of responsibility and to discharge my duties as king as I would wish to do without the help and support of the woman I love."

1939: Germany invades Poland, leading to a declaration of war.

1940: Winston Churchill becomes Prime Minister following the resignation of Neville Chamberlain.

1941: America enters the war after Japan attacks its naval base at Pearl Harbour.

THE SECOND WORLD WAR

The Great Depression of the 1930s had affected most countries in Europe. In Germany, this had led to the founding of the Nazi Party. The Nazi leader, who was called Adolf Hitler, was very ambitious and wanted to conquer Europe.

From left: Josef Stalin, Franklin D. Roosevelt and Winston Churchill

WAR BREAKS OUT

The nations of Europe began to get very nervous as they saw Germany building up its army. War was eventually declared on Germany when Hitler invaded Poland in 1939. Most European countries were involved in the war, and America and Japan joined in the fighting later on.

During the war, the United States and Russia were on the same side as Britain. The Russian President, Josef Stalin, the American President, Franklin D. Roosevelt, and the British Prime Minister, Winston Churchill, were known as "The Big Three".

Winston Churchill
Winston Churchill (1874–1965) was the British Prime Minister for most of the war. He made very famous speeches that people found inspiring and visited places that had been bombed.

EVACUATION IN BRITAIN

Big cities in Britain became targets for German bombers because this is where most of the factories were. So, many children living in cities were sent away from home to live with families in the country where it would be much safer. Sadly, many children were unhappy and missed their families.

Some people thought that the royal family should leave Britain so that they would be safe. But Queen Elizabeth famously said: "The children won't go without me. I won't leave the King. And the King will never leave." King George VI (1895–1952) and Queen Elizabeth visited bombed parts of London. This made them very popular with the British people.

1942: Rationing of coal for home use is introduced and central heating is banned in summer.

1944: Churchill visits Russia to have meetings with the Russian leaders.

1949: Clothes rationing ends but people continue to have to make do with old garments.

RATIONING

During the war Britain could not import food from abroad, so everybody had to manage with what could be produced here. To avoid a shortage, food was rationed. Other things in short supply, such as petrol and clothing, were also rationed.

Although life was very drab, there was also a "wartime spirit". People felt that they all had to work together and that eventually everything would turn out all right.

DID YOU KNOW?

American soldiers based in Britain made chewing gum popular.

Adolf Hitler (1889–1945)

MAKING DO

Sometimes, people would get hold of torn parachutes and use them to make underwear. Before the invention of nylon, silk stockings were a luxury. Instead, women would use gravy powder to colour their bare legs like a fake tan. Then they drew lines up the backs of their legs with a pencil, so that it looked as if they were wearing stockings with seams.

When people got married, everybody would put their rations together and make a small wedding cake. Then a big fake cake made from cardboard would be placed over the top of it.

AWESOME FACT

In September 1940, Buckingham Palace in London was bombed.

INTERESTING

Digging for Victory
People were encouraged to grow their own vegetables. This was called "digging for victory" because all the money saved could be spent on the war effort. Many people had a better diet during this period of food rationing than they did afterwards.

1936: The Spitfire is seen for the first time at an air display at RAF Hendon in London.

1939: The first German air attack is launched over England, but no bombs are dropped.

1940: German troops seize the port of Dunkirk in France, stranding many Allies.

FAMOUS BATTLES

Adolf Hitler invaded France during the Second World War and then planned to invade Britain as well. But this was much more difficult because Britain is an island. There were several battles fought in the air and at sea.

THE BLITZ AND AIR RAIDS

The Blitz was the name given to the air raids made by German planes on London and other big cities such as Coventry, Birmingham and Bristol. When the enemy planes were coming, sirens would sound. Everybody knew that they had to find shelter. If there was no time, some people just sheltered under the kitchen table.

BLACK OUT TONIGHT

AWESOME FACT

The Black-Out

To stop the German pilots being able to see towns and cities during air raids, everybody had to have thick curtains that could be drawn at night. Air-raid wardens would patrol the streets and let people know if they could see even a small chink of light.

DUNKIRK

In June 1940 the Germans seized the port of Dunkirk in northern France. Thousands of allied soldiers were stranded there, and it looked as if they would be captured. Britain sent all kinds of boats to rescue the soldiers – not only warships, but also fishing boats, lifeboats and yachts.

1941: The Blitz, a series of air attacks on British cities and air bases, comes to an end.

1944: The Allies attack France with the intention of pushing back the German forces.

1993: A Battle of Britain Memorial is opened at Capel-le-Ferne near Folkestone.

THE BATTLE OF BRITAIN

After Dunkirk, Hitler set his sights on Britain. The Battle of Britain began in July 1940. To start with, the Germans attacked air bases and ships in the sea that were carrying food. In September, they started to bomb London. This went on until October. But the British fighter pilots fought back bravely.

In the end, Hitler gave up and decided to invade Russia instead. This marked a turning point in the war. People now felt that Hitler could be stopped.

DID YOU KNOW?

The main British fighter planes used in the war were the Hurricane and the Spitfire.

COOL FACTS

Churchill's Famous Speech

At the end of the Battle of Britain, Churchill made a famous speech on 20 August 1940. He told the nation:

"Never in the field of human conflict was so much owed by so many to so few."

Churchill meant that all the British people owed their lives to the few brave pilots of the Royal Air Force (RAF).

INTERESTING

St. Paul's Cathedral
A famous photograph showed the streets around St. Paul's in flames. Churchill ordered that every effort should be made to save the cathedral. He saw it as a symbol of British pride.

THE D-DAY LANDINGS

In June 1944, Britain and America planned to push the Germans out of France. They started bombing German railways and bridges to slow the Germans down. The Allied invasion was nearly cancelled due to bad weather. They needed to attack under a full moon, so that they could see where they were going. Although it was cloudy, they attacked anyway, and this took the Germans by surprise. First they attacked by air, and then warships started bombing the beaches. Fighting was fierce, but the Allies were able to capture the beaches. Then they pushed inland.

1942: William Beveridge writes a report that later becomes the basis for the welfare state.

1945: Germany surrenders and Victory in Europe day is formally announced.

1946: The National Health Service Act creates a new free health service for England and Wales.

VE DAY

The liberation of Western Europe started with the D-Day landings in 1944. Although the end of the war was in sight, there were still battles to be fought before the war finally ended.

THE END OF WAR

In April 1945, seeing that he was about to be defeated, Hitler killed himself in Berlin. In May, Germany surrendered. The 8 May was declared VE Day – Victory in Europe Day – and there was a public holiday. When the announcement was made the previous evening, there was national rejoicing and boats along the River Thames honked their horns. In London, people went on the streets to celebrate. Just before midnight there was a thunderstorm, and everybody got drenched.

The next day there were street parties throughout the country. Large crowds gathered around Buckingham Palace and shouted, "We want the king!" In the late afternoon, the royal family came out onto the balcony. George VI wore his Royal Navy uniform and Princess Elizabeth wore her ATS (Auxiliary Territorial Service) uniform. They were joined by Winston Churchill.

The war was not completely over, however, as there was still fighting going on in the Pacific, mainly involving America and Japan. Victory in the region was not won until August.

CELEBRATING VICTORY

To celebrate the end of the black-out, the government said that bonfires could be lit as long as nothing was burnt that could be used again. Some fires got out of hand, and the fire brigades were kept very busy. Two searchlights were shone over St. Paul's Cathedral, making a great "V" in the sky – which stood for Victory.

People were also allowed to buy cotton bunting without using their rationing coupons, but only as long as it was red, white and blue, the colours of the Union Jack.

1948: The Park Hospital, the first NHS hospital, begins treating patients in Manchester.

1952: Charges are introduced for medicines prescribed by doctors.

1995: The May Day holiday is switched to 8 May to mark the 50th anniversary of VE Day.

THE GENERAL ELECTION OF 1945

In July, there was a general election. Winston Churchill, the Conservative leader, was confident that he would win, as he had been such a strong leader during the war. However, people were in the mood for change, and the Labour party, led by Clement Attlee, swept to power.

Attlee wanted to rebuild Britain after the war. He wanted everybody to have a job but also thought that people who could not work or were sick should be properly looked after. He set up the welfare state and the National Health Service.

Winston Churchill celebrates the end of the Second World War.

AWESOME FACT

In 1948, the first free hospital, called the Park Hospital, was opened in Manchester.

INTERESTING

The National Health Service

Before the start of the National Health Service (NHS), people had to pay to see a doctor or dentist. The new plan was to bring hospitals, doctors, nurses, pharmacists, opticians and dentists into a single organisation that would be free for everybody to use. The service is funded by the taxes that people pay.

10
50
100

MODERN
BRITAIN
1945–2013

1947: Heavy snow brings Britain to a standstill and causes huge problems.

1949: Clement Attlee lays the foundation stone of the Royal Festival Hall.

1951: The Festival of Britain takes place, opened by the king and queen.

THE POST-WAR YEARS

After the Second World War ended, it took Britain time to get back to normal again. In fact, most people had forgotten what normal life was like, and things continued to be difficult for several years.

THE WINTER OF 1947

In January 1947, there was heavy snow in Britain. The snow formed drifts, cutting off many roads and railway tracks. There was a shortage of coal and many power stations were shut down. The cold weather continued with no sign of a thaw. There were fears of a food shortage, as many vegetables were frozen in the ground. It was just like the war all over again.

In March, the snow began to melt. But because the ground underneath was still frozen, the melted snow just ran into rivers and caused flooding. Although the weather eventually got back to normal, the British economy took a long time to recover.

COOL FACTS

The End of Rationing

Rationing finally came to an end in 1954. Although luxury goods were available again, not many people could afford them. Bananas and other imported fruits were still considered exotic novelties. Some people continued to keep stocks of tinned food and sugar just in case there was a shortage again.

1952: Thick fog in London results in death for some and leads to new pollution laws.

1954: Rationing, which had begun in 1939, finally comes to an end.

1968: The Hayward Gallery is opened on London's South Bank by the River Thames.

THE FESTIVAL OF BRITAIN

It was decided that a big celebration was needed to cheer everybody up. It would mark the centenary of the Great Exhibition of 1851 and promote British art, design and industry. On 3 May 1951, there was a special service in St. Paul's Cathedral, attended by George VI and Queen Elizabeth. The king then declared the festival open in a broadcast from the cathedral steps. Later in the afternoon, the king and queen attended a service of dedication led by the Archbishop of Canterbury at the newly built Royal Festival Hall on London's South Bank.

Battersea Park was transformed into the Festival Gardens, laid out as a pleasure garden with a tree walk, fountains and a grotto. There were also exhibitions of art and design all over the country and 2,000 campfires were lit across Britain.

LONDON

19 51

FESTIVAL OF BRITAIN

GUIDE PRICE 2/6

The South Bank

The South Bank became a new home for the arts. The National Film Theatre was added in 1952, then the Royal National Theatre in 1963, and the Hayward Gallery in 1968.

The Great Smog

On 5 December 1952, London was engulfed in a thick fog. The fog mixed with smoke from fires in homes and factories to create a deadly smog. Transport came to a standstill. In some places, you could only see about 30cm (12in) in front of you. The smog lifted on 9 December, but many people who suffered from breathing problems died. The smog led to the Clean Air Acts of 1956 and 1968, and started the environmental movement.

1926: Elizabeth is born in Bruton Street in Mayfair in London. She goes on to become Elizabeth II.

1930: Elizabeth's sister, Margaret, is born at Glamis Castle in Scotland.

1947: Elizabeth marries Prince Philip of Greece in Westminster Abbey.

QUEEN ELIZABETH II (1926–present day)

When George VI died in 1952, Princess Elizabeth and her husband, Prince Philip, were in Kenya following a visit to Australia and New Zealand. They returned to Britain immediately.

A famous photograph taken at George VI's funeral shows his mother, Queen Mary, his widow, Queen Elizabeth, and his daughter – the new Queen Elizabeth II. All three women have their faces heavily veiled.

A PROTECTED PRINCESS

Elizabeth was only 25 when she came to the throne. Although everybody was saddened by the death of her father, there was a new feeling of optimism in the country. It was thought that there would be a new Elizabethan Age that would be just like the first one. The Coronation was planned for the following year, after a period of mourning.

Elizabeth had married Philip of Greece and Denmark in 1947. With their two small children, Prince Charles and Princess Anne, they looked like the perfect family. They later went on to have two more sons. Prince Andrew was born in 1960 and Prince Edward in 1964.

1948: Prince Charles, Elizabeth's eldest child, is born at Buckingham Palace.

1953: Elizabeth is crowned Queen in a ceremony in Westminster Abbey.

1965: Queen Sālote of Tonga dies in Auckland in New Zealand.

THE CORONATION

The date of the Coronation was chosen carefully. It was thought that 2 June would be the sunniest day of the year. Unfortunately, it rained, but people were happy to line the streets and cheer on the Queen.

The whole ceremony was broadcast on television, apart from the moment when the Archbishop of Canterbury actually anointed her as Queen. There were street parties and many people bought souvenirs of the occasion.

DID YOU KNOW?

The Conquest of Everest

On the day of the Coronation, it was announced that Edmund Hillary and Tenzing Norgay had climbed to the top of Mount Everest in the Himalayas – the first people that are known to have done so. They actually reached the summit on 29 May, but the news was delayed to coincide with the Coronation.

COOL FACTS

- ❖ The Queen was taken to Westminster Abbey in the Gold State Coach pulled by eight horses.
- ❖ For the Coronation, Queen Elizabeth wore a white satin dress embroidered with the emblems of the United Kingdom and the Commonwealth.
- ❖ Other kings and queens were invited. Queen Sālote of Tonga was very popular. Despite the rain, she insisted on having an open-air carriage, and she waved back and smiled cheerfully at the crowds.

PRINCESS MARGARET

Margaret was born in 1930 and was Queen Elizabeth's younger sister. She was considered very beautiful and was often photographed. She fell in love with Group Captain Peter Townsend. However, as he had been married before, he was considered unsuitable as a husband. She later married the photographer Antony Armstrong-Jones but they divorced in 1978. She suffered a series of strokes in later life and died in 2002.

Queen Mary (1867–1953) with the young Princesses Elizabeth and Margaret

1926: The Balfour Declaration establishes the idea of the Commonwealth.

1930: The first Commonwealth Games are held in Ontario in Canada.

1932: The New Commonwealth Movement is founded.

THE COMMONWEALTH

Countries that had previously been part of the British Empire started to gain their independence in the 1940s and 1950s. However, many still kept their ties with Britain and the Commonwealth was created.

WHAT IS THE COMMONWEALTH?

The Commonwealth is a "free association of independent nations". Queen Elizabeth II is the head of all the Commonwealth countries, but does not actually rule them. Every country in the Commonwealth signs up to a shared set of values. These include holding fair and free elections and respecting human rights. Countries that do not follow these rules can be suspended.

Every two years the leaders of the Commonwealth nations meet to decide on ways to work together. These meetings are called Commonwealth Heads of Government Meetings (CHOGMs). They also discuss issues concerning the environment.

COOL FACTS

Commonwealth Facts

- There are 54 nations in the Commonwealth, spread over every continent and ocean in the world.
- The Commonwealth includes some of the richest and poorest, largest and smallest nations in the world.
- Six out of ten people living in the United Kingdom today have a relative living in another Commonwealth country.
- Namibia joined the Commonwealth in 1990, Cameroon and Mozambique in 1995, and Rwanda in 2009.
- The Commonwealth Games are called the "friendly games" because the competition is between individual sportsmen and women, and not between countries.

1961: South Africa leaves the Commonwealth because of its race laws.

1994: South Africa becomes a member of the Commonwealth again.

2009: Rwanda, in central Africa, becomes a member of the Commonwealth.

South Africa

In 1961, South Africa left the Commonwealth because of "apartheid" (which means "separation"). At that time, black people were not allowed to vote and mainly lived separately from white people, even though they outnumbered them. Apartheid ended gradually. In 1990, Nelson Mandela was released from prison. In 1994, the first elections were held with people of all races being able to vote, and South Africa was allowed back into the Commonwealth.

Nelson Mandela (b.1918)

INTERESTING

Nelson Mandela

Nelson Mandela (b.1918) campaigned for the rights of black people in South Africa. In 1962, he was put in prison simply because of his ideas. When he was released in 1990, he was hailed as a national hero. He was elected as President in 1994.

IMMIGRATION

Britain has often been seen as a safe haven for people who are persecuted in their own country. At the start of the 20th century, many Jews fled Russia to escape from riots called the "pogroms". More Jews came in the 1930s to escape from Hitler's Germany. After the Second World War, many Polish servicemen who had fought with the Allies remained in Britain instead of returning to Poland, which was now under Russian control.

In 1972, the President of Uganda, Idi Amin, expelled Indians and Pakistanis from the country. Many came to Britain. More recently, refugees have come from Afghanistan. With the expansion of the European Union, many people from EU countries have come to Britain to work.

DID YOU KNOW?

The Commonwealth Games

The Commonwealth Games are held every four years. In 2014, the games will be held in Glasgow.

1961: *The Beatles* play for the first time at the *Cavern* in Liverpool.

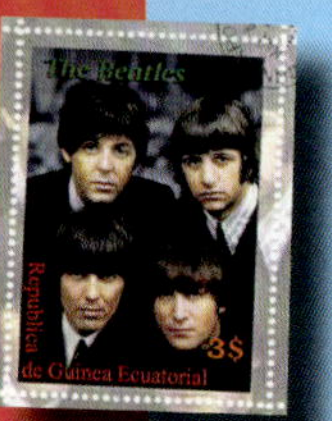

1963: Mary Quant, the fashion designer, wins the first Dress of the Year award.

1963: *Ready Steady Go!* is broadcast for the first time on ITV.

The Swinging Sixties

In the 1960s, there was a whole generation growing up that did not remember the war. They wanted to have fun. This was really the birth of high street fashion and popular culture.

FASHION

Girls started wearing much more colourful clothes. They often had bold make-up and added brightly coloured plastic jewellery. Short, geometric hairstyles that framed the face became popular.

In London, Carnaby Street, with a number of small boutiques, became the place to go for new fashion. Cathy McGowan (b.1943), who presented the pop programme *Ready, Steady, Go!* on television, was a style icon. In Kensington, Barbara Hulanicki opened Biba in 1964, which sold affordable clothes just like the ones that Cathy wore. Office girls could go shopping in their lunch hour and get a completely new look for going out that evening.

Young men started to grow their hair longer, with a fringe at the front. They had tight trousers and pointed shoes.

Mary Quant

Mary Quant (b.1934) was a key figure in setting new fashion trends. She thought that young people should dress to please themselves and treat fashion as a game.

Mary created the miniskirt, with a hemline well above the knee. This was more like sportswear, so you could run for the bus in it!

1964: Cilla Black has a No.1 hit with *Anyone Who Had A Heart.*

1966: England win the World Cup, defeating West Germany at Wembley.

1970: *The Beatles* break up in order to pursue their own personal interests.

BEATLEMANIA

In Liverpool, a club called the *Cavern* opened in 1957. In 1961, *The Beatles*, a group of four young men, gave their first performance there. They rapidly became popular and secured a record deal with EMI. Their string of hits included *She Loves You*, *I Wanna Hold Your Hand* and *A Hard Day's Night*. Unlike some boy bands today, they could play guitar and drums, as well as sing. They also became popular in America. When they played, girls would scream and often pass out in excitement.

DID YOU KNOW?

Cilla Black worked in the *Cavern* cloakroom before becoming famous.

SCAN ME

Instructions on page 5

The Twist

Before the 1960s, people enjoyed ballroom dances such as the waltz and foxtrot, always in couples. There were set steps that you had to learn, and you had to be careful not to crash into other couples on the dance floor. A new dance was made popular by a song called *The Twist* by the American singer-songwriter Chubby Checker. There were no formal steps. You kept the balls of your feet on the floor and twisted your body up and down in time to the music, trying to go as low as possible.

INTERESTING

In 1966, England hosted the FIFA World Cup – and won the trophy, defeating West Germany 4–2 in the final.

AWESOME FACT

Mods and Rockers

There were two main strands of youth culture. Mods were very interested in fashion, while rockers were into motorbikes and wore black leather clothes.

1957: The Treaty of Rome creates the European Economic Community.

1971: Decimal currency is introduced to replace the old shillings and pence.

1973: After several years of negotiating, the United Kingdom joins the Common Market.

THE EUROPEAN UNION

After the Second World War ended, many European countries decided that they would all be better off if they could work with each other in order to stop another war happening.

CO-OPERATION BETWEEN NATIONS

In 1957, the Treaty of Rome created the European Economic Community (EEC) or "Common Market". At first, this included Belgium, France, Germany, Italy, Luxembourg and the Netherlands. The United Kingdom joined in 1973.

In the late 1980s, the face of Europe changed. After the war, Russia – then usually referred to as the Soviet Union – controlled many eastern European countries. There was not much trade between them and the rest of Europe, and travel was difficult. But they all wanted their freedom and split off from Russia. This was mainly done peacefully, helped by the President of the Soviet Union, Mikhail Gorbachev (b.1931).

The European Union (EU), as it was now called, got bigger as more of these countries joined. The European Union is run from Brussels, the capital of Belgium. The European Parliament passes laws that all members have to abide by.

The signing of the Treaty of Rome (1957)

INTERESTING

The Euro

In 1992, the Maastricht Treaty set out plans for a single currency for all members. Mrs. Thatcher, the Prime Minister of Britain at the time, thought that this would not work. However, many of the member states started using the Euro in 1999.

1974: Work begins on the Channel Tunnel to link Britain with France.

1992: The Maastricht Treaty sets out ideas for a single currency, the Euro.

2007: St. Pancras Station in London reopens with a direct link to the continent.

DECIMALISATION

Until 1971, Britain had a very complicated money system. A pound was made up of 20 shillings and each shilling was made up of 12 pennies. There was a coin for three pennies called a threepenny bit and for six pennies called a sixpence. A half crown was two shillings and sixpence, while a guinea was one pound and a shilling.

This made adding up money very difficult, and people often made mistakes. It was decided that it would be much easier if a pound just had 100 pennies in it, and there were no shillings at all.

The Channel Tunnel

Being an island always gave Britain an advantage in times of war, but made travel to mainland Europe difficult. Work began on a tunnel for a railway in 1974. The English started tunnelling from one side of the English Channel and the French from the other side. The two tunnels met in 1990. The tunnel was completed in 1994.

COOL FACTS

Tunnel Facts

- The idea of a tunnel between England and France was not a new one. The first design was made in 1802.
- The Channel Tunnel is 50km (31 miles) long with an undersea section of 39km (24 miles).

AWESOME FACT

Concorde

Concorde was the first supersonic passenger aeroplane. It was built jointly by French and British manufacturers. Because it flew faster than the speed of sound, you could get from London to New York in around three hours. Concorde first flew in 1973. The last flight took place in 2003.

1925: Margaret Roberts is born in Grantham in Lincolnshire.	**1959:** Mrs. Thatcher becomes the Member of Parliament for Finchley.	**1975:** Mrs. Thatcher defeats Mr. Heath to become the leader of the Conservative Party.

MARGARET THATCHER

Margaret Thatcher became the United Kingdom's first woman Prime Minister when she was elected in 1979. She was considered very strong-minded and many people did not agree with her policies.

THE "IRON LADY"

Margaret Roberts was born in 1925 in Lincolnshire. Her father had a grocer's shop. She married Denis Thatcher in 1951 and became a Conservative Member of Parliament in 1959. In 1975, she challenged the former Prime Minister, Edward Heath (1916–2005), who had just lost a general election, and became leader of the Conservative Party.

A Russian journalist once called her the "Iron Lady". She took this as a compliment, and the term was often used to describe her.

The Winter of Discontent

In the winter of 1978–1979, there were many strikes. Rubbish piled up in the streets when the binmen went on strike. People called it "The Winter of Discontent", a phrase from Shakespeare. The Labour government, led by Jim Callaghan, became very unpopular. There was a general election, and Mrs. Thatcher was elected as Prime Minister.

Mrs. Thatcher won three general elections and was Prime Minister for eleven and a half years.

1979: Mrs. Thatcher wins the general election, becoming the first woman ever to do so.

1990: Mrs. Thatcher resigns and leaves Downing Street in tears after many years in power.

2013: Mrs. Thatcher dies and there is a funeral service at St. Paul's Cathedral.

Mrs. Thatcher working with her Cabinet.

Miners on strike in protest against the closure of the coal mines.

TRADE UNION REFORM AND THE MINERS' STRIKE

Mrs. Thatcher passed new laws that made it more difficult for unions to call strikes. In 1984, some of the coal mines were closed down and many miners lost their jobs. Arthur Skargill, the leader of the National Union of Mineworkers (NUM), called a strike. The government maintained that this was illegal.

The strike went on for a year. Eventually, the miners gave in and went back to work. More mines were closed and entire communities, where mining had been very important, were changed forever.

MRS. THATCHER'S RESIGNATION

Mrs. Thatcher was a very dominant figure and some even called her bossy. She had many arguments with her own ministers. She was opposed to the idea of a single currency within the European Union. In 1989–1990, she introduced a new tax called the Community Charge (or "Poll Tax") to change the way local government was paid for. Instead of paying rates based on how much your house was worth, everybody would pay the same. This was very expensive for many people and led to rioting in the streets.

In November 1990, Michael Heseltine (b.1933) challenged her for the leadership. Although she won more votes than him, she knew she no longer had enough support to carry on. She resigned as Prime Minister. There was a further vote for a new leader, and John Major (b.1943) became Prime Minister.

Mrs. Thatcher was given the title Baroness. Towards the end of her life she had several strokes and was rarely seen in public.

COOL FACT

Baroness Thatcher's Funeral
Baroness Thatcher died in 2013 and a big funeral service for her was held in St. Paul's Cathedral in London.

1961: Lady Diana Spencer is born in Sandringham in Norfolk.

1981: Prince Charles and Diana marry in a service at St. Paul's Cathedral.

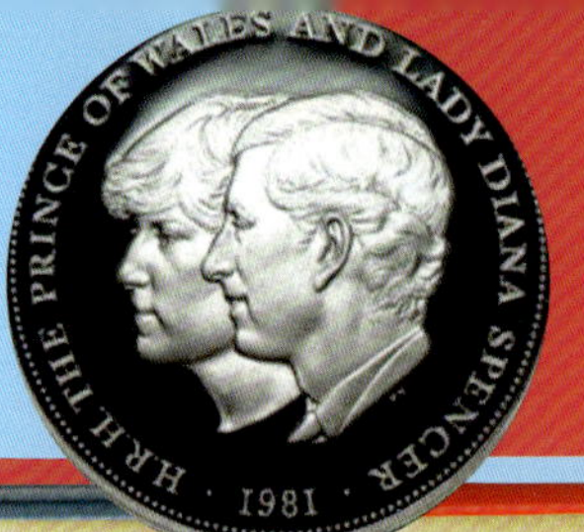

1982: Diana gives birth to Prince William at St. Mary's Hospital, in Paddington, London.

CHARLES AND DIANA

Everybody was waiting for Charles, the Prince of Wales and the heir to the throne, to get married. Eventually, he asked Lady Diana Spencer (1961–1997) to be his wife and future queen.

A ROYAL WEDDING

Charles and Diana's wedding in 1981 was probably the most lavish royal wedding ever. It was decided that Westminster Abbey was too small, so the couple got married in St. Paul's Cathedral. The wedding was watched by millions of people around the world.

Although the couple had two sons, William (b.1982) and Harry (b.1984), they became increasingly unhappy. In 1992 they separated, and in 1996 they divorced.

Later, Diana did a lot of work for charity, especially with the homeless, the young, drug addicts and the elderly. She campaigned against the use of land mines in wars.

Diana's Wedding Dress

Diana wanted to look like a princess in a fairy tale on her wedding day. Her dress was designed by David and Elizabeth Emanuel. It was made of ivory silk taffeta and had a 7.6-m (25-ft) train. It had large puff sleeves and a billowing skirt. Diana went to the cathedral in the Queen's Glass Coach.

DID YOU KNOW?

Diana loved music and dancing. She danced with John Travolta and Wayne Sleep.

Diana dancing with John Travolta.

1992: The Prince and Princess of Wales agree to separate after many unhappy years.

1996: The couple divorce, but Diana remains a member of the royal family.

1997: Diana is killed in a tragic car crash in a tunnel in Paris, France. She is only 36 years old.

Diana, Princess of Wales (1961–1997)

Camilla Parker-Bowles, The Duchess of Cornwall (b. 1947)

Queen Elizabeth, The Queen Mother (1900–2002)

Diana, The People's Princess

At first, Diana seemed shy and awkward in front of the camera. She suffered from an eating disorder and lost weight. But she gained in confidence and began to enjoy the attention. She became the world's most photographed woman, and her face often appeared on magazine covers and on television.

A TRAGIC ACCIDENT

Sadly, Diana died in a tragic car accident in Paris with her boyfriend, Dodi Fayed. Their car was speeding away to avoid some photographers and crashed in a tunnel. There was national mourning, and her funeral was probably watched by as many people as had watched her wedding. For a short time, the Queen became very unpopular, as she did not return from Balmoral to London when Diana died. But she did eventually return, and made a television broadcast that paid tribute to Diana.

Mrs. Parker-Bowles

As a young man, Charles had dated Camilla Shand. But when he was sent abroad with the Royal Navy, Camilla married Andrew Parker-Bowles.

Even though he eventually married Diana, Charles was still in love with Camilla. Camilla and Andrew divorced in 1995. Camilla and Charles were later able to marry in 2005. Because Diana had been so popular, it was decided that Camilla should be known as the Duchess of Cornwall, not the Princess of Wales.

The Queen Mother

George VI's widow, Elizabeth, was known as the Queen Mother. She was very popular. She died in 2002 at the age of 102. Many thought that Charles would not marry the divorced Camilla while his grandmother was still alive.

1981: General Galtieri becomes the President of Argentina in South America.

1982: The Argentinians invade the Falklands to claim them for Argentina.

1982: Under the leadership of Mrs. Thatcher, Britain succeeds in retaking the islands.

THE FALKLANDS CONFLICT

The Falklands are a small group of islands in the Atlantic Ocean, off the coast of Argentina. Before the conflict in 1982, many people in Britain did not even know where they were.

WHY DID THE CONFLICT START?

Although geographically the islands are only (563km) 350 miles away from Argentina, Britain had ruled them for 150 years. Thinking that Britain would not retaliate, General Galtieri, the Argentine President, launched an invasion in 1982. The islands are 12,800km (8,000 miles) from Britain. It would take days for British ships to get there.

Only 1,800 people lived on the islands, and they all thought of themselves as British. Many of them were sheep farmers. Mrs. Thatcher sent a task force to reclaim the islands. The United Nations supported Britain. The war was fought on land, at sea and in the air.

After the war, General Galtieri resigned. In Britain, Mrs. Thatcher became very popular. Many people thought she had been very courageous to take on the Argentinians. In the general election of 1983, Margaret Thatcher swept back to power with an increased majority. Some members of the government now found it difficult to argue with her.

The two countries resumed diplomatic relations in 1990. Although Argentina maintains a peaceful claim to the islands, the United Kingdom says that who governs them is not open to negotiation.

1983: General Galtieri is arrested in Argentina and put on trial.

1992: The Falklands veteran Simon Weston is awarded the OBE in recognition of his bravery.

1994: Argentina renews its claim to the Falkland Islands but does not invade again.

COOL FACTS

Falkland Facts

- 913 people were killed during the Falklands Conflict. 655 were Argentines and 255 were British. The other three were residents of the islands.
- The Falklands are also home to colonies of penguins.
- In Argentina, the Falkland Islands are called the Malvinas.

THE BELGRANO

The *Belgrano* was an Argentinian warship. Although it was sailing away from the islands, and therefore not posing an immediate danger, Mrs. Thatcher gave the order to sink it and 386 Argentinians were killed. Mrs. Thatcher was criticised for her decision, both in Argentina and in Britain. She was probably acting on advice given by military leaders, but people continued to debate the sinking for many years. A few days after the sinking, the Argentines attacked HMS *Sheffield*. The ship sank and 20 British lives were lost.

The *Belgrano*

DID YOU KNOW?

Goose Green

An important battle was fought at Goose Green on East Falkland in May 1982. The fighting was fierce. Although the British were outnumbered, after a day and night's fighting, they were victorious. Only Port Stanley remained to be recaptured. The Argentinians finally surrendered in June.

INTERESTING

Simon Weston

Simon Weston is a famous veteran of the Falklands campaign. He was on RFA *Sir Galahad* when it was bombed and he suffered horrific burns to his face. He had to undergo over 70 operations to reconstruct it. He has often been interviewed on television and radio, and supports charities that help people with disfigurements.

1990: Saddam Hussein, the Iraqi leader, invades neighbouring Kuwait.

1991: Operation Desert Storm is launched in Iraq to liberate Kuwait.

1995: An international peace-keeping force is sent to Bosnia in the Balkans.

Britain at War

Besides the Falklands Conflict, Britain has been involved in several other wars in recent decades. These have led to the deaths of many British service people overseas.

BOSNIA

Yugoslavia was a country that was created out of several smaller countries by the Allies after the First World War. In 1991, civil war broke out, as some of these countries wanted their independence again. Fighting was particularly fierce in Bosnia. Many people, including children, were killed. An international peace-keeping force, including British soldiers, was sent in 1995.

AFGHANISTAN

On 11 September 2001, a terrorist attack in New York killed nearly 3,000 people. It was believed that this was masterminded by Osama bin Laden who was being sheltered in Afghanistan, which was ruled by a group called the Taliban.

The American President, George W. Bush, wanted to invade Afghanistan to remove the Taliban and demand the handover of Osama. American troops were supported by soldiers from Britain and other countries. The war in Afghanistan still continues, despite calls for the troops to return home.

2001: A terrorist attack in New York leads to an invasion of Afghanistan.

2002: Britain and the United States invade Iraq to remove Saddam Hussein.

2006: Following a trial, Saddam Hussein is executed in Baghdad.

COOL FACTS

Saddam Hussein

Saddam Hussein (1937–2006) was President of Iraq, although he was more like a dictator. While he ruled Iraq, he was responsible for the deaths of many people who opposed him. He was captured by the Americans in December 2003 and executed in 2006.

THE GULF WAR

In 1990, Saddam Hussein invaded the neighbouring country of Kuwait in the Persian Gulf. As he refused to withdraw, a group of forces, led by the United States and including Britain, began Operation Desert Storm in January 1991.

By late February, Iraq surrendered. Although the coalition had won, Saddam Hussein remained in power.

Iraq agreed to peace terms with the coalition. These allowed the United Nations (UN) to carry out inspections in Iraq to make sure they had no "weapons of mass destruction". These are very dangerous weapons that would kill a lot of people if they were used. Success in the war helped John Major to win the general election in 1992.

THE IRAQ WAR

Iraq did not always co-operate with the inspectors. By 2002, many began to suspect that Saddam Hussein had a stash of weapons. In America, the President, George W. Bush, thought that they should invade Iraq and remove Saddam Hussein. He argued that the Iraqis would welcome this.

The British Prime Minister, Tony Blair, agreed with Mr. Bush. But the UN would not support a new war until after further inspections. In March, American and British forces invaded Iraq without the UN. Saddam Hussein's army and government collapsed and, in May 2002, Mr. Bush claimed victory.

DID YOU KNOW?

Iraq's Legacy

Many people were killed during the war and no weapons of mass destruction were ever found.

Afterwards, Mr. Blair never regained the popularity he had enjoyed before.

1991: The first series of *Big Brother* is broadcast on Channel 4.

1997: Geri Halliwell wears her famous Union Jack dress at the BRIT awards.

1997: Tony Blair wins the first of three elections and creates the New Labour government.

COOL BRITANNIA

There was a feeling that life under John Major's government was rather dull. Tony Blair's victory at the general election in 1997 brought a change of mood. It was cool to be British again.

NEW LABOUR

Leaders of the Labour Party thought that many people were put off voting for them because of their links with the trade unions. Tony Blair (b.1953) and others decided to rebrand the party, which they now started calling "New Labour". However, many people felt that he was making the Labour party more like the Conservatives.

Tony Blair – a Charismatic Leader
Compared with other politicians, Mr. Blair seemed very young and in tune with youth culture. Like Mrs. Thatcher, he won three elections. He was in office for ten years.

POPULAR MUSIC

Just as in the 1960s, Britain started producing music that became popular all over the world. Boy bands included *Take That*. Robbie Williams and Gary Barlow later had successful solo careers. The *Spice Girls* had a string of hits and promoted the idea of "girl power". Some sportspeople began to enjoy the same sort of adulation. The footballer David Beckham married Spice Girl Victoria Adams and they became a noted celebrity couple in Britain and around the world.

2001: The first series of *Pop Idol* is broadcast and is hugely successful.

2007: Tony Blair resigns as Prime Minister and hands over to Gordon Brown.

2013: David Beckham announces his retirement from football at the age of 38.

Brit Art

Young British Artists was the name given to a group of artists who had studied at Goldsmiths College in the 1980s. They began to exhibit together in 1988. They were supported by the millionaire Charles Saatchi. Their work was meant to be shocking.

❖ **Damien Hirst** (b.1965) created *The Physical Impossibility of Death in the Mind of Someone Living* which is a dead shark preserved in a glass case.

❖ **Tracey Emin** (b.1963) is famous for *My Bed*, an unmade bed surrounded by clutter from the artist's bedroom.

COOL FACTS

The Financial Crisis

In 2008, there was a financial crisis that started in America and then spread around the world. Banks had been encouraging people to borrow money, usually so they could buy houses. Other people had credit cards debts. Then it was realised that many people were unable to pay the money back.

This led to the collapse of several banks. Other banks stopped lending, which caused problems for businesses. The value of people's savings dropped.

REALITY TELEVISION

A new form of television was created that featured real people rather than actors. The programme was *Big Brother*, which first aired in 1999. Members of the public were locked in a house and were observed on camera. This turned ordinary members of the public into media stars.

Simon Cowell (b.1959) created *Pop Idol* in 2001. Young people who could sing were auditioned and then coached to become pop stars. In the final rounds, they were eliminated one by one until a winner was chosen. The winner was then given a record deal. This format morphed into the *X-Factor*, where all the auditions were done in huge public arenas around the country. *Britain's Got Talent* has a similar format but includes acts other than singers.

These programmes became "interactive". People were invited to vote, at first by phone. Nowadays comments are invited via mobile phones, email and Twitter.

DID YOU KNOW?

The term "Big Brother" comes from a novel called *Nineteen Eighty-Four* by George Orwell. It appears in the phrase "Big Brother is watching you".

1921: The southern part of Ireland becomes the Republic of Eire.

1998: The Good Friday Agreement is signed to bring peace to Northern Ireland.

2004: A new building for the Scottish Parliament is opened at Holyrood.

New Independence

The United Kingdom is actually made up of four different countries – England, Scotland, Northern Ireland and Wales. They each have their own identity but Parliament has always been in London.

DEVOLUTION

In the latter part of the 20th century, many people in each country, apart from England, wanted to have their own Parliaments. These Parliaments would be able to make laws that would affect only the people who lived in that country.

This process is called devolution. Central government in London still makes the laws for everybody, but some powers are "devolved" to these smaller parliaments.

The devolved parliaments cannot decide how much tax people pay and have no control over the armed forces. Decisions on these and other important matters are still taken by the Parliament in London. All the smaller countries still elect MPs that go to Westminster, so everybody still has a say in important decisions.

INTERESTING

Nationalism
Nationalists often want to go one step further and become independent countries in their own right. Many people are opposed to this, believing that the United Kingdom works best as a single country.

DID YOU KNOW?

Welsh National Assembly
The National Assembly for Wales was set up in 1998. In 2006, the Government of Wales Act allowed the Assembly to pass laws.

The Northern Ireland Assembly
At the end of 1998, an agreement was made that would put an end to all the fighting. This was called the Good Friday Agreement (or the Belfast Agreement). The Northern Ireland Assembly was set up to make laws and run government departments in Northern Ireland.

2006: The Government of Wales Act gives powers to the Welsh National Assembly.

2007: Alex Salmond becomes the First Minister of Scotland.

2009: Carwyn Jones becomes the First Minister of Wales.

NORTHERN IRELAND

Northern Ireland has had a troubled history. In 1801, the whole of Ireland was part of the United Kingdom. The southern part of Ireland became the republic of Eire in 1921, with the northern part remaining part of the United Kingdom.

For many years, the capital of Northern Ireland, Belfast, was like a war zone. Irish nationalists, who were mainly Catholics, wanted to be part of Eire. Unionists, who were mainly Protestants, wanted to stay in the United Kingdom. There was fighting between the two groups and British soldiers were sent to Belfast to keep the peace.

Independent Assemblies

- ❖ The Northern Ireland Assembly has 108 members called Members of the Legislative Assembly.
- ❖ Technically, Wales is a principality that is ruled over by the Prince of Wales.
- ❖ The Welsh National Assembly has 60 members.
- ❖ There are 129 members of the Scottish Parliament. They are called MSPs for short.

Scotland and the Scottish Parliament

For a long time, Scotland was a separate country with its own kings and queens. This often led to wars with England until the United Kingdom was formed during the reign of Queen Anne. In 1999, the Scottish Parliament was opened. The new building for the Scottish Parliament was opened by the Queen at Holyrood in 2004.

1982: Catherine (Kate) Middleton is born in Reading in Berkshire.

2001: Prince William meets Kate Middleton at the University of St. Andrew's in Scotland.

2007: The couple separate for a while but keep on good terms with each other.

THE ROYAL WEDDING

In 2011, the wedding of Prince William, Prince Charles's elder son, and Kate Middleton took place. It was a time of national celebration and was declared a public holiday.

A TIME OF CELEBRATION

At the time of the wedding, Britain was in recession. Some businesses were forced to close, people were losing their jobs, and it was difficult to borrow money. The royal wedding cheered everybody up, but the royal family were very concerned that it should not be too lavish. The wedding was meant to be very traditional and simple. Unlike previous royal brides, Kate arrived at the abbey in a car, not a horse-drawn coach.

WILLIAM AND KATE

William and Kate had a long courtship. They met in 2001 while they were both students at the University of St. Andrew's and began dating the following year. They separated for a while in 2007. This was probably because Kate needed time to decide whether she really wanted to become a member of the royal family and the future queen. Everybody was pleased when they got back together, as it was obvious they were in love.

The couple were engaged in October 2010 and married on 29 April 2011. Unlike many royal brides, Kate was a commoner. She did not have a title and was not a member of the aristocracy.

Although all eyes were on the young couple, Kate's younger sister Pippa almost stole the show. She was the maid of honour and wore a simple white shift dress with buttons down the back.

After the wedding, the couple was taken from the abbey to Buckingham Palace in the 1902 State Landau – a kind of open-top coach. The couple were made Duke and Duchess of Cambridge.

2010: William and Kate announce their forthcoming engagement.

2011: The couple are married in Westminster Abbey.

2012: The Duchess of Cambridge announces she is expecting her first child.

AWESOME FACT

The Making of a Dress
The dressmakers who made Kate's wedding dress washed their hands every half an hour to avoid staining the fabric.

INTERESTING

Men in Uniform
William wore an Irish Guards mounted officer's uniform. As his best man, Harry wore the uniform of a captain of the Blues and Royals.

DID YOU KNOW?

The bells of Westminster Abbey were rung for three hours after the wedding.

The Mayor of London, Boris Johnson, gave the couple a tandem bike as a wedding present.

Kate's Wedding Outfit

- **Kate's wedding dress** This was designed by Sarah Burton. It was made from ivory and white satin. The bodice had a V-neck with lace detailing and the full skirt had a train measuring 270cm (110in).
- **Something borrowed** The very simple veil was held in position by a diamond tiara lent to the bride by the Queen. This tiara was originally given by George VI to the Queen Mother in 1936. They then gave it to the Queen on her eighteenth birthday.
- **Something blue** According to reports, a blue ribbon was stitched inside the dress.

1897: Queen Victoria celebrates her Diamond Jubilee.

1977: Queen Elizabeth II celebrates her Silver Jubilee.

2002: Nationwide celebrations are held for the Queen's Golden Jubilee.

The Diamond Jubilee

Elizabeth II has reigned for nearly as long as Queen Victoria, who was the longest-reigning monarch so far. In 2012, Elizabeth celebrated sixty years on the throne, being only the second monarch to do so.

A YEAR OF CELEBRATIONS

There had already been a big celebration in 1977 to mark the Queen's Silver Jubilee and another one in 2002 for her Golden Jubilee. For 2012, a celebration was planned that would be even bigger than the earlier ones. Celebrations went on throughout the year, but the focal point was the Jubilee Weekend in June.

A special bank holiday was declared on Tuesday 5 June, so that everyone had a four-day weekend. Celebrations were held in Britain and also throughout the Commonwealth. The Queen and the Duke of Edinburgh made special visits around the country.

INTERESTING

The Jubilee Concert

The concert was held outside Buckingham Palace. It was a joint venture by the BBC and Gary Barlow. Gary and the composer Andrew Lloyd Webber co-wrote a special anthem *Sing*, which was performed by a choir from many Commonwealth countries. Other artists who appeared at the concert included Robbie Williams, the pianist Lang Lang, Tom Jones, Shirley Bassey and Elton John.

INTERESTING

The Jubilee Weekend

The Jubilee weekend itself was marked by the following events:

- **Saturday 2 June** The Queen goes to the Epsom Derby horse race.
- **Sunday 3 June** The Thames Diamond Jubilee Pageant.
- **Monday 4 June** BBC Concert at Buckingham Palace.
- **Tuesday 5 June** Service of Thanksgiving at St. Paul's Cathedral followed by lunch at Westminster Hall, a carriage procession to Buckingham Palace and a balcony appearance.

2011: The Queen Elizabeth Diamond Jubilee Trust is created.

2012: Celebrations throughout the Commonwealth mark the Diamond Jubilee.

2013: A Buckingham Palace exhibition marks the 60th anniversary of the Coronation.

Jubilee Facts

- Prince Philip was unable to take part in the events on the Monday and Tuesday. He was rushed to hospital for treatment for a bladder infection.
- During her reign, the Queen has had twelve Prime Ministers.
- In keeping with the diamond theme, Shirley Bassey sang *Diamonds Are Forever*.
- 10,000 free tickets were made available for the Buckingham Palace Concert and 1.2 million people applied. Ticket holders were able to go to a special picnic in the palace garden in the afternoon.

DID YOU KNOW?

Jubilee Beacons

2,012 beacons were lit by communities and individuals throughout the United Kingdom, as well as in the Channel Islands, the Isle of Man and the Commonwealth. The Queen herself lit the National Beacon in central London.

River Thames Flotilla

The flotilla was made up of nearly 1,000 boats from around the United Kingdom, the Commonwealth and other parts of the world. The Queen and the Duke of Edinburgh travelled in the Royal Barge, which formed the centrepiece of the flotilla.

2005: London wins the bid to host the 30th Olympic Games – this is a great achievement.

2007: The much-anticipated official logo for the London Olympics is revealed.

2008: At the Beijing Olympics closing ceremony, the Olympic flag is handed over.

The Olympic Games 2012

Everybody was very excited when Britain won the bid to host the Olympic Games in 2012. It would add to the national celebrations for the Queen's Diamond Jubilee.

WINNING THE BID

Hosting the Olympic Games is considered a great honour. Important cities throughout the world make bids – they have to persuade the International Olympic Committee (IOC) that they can provide big enough sports stadiums and house all the visiting athletes.

London won the bid on 6 July 2005, which allowed seven years to build all the facilities. A special Olympic village was to be built in Stratford, in east London.

The Olympic Games in Beijing in 2008 was very spectacular, and some people were afraid that Britain would not be able to provide anything as lavish during a recession. There was also a worry that the British summer would be unpredictable.

As it turned out, the games were a huge success. They were well organised, and were enjoyed by everyone.

2010: Official Olympic mascots Wenlock and Mandeville are unveiled.

2011: People are allowed to apply for tickets for the opening ceremony.

2012: After much preparation, the Games take place to universal acclaim.

THE OPENING CEREMONY

The opening ceremony was devised by the film director Danny Boyle. Although it celebrated British achievement, it was full of jokes that only British people would really understand. Everybody gasped when they saw the Queen taking part. This had been kept a closely guarded secret. When Daniel Craig as James Bond was shown walking the corridors of Buckingham Palace, everybody expected the Queen to be played by an actress such as Helen Mirren or Judi Dench.

However, Queen Elizabeth appeared as herself. She was shown getting into a helicopter with James Bond and then a stand-in parachuted into the stadium wearing the same dress. The real Queen then appeared on the stand to declare the Olympic Games officially open.

AWESOME FACT

In December, Bradley Wiggins was named BBC Sports Personality of the Year. He was knighted in 2013.

COOL FACTS

Gold Medal Winners

- In cycling, Bradley Wiggins ("Wiggo"), who had just won the Tour de France cycle race, won gold for the time trial. This brought his total of Olympic medals to seven, a record shared with Chris Hoy, who won gold in the team sprint.
- Jessica Ennis won gold in the heptathlon, a combination of seven track and field events.
- Mo Farah won gold in the 10,000 metres.
- In tennis, Andy Murray beat Roger Federer in the final. It made up for losing the Wimbledon final to Federer a few weeks before.

The Kings and Queens of Great Britain

This list of the kings and queens of Great Britain is given in chronological order, with each monarch's date of ascension appearing next to their name.

Iron Age Britain 750 BC–43 AD
Roman Britain 43–450 AD
The Anglo-Saxons and Vikings 450–1017 AD

The Danes
King Canute 1017
Harold I 1035
Hardicanute 1040

The Saxons
Edward the Confessor 1042
Harold II 1066

The Normans
William I 1066
William II 1087
Henry I 1100
Stephen 1135

The Plantagenets
Henry II 1154
Richard I 1189
John 1199
Henry III 1216
Edward I 1272
Edward II 1307
Edward III 1327
Richard II 1377

The House of Lancaster
Henry IV 1399
Henry V 1413
Henry VI 1422

The House of York
Edward IV 1461
Edward V 1483
Richard III 1483

The Tudors
Henry VII 1485
Henry VIII 1509
Edward VI 1547
Jane Grey 1553
Mary I 1553
Elizabeth I 1558

The Stuarts
James I 1603
Charles I 1625

The Commonwealth
Oliver Cromwell 1649
Richard Cromwell 1658

The Stuarts
Charles II 1660
James II 1685
William III & Mary II 1689
Anne 1702

The House of Hanover
George I 1714
George II 1727
George III 1760
George IV 1820
William IV 1830
Victoria 1837

The House of Saxe-Coburg-Gotha
Edward VII 1901

The House of Windsor
George V 1910
Edward VIII 1936
George VI 1936
Elizabeth II 1952

Index

MP
NAZIS OUT
NAZIS OUT